Introduction to Internet Programming

CS-74

For

Bachelor of Computer Applications [BCA]

By

Dinesh Verma
Sun Microsystems Certified JAVA(TM) Programmer,
MCA, BCA, 'A' & 'O' Level, JP

S.ROY
MCA, B.SC., DECM, DCPA,DECOM
Academic Counsellor - ARSD College, Delhi University
Guest Lecturer - Delhi College, Delhi University
Visiting Faculty - Punjab Technical University

CLOSER TO NATURE
WE USE RECYCLED PAPER

Useful For

IGNOU, Nalanda University, Kurushetra University, Lalit Narayan Mithila University, Andhra University, Pt. Sunderlal Sharma (Open) University (Bilaspur), Annamalai University, Bangalore University, Bharathiar University, Bharathidasan University, HP University, Jamia Millia Islamia, Kakatiya University (Andhra Pradesh), KSOU (Karnataka), KOU (Rajasthan), MPBOU (MP), MDU (Haryana), Punjab University, Tamilnadu Open University, Sri Padmavati Mahila Visvavidyalayam (Andhra Pradesh), Sri Venkateswara University (Andhra Pradesh), UCSDE (Kerala), University of Jammu, YCMOU, Rajasthan University, UPRTOU (UP) and all other Indian Universities.

GPH BOOK™

GULLYBABA PUBLISHING HOUSE (P) LTD.

AN ISO 9001:2008 CERTIFIED CO.

Developed and Produced by:
GullyBaba Publishing House (P) Ltd.
Regd. Office:
2525/193, 1st Floor,
Onkar Nagar-A, Tri Nagar,
New Delhi-110035
Landmark: Kanhaiya Nagar Metro Station

Branch Office:
1A/2A, 20, Hari Sadan,
Ansari Road, Daryaganj,
New Delhi-110002

E-mail: info@gullybaba.com, Website: GullyBaba.com

Edition: 2014

ISBN: 978-81-89086-30-5

Preface

This book is mainly targeted for BCA exam of Introduction to Internet Programming. It has been introduced in market after seeing the huge demand of ready to grasp material for exams with high level of quality, and its un-availability in market. We the GullyBaba Publishing House took a step ahead to publish the quality material focusing on exams at the same time giving you indepth knowledge about the subject.

GPH Book is the pioneer effort that provides a unique methodology so as to perform better in exams. If your goal is to attain higher grade use this powerful study tool independently or along with your text.

On the Web : ***www.gullybaba.com*** *is the vital resource for your exams acting as catalyst to boost up your preparation. Gullybaba.com has been Listed* ***no.1*** *in www.google.com and www.yahoo.com when you search "IGNOU MCA BCA MBA". Now you can access us on the net through* ***www.doctorignou.com, www.doeacconline.com, www.gphindia.com, and www.gullybabapublishinghouse.com.***

Feedback about the book can be sent at **cs74writers@gullybaba.com.**

Acknowledgments :

We appreciate the staff and facility support provided by GullyBaba Publishing House. In particular, we appreciate the encouragement and professional advises received from Mr. Ajay Saini, Mr. Tarun Sharma, B. K. Krishna and many more.

Also we would like to thank typesetting and designing team Mrs. Bhawna Verma, Mr. Shravan Vats, Mr. Parveen Kumar, and Mr. Mukesh.

We gratefully acknowledges the significant contributions of Mr. Mahesh Chand, Mrs. Bimla Devi, Mrs. Bhawna Verma and our experts in bringing out this publication.

New Delhi ***Publisher***

Feedback is the breakfast of Champions.

Ken Blanchard

You can Help other students.
"Inform any error or mistake in this book."

We and Universe
will reward you for Your Kind act.

Email at : feedback@gullybaba.com
or
WhatsApp on 9350849407

Contents

Question Papers

CHAPTER 1

BASIC FOUNDATION OF OOP

Q1. Java is object-oriented. What are the advantages of object-oreinted programming compared to procedural oriented programming ? [DEC01,Q1(ii)]
 # What is Object Oriented Programming? How is it different from procedural programming?

ANS : JAVA IS OBJECT-ORIENTED :

Although influenced by its predecessors, Java was not designed to be source-code compatible with any other language. This allowed the Java team the freedom to design with a blank state. Once outcome of this was a clean, usable, pragmatic approach to objects. Borrowing liberally from many seminal object-software environment of the last few decades, Java manages to strike a balance between the purist's "everything is an object" paradigm and the pragmatist's "stay out of my way" model. The object model in Java is simple and easy to extend, while simple types, such as integers, are kept as high-performance nonobjects.

Procedural languages are the languages where each statement in the language tells the computer to do something. Get some input add these numbers, divided by 6, display that output. A program in a procedural language is a list of instructions. For very small programs no other organizing principle (often called a paradigm) is needed. The programmer creates the list of instructions, and the computer caries them out. Pascal, C, BASIC, Fortran, and similar languages are procedural languages.

🗁 DIVISION INTO FUNCTIONS :

When programs become larger, a single list of instructions becomes unwieldy. Few programmers can comprehend a program of more than a few hundred statements unless it is broken down into smaller units. For this reason the function was adopted as a way to make programs more comprehensible to their human creators. (The term function is used in C++ and C. In other languages the same concept may be referred to as a subroutine, a subprogram, or a procedure)

🗁 PROBLEMS WITH STRUCTURED PROGRAMMING

The principal idea behind structured programming was as simple as the idea of "divide and conquer." A computer program could be regarded as consisting of a set of tasks. Any task that was too complex to be simply described would be broken into a set of smaller component tasks, until the tasks were sufficiently small and self-contained to be easily understood. As programs grow ever larger and more complex, even the structured programming approach beings to show signs of strain. You may have heard about, or been involved in, horror stories of program development. The project is too complex, the schedule slips, more programmers are added, complexity increases, cost skyrocket, the schedule slips further, and finally disaster. Analyzing the reasons for these failures reveals that there are weakness in the procedural paradigm itself. No matter how well the structured programming approach is implemented, large programs become excessively complex.

What are the reason for this failure of procedural languages? One of the most crucial is the role played by data.

DATA IS UNDERVALUED

In a procedural language, the emphasis is on doing things--read the keyboard, add the values, check for error, and so on. The subdivision of a program into functions continues this emphasis. Functions do thing as single program statements do. What they do may be more complex or abstract, but the emphasis is still on the action.

WHAT HAPPENS TO THE DATA IN THIS PARADIGM?

Data is, after all, the reason for a program's existence. Data is given second-class status in the organization of procedural languages.

For example, in an inventory program, the data that makes up the inventory is probably read from a disk file into memory, where it is treated as a global variable. By global we mean that the variables that constitute the data are declared outside of any function, so they are accessible to all functions. These functions perform various operations on the data. They read it, analyze it, update it, rearrange it, display it, write it back to the disk, and so on.

We should note that most languages, such as pascal and C, also support local variables, which are hidden within a single function. But local variables are not useful for important data that must be accessed by many different functions. Figure below shows the relationship between global and local variables.

Global and Local Variables

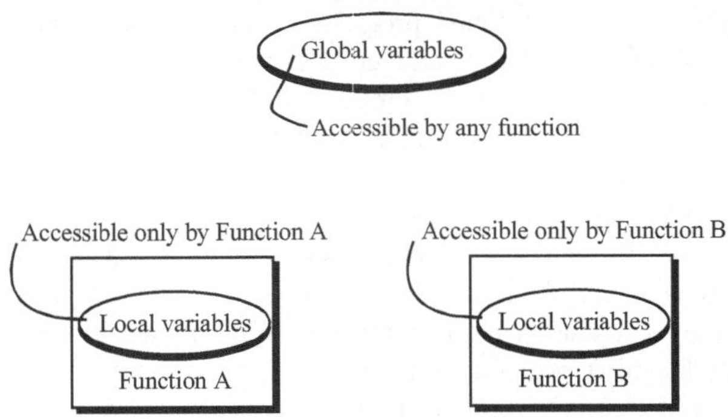

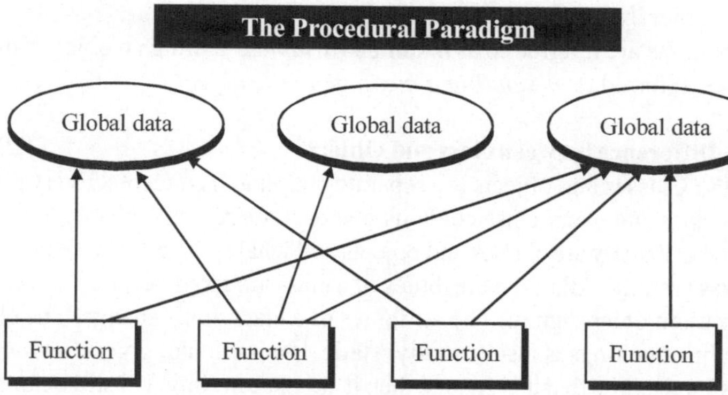

Now suppose a new programmer is hired to write a function to analyze this inventory data in a certain way. Unfamiliar with the subtitles of the program, the programmer creates a function which has complete access to the data. It's like leaving your personal papers in the lobby of your apartment building: Anyone can change or destroy them. In the same way. Global data can be corrupted by functions that have no authorization to change it. What is needed is a way to restrict access to the data, to hide it from all but a few critical functions. This will Protect the data, simplify maintenance, and offer other benefits as well.

TRADITIONAL LANGUAGES DOES NOT PROVIDE EXTENSIBILITY.

One is the difficulty of creating new data types. Computer languages typically have several built-in data types: your own data type? Perhaps you want to work with complex numbers, or two-dimensional coordinates or dates-quantities the built-in-data types don't handle easily. Being able to create your own types is called extensibility; you can extend the capabilities of the language. Traditional languages are not usually extensible. Without unnatural convolutions, you can't bundle together both X and Y coordinates into a single variable called point, and then add subtract values of this type. The result is that traditional programs are more complex to write and maintain.

The object-oriented approach : Solution to all these problems.

The fundamental idea behind object-oriented languages is to combine both data and the functions that operate on that data into a single unit called ***an object***. An object's functions, called member functions in Java typically provide the only way to access its data. If you want to read a data item in an object, you call only way to access its data. If you want to read a data item in an object, you call a member function in the object. It will read the item and return the value to you it can't access the data directly. The data is hidden, so it is safe to accidental alterations. Data and its functions are said to be encapsulated into a single entity, ***data encapsulation and data hiding*** are key terms in the description of object-oriented languages.
No other functions can access the data. This simplifies writing, debugging, and maintaining the program.

A Java program typically consist of a number of objects, which communicates with each other by calling one another's member functions.
Data items are referred to as ***instance variables***. Calling an object's member function is referred to as ***sending a message to the object***.

Q2. Difference between class and Object. [JUN03,Q3(iii)]

ANS : Classes and objects are separate but related concepts. Every object belongs to a class and every class contains one or more related objects.
So what exactly are classes and objects and what is the difference between them? A **Class** is static. All of the attributes of a class are fixed before, during, and after the execution of a program. The attributes of a class don't change. The class to which an object belongs is also (usually) static. If a particular object belongs to a certain class at the time that it is created then it almost certainly will still belong to that class right up until the time that it is destroyed.
An **Object** on the other hand has a limited lifespan. Objects are created and eventually destroyed. Also during that lifetime, the attributes of the object may undergo significant change.
So let's now use an example to clarify what the differences are between a class and an object.
Let us consider the class **car**. Cars have a body, wheels, an engine, seats, are used to transport people between locations, and require at least one person in the car for it to move by its own power. These are some of the attributes of the class - car - and all members that this class has ever or will ever have share these attributes. The members of the class - car - are objects and the objects are **individual and specific** cars. Each individual car has a creation date (an example of an object having an attribute that is static), an owner, a registered address (examples of attributes that may or may not change), a current location, current occupants, current fuel level (examples of attributes that change quickly), and it may be covered by insurance (an example of an attribute that may or may not exist).
Or A class can be thought as an architectural drawing of a building, by using that drawing we can make as many as buildings to live in. Architechtural Design is of no use until the buildings are made on the basis of this drawing. And building can differ in color, size, number of rooms, etc. Here, Architechral design is *class* and Building is an *object.*
So basically the difference between a class and an object is that a class is a general concept while objects are the specific and real instances that embody that concept. When creating an object oriented program we define the classes and the relationships between the classes. We then execute the program to create, update, and destroy the objects which are the specific realization of these classes.

Q3. What are the Characteristics of object-oriented languages ?

ANS : Let's briefly examine a few of the major elements of object-oriented languages in general and Java in particular.

OBJECTS

When you approach a programming problem in an object-oriented language you no longer ask how the problem will be divided into functions, but how it will be divided into object. Thinking in term of object, rather than functions has a suprisingly helpful effect on how easily programs can be designed. This results from the close match between objects in the programming sense and objects in the real world. What kinds of things become objects in object-oriented programs? The answer to this is limited only by your imagination, but here are typical categories to start you thinking:

PHYSICAL OBJECTS

Automobiles in a traffic-flow simulation
Electrical components in a circuit-design program
Countries in an economics model
Aircraft in an-traffic-control system

ELEMENTS OF THE COMPUTER-USER ENVIRONMENT

Windows
Menus
Graphics object (lines, rectangles, circles)
The mouse and the keyboard

PROGRAMMING CONSTRUCTS

Customized arrays
Stacks
Linked lists
Binary trees

COLLECTIONS OF DATA

An inventory
A personnel file
A dictionary
A table of the latitudes and longitudes of world cities

USER-DEFINED DATA TYPES

Time Angles
Complex numbers
Points on the plane
Components in computer games
Positions in a board game (chess, checkers)
Animals in an ecological simulation

The match between programming objects and real-world object is the happy results of combining data and functions: The resulting objects offer a revolution in program design. No such close match between programing constructs and the items being modeled exists in a procedural language.

Q4. DEFINE CLASS VARIABLE. **[DEC03,Q2(IV)]**

ANS : In OOP we say that objects are members of classes. What does this mean? Let's look at an analogy. Almost all computer languages have built-in data types. For instance a data type int. Meaning integer, is predefined in Java. You can declare as many variables of types int as you need in your program:

int day;
int count;
int divisor;
int answer;

In a similar way you can make as many as objects of the same class, as shown in figure below. A class serves as a plan, or template. It specifies what data and what functions

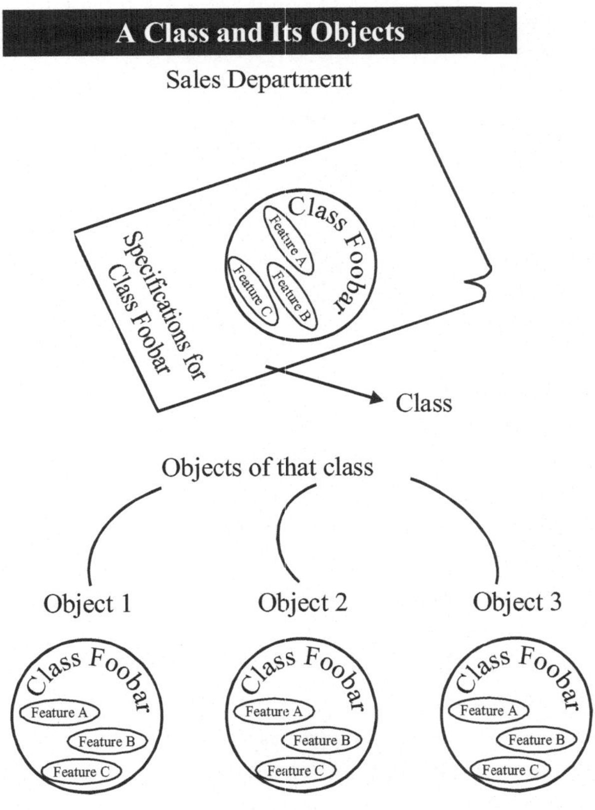

will be included in object of that class. Defining the class doesn't create any abject, just as the mere existence of a type int doesn't create any variables.

A class is thus a collection of similar objects. This fits our nontechnical understanding of the class of rock musicians. There is no one person called "rock musician" but specific people with specific names are members of this class if they posses certain characteristics.

Q5. Define Data Encapsulation. **[DEC02, Q3(i)]**

ANS : The fundamental idea behind object-oriented languages is to combine both data and the functions that operate on that data into a single unit called ***an object***. An object's functions, called member functions in Java typically provide the only way to access its data. If you want to read a data item in an object, you call only way to access its data. If you want to read a data item in an object, you call a member function in the object. It will read the item and return the value to you it can't access the data directly. The data is hidden, so it is safe to accidental alterations. Data and its functions are said to be encapsulated into a single entity, ***data encapsulation and data hiding*** are key terms in the description of object-oriented languages.
No other functions can access the data. This simplifies writing, debugging, and maintaining the program.
A class can be thought as an architectural drawing of a building, by using that drawing we can make as many as buildings to live in. Architechtural Design is of no use until the buildings are made on the basis of this drawing. And building can differ in color, size, number of rooms, etc. Here, Architechral design is *class* and Building is an *object*.

Q6. Write short note on instance variable and sending message to the object.

ANS : A Java program typically consist of a number of objects, which communicates with each other by calling one another's member functions.
Data items are referred to as ***instance variables***. Calling an object's member function is referred to as ***sending a message to the object***. Refer the following diagram to understand the concept of data encapsulation.

The Object-oriented Paradigm

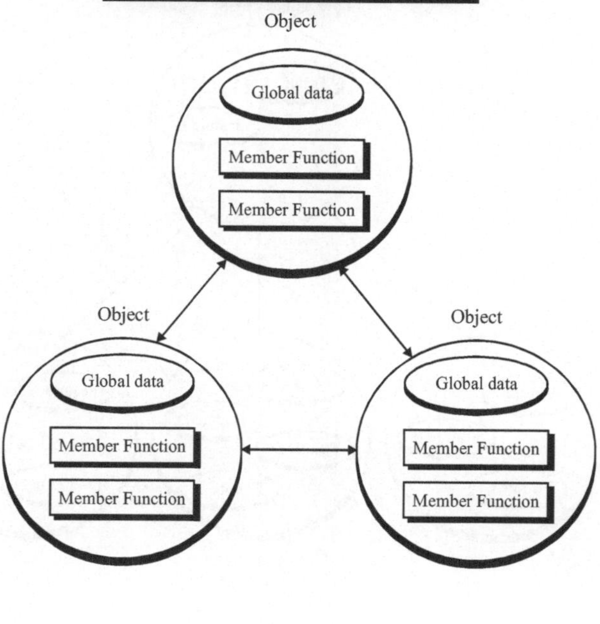

INHERITANCE

Q7. What is inheritance ? Explain diagrammatically.

ANS : The idea of classes leads to the idea of inheritance. In our daily lives, we use the concept of classes being divided into subclasses. We know that the class of animals is divided into mammals, amphibians, insects, bird, and so on. The class of vehicles is divided into cars, truck, buses, and motorcycles.

The principle in this sort of division is that each subclass shares common characteristics with the class from which it's derived. Cars, truck, buses, and motorcycles all have wheels and a motor; these are the defining characteristics of vehicles. In addition to the characteristics: buses, for instance, have seats for many people, while trucks have space for hauling loads.

This ideas shown in the next figure notice in the figure that features of A and B, which are part of the base class, are common to all derived classes, but that each deriver class also has features of its own.

In a similar way, an OOP class can be divided into subclass. In Java the original class is called the **base class**: other classes can be defined that share characteristics, but add their own as well. These are called **derived classes**.

Don't confuse the relation of objects to classes, on the one hand with the relation of a base class to deriver classes, on the other. Objects, which exit in the computers memory, embody the exact characteristics from their base class, but add new ones of their own.

Inheritance is somewhat analogous to using functions to simplify a traditional procedural program. If we find that three different sections of a procedural program do almost exactly the same thing, we recognize an opportunity to extract the common elements of these three sections and put them into a single function . As functions do in a procedural program, inheritance shortens an object-oriented program and clarifies the relationship among program elements.

Inheritance

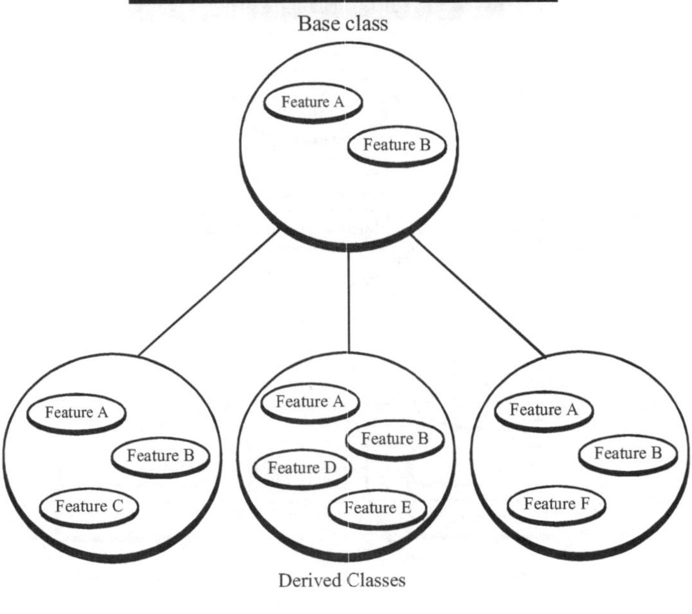

REUSABILITY

Q8. Explain the concept of reusability.

ANS : Once a class has been written, created, and debugged, it can be distributed to other programmers for use in their own programs. This is called reusability. It is similar to the way a library of functions in a procedural language can be incorporate into different programs.

In OOP the concept of inheritance provides an important extension to the idea of reusability. A programmer can take an existing class, and,without modifying it. This is done by deriving a new class from the existing one. The new class will inherit the capabilities of the old one but is free to add new features of its own.

For example, you might have written (or purchased from someone else) a class that creates a menu system, such as that used in the Java's Integrated Development Environment (IDE). This class works fine, and you don't want to change it but you want to add the capability to make some menu entries flash on and off to do this you simply create a new class that inherits all the capability of the existing one but adds flashing menu entries.

ABSTRACTION

Q9. Define the term abstraction. **[DEC03,Q2(ii)]**

ANS : The most important term is '***Abstraction***'. Abstraction means ignoring those aspects of a subject that are not revealed to the current purpose in order to concentrate more fully on those that are relevant. To an analyst who is as good as a subject expert it means choosing certain things or aspects of the system over others at a time. Most of the things in the real world are intrinsically complex, far more complex than one can comprehend at a time. By using abstraction one selects only a part of the whole complex instead of working with the whole thing. It does not mean ignoring the details altogether but only temporarily, the details are embedded inside and are dealt with at a later stage. Abstraction is used by OOP as a primary method of managing complexity.

Association is the principle by which ideas are connected together or united. Association is used to tie together certain things that happen at some point in time or under similar conditions.

Communicating with messages is the principle for managing complexity, which is used when interfaces are involved to communicate between the entities. OOP uses classes and objects have attributes, which can be exclusively accessed by services of the objects. To change the attributes of the object (a data member of the object), a message has to be sent to the object to invoke the service. This mechanism helps in implementing encapsulation and **data abstraction**.

CREATING NEW DATA TYPES

Q10. Discuss new data types in java.

ANS : One of the benefits of objects is that give the programmer a convenient way to construct new data types. Suppose you work with two-dimensional positions (such as X and Y coordinates, or latitude and longitude) in your program. You would like to express operations on these positional values with normal arithmetic operations, such as

Position1 = position2 + origin;

Where the variables position1, position2 and origin each represent a pair of independent numerical quantities. By creating a class that incorporates these two values, and declaring position1, position2 and origin to be objects of this class, we can, in effect, create a new data type. Many features of Java are intended to facilitate the creation of new data types in this manner.

Q11. Define Operator Overloading. [JUN02,Q3(c)]

ANS : POLYMORPHISM & OVERLOADING : Note that the = (equal) and + (plus) operators, used in the position arithmetic don't act the same way they do in operations on built-in types like int. The object position1(in previous question) and so on are not predefined in Java, but are programmer-defined objects of class position. How do the = and + operations know how to operate on objects ? The answer is that we can define new operations for these operators. These operators will be member functions of the position class.

Using operators or functions in different ways, depending on what they are operating on , is called **polymorphism**. One thing with several distinct forms. When an existing operator, such as + or = is given the capability to operate on a new data type, it is said to be overloaded. **Overloading** is a kind of polymorphism; it is also an important feature of OOP.

CHAPTER 2

INTRODUCTION TO JAVA

- JAVA
  - OBJECT ORIENTED LANGUAGE
  - JAVA APPLET & APPLICATION ()
  - SECURITY
  - PORTABILITY
  - SIMPLE
  - OBJECT ORIENTED
  - ROBUST
  - ARCHITECTURE NEUTRAL
  - MULTITHREADED
  - DISTRIBUTED
  - DYNAMIC
- ABTRACTION
- ENCAPSULATION
- INHERITANCE
- POLYMORPHISM
- HELLOWORD
- ATOMIC ELEMENTS OF JAVA
  - WHITESPACE
  - IDENTIFIERS
  - LITERALS
  - COMMENTS
  - SEPARATORS
  - JAVA KEYWORDS

The Creation of Java

Java was conceived by James Glosing, Patrick Naughton, Chris Warth, EdFrank, and Mike Sheridan at Sun Microsystems, Inc. in 1991. It took 18 months to develop the first working version. This language was finally called "Oak" but was renamed "Java" in 1995.

Java derives much of its character form C and C++. This is by intent. The Java designgers knew that using the familiar syntax of C and echoing the object-oriented features of C++ would make their language appealing to the community of experienced C/C++ programmers.

The environment change there was the need for platform-independent programs destined for distribution on the Internet. Then Java fulfilled this need. However, Java also embodies changes in the way that people approach the writing of program. *"Java is to Internet programming what C was to systems programming: a revolutionary force that will change the world."*

Q1. What is the difference between an Applet and an Application ?
[JUN03,Q1(v) ; DEC03,Q3(i) ; JUN02,Q2(i) ; JUN01,Q5(a)]

ANS : Java can be used to create two types of programs: applications and applets. An *application* is a program that runs on your computer, under the operating system of that computer. When used to create applications, Java is not much different from any other computer language. Rather, it is Java's ability to create applets that makes it important. An *applet* is an application designed to be transmitted over the Internet and executed by a Java-compatible Web browser. An applet is actually a tiny Java program, dynamically downloaded across the network, just like an image, sound file, or video clip. The important difference is that an applet is an *intelligent program*, not just an animation or media file. In other words, an applet is a program that can react to user input and dynamically change-not just run the same animation or sound over and over.

As exciting as applets are, they would be nothing more than wishful thinking if Java were not able to address the two fundamental problems associated with them: security and portability. Let us define difference between them.

Java Application	Java Applet
1. GUI (Graphical User Interface)	
Optional	Inherently graphical
2. Memory Requirements	
Minimal Java Application requirements	Java Application requirements plus web browser requirements
3. Distribution	
Loaded from the file system or by a custom class loading process.	Linked via HTML and transported via HTTP.
4. Environmental Input	
Command-Line Parameters	Browser client location and size; parameters embedded in the host HTML document.
5. Method Expected by Virtual Machine	
"main( )"- startup method.	int( ) - initialize method. start( ) - startup method stop( ) - pause/deactivate method destroy( ) - termination method paint( ) - drawing method.
6. Typical Applications	
Network server; multimedia kiosks,	public-access order-entry system for the developer tools; appliance and

consumer web; online multimedia presentations; electronics control. web based animations and navigations.

Q2. Difference between Interpreter and Compiler. [JUN03,Q3(ii)]

ANS : A *compiler* is a program that translates a source program written in some high-level programming language (such as Java) into machine code for some computer architecture (such as the Intel Pentium architecture). The generated machine code can be later executed many times against different data each time.

An *interpreter* reads an executable source program written in a high-level programming language as well as data for this program, and it runs the program against the data to produce some results. One example is the Unix shell interpreter, which runs operating system commands interactively.

Note that both interpreters and compilers (like any other program) are written in some high-level programming language (which may be different from the language they accept) and they are translated into machine code. For example, a Java interpreter can be completely written in Pascal, or even Java. The interpreter source program is machine independent since it does not generate machine code. (Note the difference between *generate* and *translated into* machine code.) An interpreter is generally slower than a compiler because it processes and interprets each statement in a program as many times as the number of the evaluations of this statement. For example, when a for-loop is interpreted, the statements inside the for-loop body will be analyzed and evaluated on every loop step. Some languages, such as Java and LISP, come with both an interpreter and a compiler. Java source programs (Java classes with `.java` extension) are translated by the `javac` compiler into byte-code files (with `.class` extension). The Java interpreter, `java`, called the Java Virtual Machine (JVM), may actually interpret byte codes directly or may internally compile them to macine code and then execute that code.

Typically, when used in that generic manner, the term *Java* ***compiler*** refers to a program which translates Java language source code into the Java Virtual Machine (JVM) *bytecodes*. The term Java ***interpreter*** refers to a program which implements the JVM specification and actually executes the bytecodes (and thereby running your program).

Q3. What is Java Virtual Machine(JVM) ? Explain it.

[JUN02,Q1(b) ; JUN03,Q1(ii)]

ANS : The core of Java technology, the Java Virtual Machine(JVM) is an abstract computing machine that enables the Java platform to host applications on any computer or operating system without rewriting or recompiling. Anyone interested in designing a language or writing a compiler for the Java Virtual Machine must have an in-depth understanding of its binary class format and instruction set. If you are programming with the Java programming language, knowledge of the Java virtual machine will give you valuable insight into the Java platform's security capabilities and cross-platform portability. It will increase your understanding of the Java programming language, enabling you to improve the security and performance of your programs.

Q4. How Java Works ?

 # What is bytecode in Java ? **[JUNE04,Q1(a)]**

ANS : As with many other programming languages, Java uses a compiler to convert human-readable source code (.java) files into executable code (.class) files. Traditional compilers produce code that can be executed by specific hardware; for example, and Windows 98, C++ compiler creates executable program that works with Intel x^{86} compatible processors. In contrast the Java compiler (javac.exe) generates architecture - independent "bytecodes".

This bytecode can be executed by only a Java Virtual Machine (JVM), which is an idealized Java processor chip usually implemented in software rather than hardware.

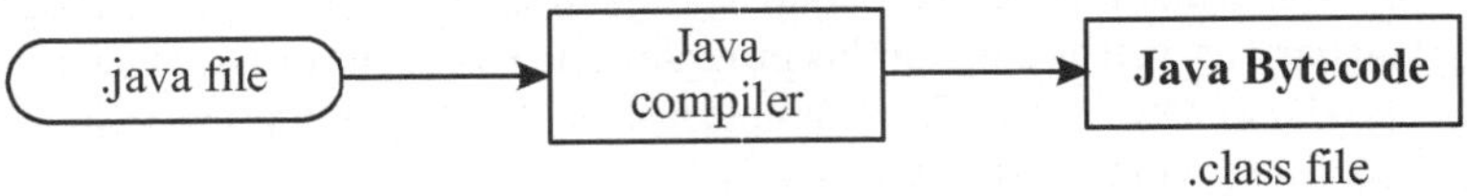

A Java source code file that can contain more than one class, on compilation will produce different ".class" file for each class in the source code.

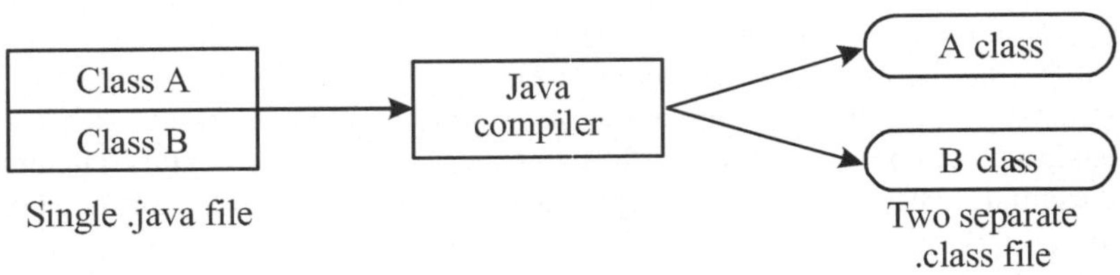

Remember, although the details of the JVM will differ from platform to platform, all interpret the same Java bytecode.

The execution unit of the VM carries out the instructions specified in the bytecodes. The simplex execution unit is an "interpreter", which is a program that reads the bytecodes, interprets their meaning, and then performs the associated function.

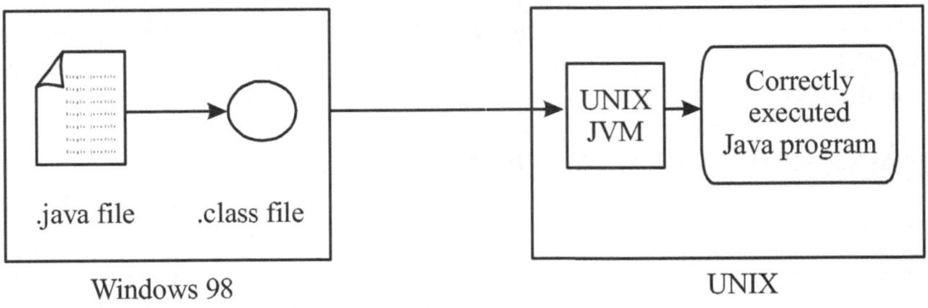

Q5. Describe main features of Java Programming Language. **[JUNE01,Q1(iii)]**

ANS : Although the fundamental forces that necessitated the invention of Java are portability and security, other factors also played an important role in molding the final form of the language.

- Simple

- Secure [DEC02,Q3(v) ; JUN03, Q2(f) ; JUN02,Q3(b)]
- Portable
- Object-oriented [JUNE03,Q2(c)]
- Robust [DEC02,Q1(e) ; DEC01,Q3(iv)]
- Multithreaded [JUNE02,Q3(a) ; JUNE03,Q2(a)]
- Architecture-natural
- Intepreted [DEC01,Q3(v)]
- High performance
- Distributed [DEC01,Q3(iii) ; JUNE03,Q2(b)]
- Dynamic

Simple

Because Java inherits the C/C++ syntax and many of the object-oriented features of C++, most programmers have little trouble learning Java. Also, some of the more confusing concepts from C++ are either left out of Java or implemented in a cleaner, more approachable manner.

Beyond its similarities with C/C++, Java has another attribute that makes it easy to learn: It makes an effort not to have *surprising* features. In Java, there are a small number of clearly defined ways to accomplish a given task.

Secure

As you are likely aware, every time that you download a "normal" program, you are risking a viral infection. Prior to Java, most users did not download executable programs frequently, and those who did scanned them for viruses prior to execution. Even so, most users still worried about the possibility of infecting their systems with a virus. In addition to viruses, another type of malicious program exists that must be guarded against. This type of program can gather private information, such as credit card numbers, bank account balances, and passwords, by searching the contents of your computer's local file system.

When you use a Java-compatible Web browser, you can safety download Java applets without fear of viral infection or malicious intent. Java achieves this protection by confining a Java program to the Java execution environment and not allowing it access to other parts of the computer. The ability to download applets with confidence that no harm will be done and that no security will be breached is considered by many to be the single most important aspect of Java.

Portable

There are many types of computers and operating systems are in use throughout the world-and many are connected to the Internet. For programs to be dynamically downloaded to all the various types of platforms connected to the Internet, some means of generating portable executable code is needed.

Translating a Java program into bytecode (Binary coded classes) help makes it much easier to run a program in a wide variety of environment. The reason is straightforward: only the JVM needs to be implemented for each platform. Once the run-time package exists for a given system, any Java program can run on it. Remember, although the details of the JVM will differ from platform to platform, all interpret the same Java bytecode. If a Java program were compiled to native code, then different versions of the same program would have to exist for each type of

CPU connected to the Internet. This is, of course, not a feasible solution. Thus, the interpretation of bytecode is the easiest way to create truly portable programs.

Object-oriented

Although influenced by its predecessors, Java was not designed to be source-code compatible with any other language. This allowed the Java team the freedom to design with a blank state. Once outcome of this was a clean, usable, pragmatic approach to objects. Borrowing liberally from many seminal object-software environment of the last few decades, Java manages to strike a balance between the purist's "everything is an object" paradigm and the pragmatist's "stay out of my way" model. The object model in Java is simple and easy to extend, while simple types, such as integers, are kept as high-performance nonobjects.

Robust

The multiplatformed environment of the Web places extraordinary demands on a program, because the program must execute reliably in a variety of systems. Thus, the ability to create robust programs was given a high priority in the design of Java. Because Java is a strictly typed language, it checks your code at compile time.

To understand how Java is robust, consider two of the main reasons for program failure: memory management mistakes and mishandled exceptional conditions (that is, run-time errors). Memory management can be a difficult, tedious task in traditional programming environments. For example, in C/C++, the programmer must manually allocate and free all dynamic memory. This sometimes leads to problems, because programmer will either forget to free memory that has been previously allocated or, worse, try to free some memory that another part of their code is still using. Java virtually eliminates these problems by managing memory allocation and deallocation for you. (In fact, deallocation is completely automatic, because Java provides garbage collection for unused objects.) Exceptional conditions in traditional environment often arise in situation such a division by zero or "file not found," and they must be managed with clumsy and hard-to-read constructs. Java helps in this area by providing object-oriented exception handling. In a well-written Java program, all run-time errors can-and should-be managed by your program.

Multithreaded

Java was designed to meet the real-world requirement of creating interactive, networked programs. To accomplish this, Java supports multithreaded programming, which allows you to write programs that do many things simultaneously. The Java run-time system comes with an elegant yet sophisticated solution for multiprocess synchronization that enables you to construct smoothly running interactive systems. Java's easy-to-use approach to multithreading allows you to think about the specific behavior of your program, not the multitasking subsystem

Architecture-netural

A central issue for the Java designers was that of code longevity and portability. One of the main problems faced by programmers is that no guarantee exists that if you write a program today, it will run tomorrow-even on the same machine. Operating system upgrades, processor upgrades, and changes in core system resources can all combine to make a program malfunction. The Java designers made several hard decisions in the Java language and the Java Virtual Machine in an attempt to alter this situation. Their goal was "write once; run anywhere, any time, forever." To a great extent, this goal was accomplished.

Interpreted

As described earlier, Java enables the creation of cross-platform programs by compiling into an intermediate representation called Java bytecode. This code can be interpreted on any system that provides a Java Virtual Machine.

High performance

Java was designed to perform well on very low-power CPUs. The Java bytecode was carefully designed so that it would be easy to translate directly into native machine code. It is of very high performance by using a just-in-time compiler. Java run-time systems that provide this feature lose none of the benefits of the platform-independent code.

Distributed

Java is designed for the distributed environment of the Internet, because it handles TCP/IP protocols. In fact, accessing a resource using a URL is not much different from accessing a file. The original version of Java (Oak) included features for intra-address-spaces messaging. This allowed objects on two different computers to execute procedure remotely. Java has recently revived these interfaces in a package called *Remote Method Invocation* (*RMI*). This feature brings an unparalleled level of abstraction to client/server programming.

Dynamic

Java programs carry with them substantial amounts of run-time types information that is used to verify and resolve accesses to objects at run time. This makes it possible to dynamically link code in a safe and expedient manner. This is crucial to the robustness of the applet environment, in which small fragments of bytecode may be dynamically updated on a running system.

Q6. What is the relationship between Java and HTML ? [DEC02,Q1(ii)(a)]

ANS : HTML(Hypertext Markup Language) is, in essence, a means of defining the logical organization of information and providing links, called hypertext links, to related information. Although HTML allows a user to read documents in a dynamic manner, HTML is markup language, and never has been, a programming language. As to be a programming language the language must have support for "conditional", "looping" and "branching" statements which all are not supported by HTML. The only connection that HTML has to Java is that it provides the applet tag, which executes a Java applet. Thus, it is possible to embed instructions in a hypertext document that cause a Java applet to execute.

Q7. Write a simple program in Java. Explain all the keywords used.

"Hi Students, Welcome to GullyBaba" Program

ANS :
```
/* This is a simple Java Program*/
class HiStudents
{
    public static void main(String args[ ])
```

```
    {
      System.out.printin("Hi Students, Welcome to GullyBaba");
    }
}
```

Save this text file as "hi.java" in JDK's |bin| folder.
Go to Command prompt and follow these steps.

1. Compile Java file.

bin > javac hi.java

2. Run your Class file.

bin > java hi

All Java applications begin execution by calling main( ). (This is just like C/C++). The public keyword is an access specifier, which allows the programmer to control the visibility of class members. When a class member is preceded by public, then that member may be accessed by code outside the class in which it is declared. (The opposite of public is private, which prevents a member from being used by code defined outside of its class). In this case, main( ) must be declared as public, since it must be called by code outside of its class when the program is started. The keyword static allows main( ) to be called without having to instantiate a particular instance of the class. This is necessary since main( ) is called by the Java interpreter before any object is made. The keyword void simply tells the compiler that main( ) does not return a value. As you will see, methods may also return values.
In main( ), there is only one parameter, albeit a complicated one. String args[ ] declares a parameter named args, which is an array of instances of the class String. (Array are collections of similar objects.) Objects of type String store character strings. In this case, args receives any command-line arguments present when the program is executed.

Q8. Discuss all Atomic Elements used in JAVA.

ANS : Java programs are a collection of whitespace, identifiers, comments, literals, separators and keywords.

Whitespace → Java is a free-form language. This means that you do not need to follow any special indentation rules. For example, the Example program could have been written all on one line or in any other strange way you felt like typing it, as long as there was at least one whitespace character between each token that was not already delineated by an operator or separator. In Java, whitespace is a space, tab or newline.

Identifiers →

(a) Identifiers are used for class names, method names and variable names.

(b) An identifier may be any descriptive sequence of uppercase and lowercase letters, numbers, or the underscore and dollar-sign characters.

(c) They must not begin with a number, lest they be confused with a numeric literal.

(d) Java is case-sensitive, so VALUE is a different identifier than Value.

Some examples of valid identifiers are:

AvgTemp count a4 $test
this_is_ok

Invalid variable names include:

2count high-temp Not/ok

Literals → A literal is an actual value such a 35 or "Hello". A constant value in Java is created by using a literal representation of it. For example, here are some literals:

100 98.6 'X' "This is a test"

Left to right, the first literal specifies an integer, the next is a floating-point value, the third is a character constant, and the last is a string. A literal can be used anywhere a value of its type is allowed.

Comment → There are three types of comments defined by Java. You have already seen two: single-line and multiline. The third type is called a documentation comment. This type of comment is used to produce an HTML file that documents your program. The documentation comment begins with a /** and ends with a */.

Separators → In Java, there are a few characters that are used as separators. The most commonly used separator in Java is the semicolon. As you have seen, it is used to terminate statements. The separators are shown in the following table.

Symbol	Name	Purpose
()	Parentheses	Used to contain lists of parameters in method definition and invocation. Also used for defining precedence in expressions, in control statements, and surrounding cast types.
{}	Braces	Used to contain the values of automatically initialized arrays. Also used to define a block of code, for classes, methods, and local scopes.
[]	Brackets	Used to declare array types. Also used when dereferencing array values.
;	Semicolon	Terminates statements.
,	Comma	Separates consecutive identifiers in a variable declaration. Also used the chain statements together inside a for statement.
.	Period	Used to separate package names from subpackages and classes. Also used from subpackages and classes. Also used to separate a variable or method from a reference variable.

The Java Keywords

There are 48 reserved keywords currently defined in the Java languages (see following table). These keywords, combined with the syntax of the operators and separators, form the definition of the Java language. These keywords cannot be used as names for a variable, class, or method.

abstract	const	finally	int	public	this
boolean	continue	float	interface	return	throw
break	default	for	long	short	throws
byte	do	goto	native	static	tansient
case	double	if	new	strictfp	try
catch	else	implements	package	super	void
char	extends	import	private	switch	volatile
class	final	instanceof	protected	synchronized	while

Table : Java Reserved Keywords

The keywords const and goto are reserved but not used. In the early days of Java, several other keywords were reserved for possible future use. However, the current specification for Java only defines the keywords shown in table.

In addition to the keywords, Java reserves the following: true, false, and null. These are values defined by Java. You may not use these words for the names of variables, classes and so on.

CHAPTER 3

DATA TYPES

- SIMPLE DATA TYPES
  - INTEGER
  - BYTE
  - SHORT
  - INT
  - LONG
  - FLOATING POINT
  - FLOAT
  - DOUBLE
  - CHARACTERS
  - BOOLEAN
  - SIMPLE
  - OBJECT
- OTHERS DATA TYPES
  - STRING
  - STRING BUFFER
  - ARRAYS
- OPERATORS
  - RELATIONAL & EQUALITY OPERATORS
  - ASSIGNMENT OPERATORS
  - ARITHMATIC
  - BITWISE
  - INCREMENT & DECREMENT (UNARY OPERATORS)
  - LOGICAL
- JAVA VARIABLE DECLARATION RULES
- ARRAYS
  - ONE DIMENSIONAL
  - MULTI DIMENSIONAL

Q1. List all primitive data types, size and range of values they accept.

[JUNE03,Q1(v)]

 # List all primitive data types with their sizes as defined in Java. [DEC03,Q1(iii)]

ANS : Java defines eight simple (or elemental) types of data: byte, short, int, long, char, float, double and boolean. these can be put in four groups :

✓ ***Integers :*** This group includes byte, short, int and long, which are for whole-valued signed number.

✓ ***Floating-point numbers :*** This group includes float and double, which represent numbers with fractional precision.

✓ ***Characters :*** This group includes char, which represents symbols in a character set, like letters and numbers.

✓ ***Boolean :*** This group includes boolean, which is a special type for representing true/false values.

Integers : Java defines four integer types: byte, short, int and long. All of these are signed, positive and negative values. The width and ranges of these integer types vary widely, as shown in this table:

Name	Width	Range
long	64	-9,223,372,036,854,775,808 to 9,223,372,036,854,775,807
int	32	-2,147,483,648 to 2,147,483,647
short	16	-32,768 to 32,767
byte	8	-128 to 127

Floating-Point Types : Floating-point numbers, also known as real numbers, are used when evaluating expressions that require fractional precision.

Name	Width in Bits	Range
double	64	1.7e-308 to 1.7e+308
float	32	3.4e-038 to 3.4e+038

Q2. Discuss characters in Java.

#. What is the difference between ASCII code and Unicode ? [JUNE03,Q3(v)]

ANS : For character data, each character is assigned a unique code. We can have a character set of 26 capital letters, 10 digits, 0 through 9, and a few punctuation marks such as space, period, minus sign, comma and carriage return. More sophisticated character sets include capital letters and small letters, the 10 digits, a wide set of punctuation characters, a collection of special characters useful in mathematics and even greek letters. Once such widely used code is ASCII (American Starndard Code for Information Interchange). Most of the present day computers use this code for storing data in memory. The ASCII character set cosists of 128 characters and 7 bits are used to code each character. e.g. a=1100001 (141 octal). Now even more sophisticated character representation supported by Unicode. Java uses Unicode to represent characters. Unicode define a fully international character set that can represent all of the characters found in all human languages. It is a unification of dozens of character sets, such as Latin, Greeek, Arbic, Cyrillic,

Hebrew, Katakana, Hangul and many more. For this purpose, it requires 16 bits. Thus, in Java char is a 16-bit type. The range of a char is 0 to 65,536. There are no negative chras. The standard set of chracters known as ASCII still ranges from 0 to 255.

Booleans

Q3. What is Boolean?

ANS : Java has a simple type, called boolean, for logical values. It can have only one of two possible values, true or false. This is the type returned by all relational operators, such as a < b. Boolean is also the type required by the conditional expressions that govern the control statements such as if and for.

Q4. List some Derived Data Types.

Q#. Discuss the difference between String and StringBuffer class as defined in Java. **[DEC03,Q6(b)]**

ANS : String & String Buffer : A string is a sequence of character. The ***String*** datatype is actually a class of the core API (java.lang.string), rather than a built-in type, but it is used so frequently that it is appropriate to cover here. Java compiler recognizes characters within double quotation marks as "String" literals. String can contain as many characters as one wish, there is no maximum string length restriction. Strings are immutable in Java; that is, you cannot change the contents of a string, although you can redefine a ***String*** object variable.

For instance, as the string variable *message* is initially defined as

string message = "Hello Java";

There is no way to change the contents of the object pointed to by *message* by, say, passing it to another method: change(S);

//Impossible to change object pointed to by S

However, we can make the string variable *message* refer to a new string object;

message = message + "Language";

Some useful methods provided by "String" class

Method	Description
boolean equals (String S)	Text two strings for equality
int Length( )	Obtain the length of the String
char charAt (int index)	Obtain the character at a specified index within a String

Examples:

```
//Demostrating some string class methods
Class StringDemo
{
```

```
    public static void main (String args[ ])
    {
      String S1 = "First";
      String S2 = "Second";
      String S3 = S1;
    System.out.println("Length of S1: " + S1.Length( ));
    System.out.println("char at index 2 in S2: " + S2.charAt(3));
    System.out.print("Is S1 same as S2 : " + S1.equals(S2));
    System.out.print("Is S1 equals to S3 : " + S1.equals(S3));
    }
}
```

StringBuffer is a peer class of String that provides much of the functionality of strings. String represents fixed-length, immutable character sequences. In contrast, StringBuffer may have characters and substrings inserted in the middle or appended to the end. StringBuffer will automatically grow to make room for such additions and often has more characters preallocated than are actually needed, to allow room for growth.

StringBuffer defines the below three constructors :

StringBuffer()
StringBuffer(int size)
StringBuffer(String str)

Methods in this class :

length()
capacity()
setLength()
insert()
reverse()
replace() etc.

Q5. Discuss various operators available in Java.

ANS : Arthmetic Operators

Java's arithmetic operators are summarized in following table. These operators accept integer or floating-point operands and produce integer or floating-point results. The auto-increment and auto-decrement operators are included as arithmetic operators.

Arithmetic Operators

Operator	Purpose
++, –	Auto-increment, auto-decrement
+, -	Unary plus, unary minus
*	Multiplication
/	Division
%	Remainder (modulo division)
+, -	Addition, subtraction

The remainder operator (%) returns the remainder of dividing the first operand by the second, so 24 % 10 is the remainder left over after dividing 24 by 10, namely 4. This operator also works with floating-pont operands.

Relational Operators

Relational Operators compare two quanitites to determine if they are equal or if one is greater than the other. Java has kept C's question/colon, or conditional, operator that takes three operands (it is ternary operator). The first operand is boolean, and the two other operands may be of any type. If the boolean operand is true, the result is the second operand; if it is false, the result is the third operand:

```
boolean b;
int c;
b = true;
c = (b ? 1 : 2); //1 will be assigned to c because b is true
b = false;
c = (b ? 1 : 2);  //2 will be assigned to c because b is false.
```

These comparison operators are usually used in conjuction with conditional statements. The relational operators are summarized in following table.

Relational Operators

Operator	Purpose
>, <, >=, <=	Tests relative magnitude
==	Tests equality
!=	Tests inequality
?:	Conditional-returns one of two operands based on a third

Boolean Operators or Logical Operators

Boolean operators act on boolean operands and return a boolean result. They implement the standard boolean algebraic operations:

AND, OR, NOT and XOR (eXclusive OR).

Boolean operators are shown in following table:

Boolean Operators

<table>
<tr><th>Operator</th><th>Purpose</th></tr>
<tr><td>!</td><td>NOT</td></tr>
<tr><td>&</td><td>Boolean AND</td></tr>
<tr><td>^</td><td>XOR</td></tr>
<tr><td>|</td><td>boolean OR</td></tr>
<tr><td>&&</td><td>Conditional AND</td></tr>
<tr><td>||</td><td>Conditional OR</td></tr>
</table>

Bitwise Operators

The integral types (byte, short, int, and long) are represented in the computer's memory as a sequence of bits (binary digits). Just like decimal numbers, binary numbers have their most significant digits to the left. In decimal, the most significant digit in the number 325 is the 3 because it represents 300, and the least significant digit is the 5. Written as a binary number, 325 is 101000101. The leftmost digit represents 100000000 binary (256 decimal) and is the most significant digit. Java's integers are signed numbers, so Java must use the leftmost bit of storage to represent the sign of the integer. For Java's integer datatypes, the high bit is used to represent the sign of the number, as shown in the next figure.

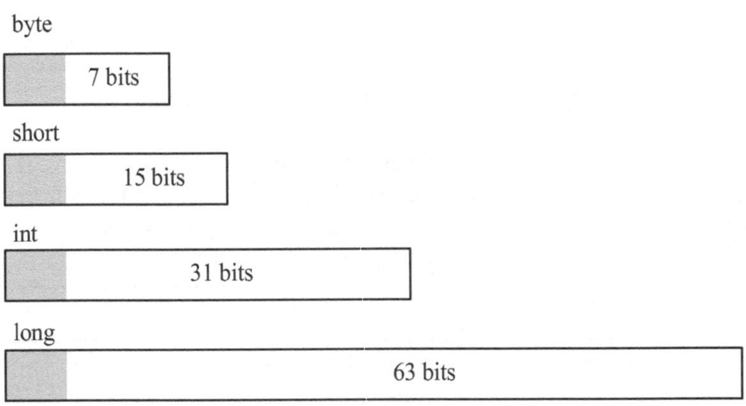

Figure : Java's integral datatypes use the high bit to indicate the sign of the number. If high bit is 1, the number is negative.

Java uses the same operators as the C language to manipulate the bits of integers. Because all of Java's integral datatypes are signed, Java supplements the C operators with an additional operator. Bit-manipulation operators are referred to as bitwise operators. The bitwise operators perform the same sort of functions as the boolean operators, as well as bit shifts.

The bitwise AND operator applies the AND operator to the corresponding bits of each operand. The bitwise OR, XOR and NOT operators work in a similar fashion.

The bitwise operators are illustrated in following figure.

1	0	0	1	0	0	1	1

AND &

1	0	1	0	1	0	1	0

=

1	0	0	0	0	0	1	0

1	0	0	1	0	0	1	1

OR |

1	0	1	0	1	0	1	0

=

1	0	1	1	1	0	1	1

1	0	0	1	0	0	1	1

NOT ~

=

0	1	1	0	1	1	0	0

1	0	0	1	0	0	1	1

XOR ^

1	0	1	0	1	0	1	0

=

0	0	1	1	1	0	0	1

Figure : Boolean bitwise operators

The shift operators shift all the bits in an integral type to the left or the right, as shown in figure. The shift operators are binary operators. The second operand is an integer that determines the number of bits to shift. The standard C shift operators act slightly differently in Java. In Java, all numbers are signed, and the sign bit is preserved through all shifts. Even though this sign bit is shifted, it is also copied, so that the resulting number will have the same sign as the original. Java adds the >>> operator, which shifts all bits to the right as if the integer were unsigned.

1	0	0	1	0	0	1	1

Right shift >>>

2

=

0	0	1	0	0	1	0	0

1	0	0	1	0	0	1	1

Signed left-shift <<

2

=

1	1	0	0	1	1	0	0

1	0	0	1	0	0	1	1

Signed right-shift >>

1

=

1	1	0	0	1	0	0	1

Figure : Examples of Java's bit-shifting operators

Bitwise Operators

Operator	Purpose
~	NOT (bitwise complement)
<<, >>	Left shift, Right shift
>>>	Right shift as if unsigned
&	Bitwise AND
^	Bitwise XOR
|	Bitwise OR

Assignment Operators

The assignment operator is an operator that assigns the second operand to the first and returns the second operand as a result.

Other assignment operators serve as shorthand for combined operation and assignment. If you wanted to add 5 to a number, you could write:

```
int i;
i = i + 5;
```

You could also use the assignment operator +=:

```
int i;
i += 5;                    //this is the same as i = i + 5
```

Assignment operators exist for most of the operators already mentioned. They are summarized in following table.

Assignment Operators

Operator	Purpose
=	Assignment
*=	Assignment with operation
/=	Assignment with operation
%=	Assignment with operation
+=	Assignment with operation
-=	Assignment with operation
>>=	Assignment with operation
<<=	Assignment with operation
>>>=	Assignment with operation
|=	Assignment with operation
&=	Assignment with operation

Q6. Define Variables. How to declare varaiable ?

ANS : Variable : The variable is the base unit of storage in a Java program. A variable is defined by the combination of an identifier, a type, and an optional initializer. In addition, all variables have a scope, which defines their visibility, and a lifetime.

Declaring a Variable :

In Java, all variables must be declared before they can be used. The basic form of a variable declaration is shown here:

type identifier [= value][, identifier [= value] ...];

The type is one of Java's atomic types, or the name of a class or interface. The identifier is the name of the variable. You can initialize the variable by specifying an equal sign and a value. Keep in mind that the initialization expression must result in a value of the same (or compatible) type as that specified for the variable. To declare more than one variable of the specified type, use a comma-separated list.

Here are several examples of variable declarations of various types. Note that some include an initialization.

```
int a, b, c;              // declares three ints, a, b, and c.
int d = 3, e, f = 5;  // declares three more ints, initializing
                                    // d and f.
byte z = 22;              //initializes z.
double pi = 3.14159;      // declares an approximati on of pi.
char x = 'x' ;            // the variable x has the value 'x'.
```

The identifiers that you choose have nothing intrinsic in their names that indicates their type.

Dynamic Initialization

Java allows variables to be initialized dynamically, using any expression valid at the time the variable is declared.

For example, here is a short program that computes the length of the hypotenuse of a right triangle give the lengths of its two opposing sides:

```
// Demonstrate dynamic initialization.
class DynInit {
    public static void main(String args []) {
      double a = 3.0, b = 4.0;
      // c is dynamically initialized
      double c = Math.sqrt(a * a + b * b);
      System.out.print1n("Hypotenuse is " + c);
      }
}
```

Here, three local variables-a, b, and c are declared. The first two, a and b, are initialized by constants. However, c is initialized dynamically to the length of the hypotenuse (using the Pythagorous theorem). The program uses another of Java's built-in methods, sqrt(), which is a member of the Math class, to compute the square root of its argument. The key point here is that the initialization expression may use any element valid at the time of the initialization calls to methods, other variables, or literals.

Q7. Discuss in detail "type casting".

 # What is typecasting ? Give two examples of typecasting in Java.

[JUNE04,Q4(b)]

ANS : Type Casting Rules :

When one type of data is assigned to another type of variable, an automatic type conversion will take place if the following two conditions are met:

· The two types are compatible.

· The destination type is larger than the source type.

When these two conditions are met, a widening conversion takes place. For example, the int type is always large enough to hold all valid byte values, so an explicit cast statement is required.

For widening conversions, the numeric types, including integer and floating-point types, are compatible with each other. However, the numeric types are not compatible with char or boolean. Also, char and boolean are not compatible with each other.

As mentioned earlier, Java also performs an automatic type conversion when storing a literal integer constant into variables of byte, short, or long.

Casting Incompatible Types :

Although the automatic type conversions are helpful, they will not fulfill all needs. For example, what if you want to assign an int value to a byte variable? This conversion will not be performed automatically, because a byte is smaller than an int. This kind of conversion is sometimes called a narrowing conversion, since you are explicitly making the value narrower so that it will fit into the target type.

To create a conversion between two incompatible types, you must use a cast. A cast is simply an explicit type conversion. It has this general form:

- (target-type) value

Here, target-type specifies the desired type to convert the specified value to. For example, the following fragment casts an int to a byte. If the integer's value is larger than the range of a byte, it will be reduced modulo (the remainder of an integer division by) the byte's range.

```
int a;
byte b;
// ...
b = (byte)a;
```

A different type of conversion will occur when a floating-point value is assigned to an integer type: truncation. As you know, integers do not have fractional component. For example, if the value 1.23 is assigned to an integer, the resulting value will simply be 1. The 0.23 will have been truncated. Of course, if the size of the whole number component is large to fit in the target integer type, then that value will be reduced modulo to the target type's range.

The following program demonstrates some type conversions that require casts:

```
// Demonstrate casts.
class Conversion {
    public static void main(String args[] ){
    byte b;
    int i=257;
```

```
double d = 323.142;
System.out.println("\nConversion of int to byte.");
  b = (byte)i;
System.out.println("i and b " + i + " " + b);
System.out.println("\nConversion of double to int.");
  i = (int)d;
System.out.println("d and i " + d + " " + i);
System.out.println("\nConversion of double to byte.");
  b = (byte)d;
System.out.println("d and b " + d + " " + b);
}
}
```

```
Conversion of int to byte.
    i and b 257        1
Conversion of double to int.
    d and i 323.142    323
Conversion of double to byte.
    d and b 323.142    67
```

Let's look at each conversion. When the value 257 is cast into a byte variable, the result is the remainder of the division of 257 by 256 (the range of a byte), which is 1 in this case. When the d is converted to an int, its fractional component is lost. When d is converted to a byte, its fractional component is lost, and the value is reduced modulo 256, which in this case is 67.

Automatic Type Promotion

In addition to assignments, there is another place where certain type of conversions may occur: To see why, consider the following. In an expression, the precision required of an intermediate value will sometimes exceed the range of either operand. For example, examine the following expression:

```
byte a = 40;
byte b = 50;
byte c = 100;
int d = a * b / c;
```

The result of the intermediate term a * b easily exceeds the range of either of its byte operands. To handle this kind of problem, Java automatically promotes each byte or short operand to int when evaluating an expression. This means that the subexpression a * b is performed using integers-not bytes. Thus, 2,000, the result of the intermediate expression, 50 * 40, is legal even though a and b are both specified as type byte.

As useful as the automatic promotions are, they can cause confusing compile-time errors. For example, this seemingly correct code causes a problem:

```
byte b = 50;
  b = b*2; // Error! Cannot assign an int to a byte!
```

The code is attempting to store 50 * 2, a perfectly valid byte value, back into a byte variable. However, because the operands were automatically promoted to int when the expression was evaluated, the result has also been promoted to int. Thus, the result of the expression is now of type int, which cannot be assigned to a byte without the use of a cast. This is true even if, as in this particular case, the value being assigned would still fit in the target type.

In cases where you understand the consequences of overflow, you should use an explicit cast, such as

```
byte b = 50;
b = (byte) (b*2);
```

which yields the correct value of 100.

Q8. Write some programs showing Java's Variable Declaration and use of literals.

ANS : class testVar

```
class testVar
{
    public static void main(String args[])
    {
     int a;          //Declaring an int type variable that store
                     //int type of data
     char b;         //Declaring an char type variable that store
                     //char type of data
     float c;        //Declaring an float type variable that store
                     //float type of data
     a=10;
     b='a';
     c=10.2f;
       System.out.println(a + " , " + b + " , " + c);
     a=20;
     b='b';
     c=13.2f;
       System.out.println(a + " , " + b + " , " + c);
     ++a;
     ++b;            //Integer value of char 'b' is incremeted by 1
     ++c;
    System.out.println(a + " , " + b + " , " + c);
    }
}

/**************************************************************/
class chardemo
{
    public static void main(String args[])
    {
      char ch1,ch2;
      ch1=88;
      ch2='Y';
      System.out.println(ch1 +" "+ ch2);
    }
```

```
}
/**************************************************************/
class testfloatVar
{
    public static void main(String args[])
    {
     float pi=3.14f;
     double area;
     float radius=9;
    area=pi*radius*radius;
   System.out.println("Area of the circle : " + area);
  }
}
```

In the given example to initialize a float varible 'f' is added at end of float literal, also, we achieve the same by adding '(float)' before the literal.

```
/*************************************************************/

class booltest
{
   public static void main(String args[])
   {
     boolean b;
     b=false;
     if(b)    // same as if(b==true)
        System.out.println("b is true");
     else
        System.out.println("b is false");
   }
}
```

Q9. Define array. Write short note on One Diamensional Arrays.

ANS : An array is a group of variables of same type that can be refered to by a common name. The type can be either primitive datatype (int, short, char, boolean), or an object type like "String."

One Dimensional Array :

To create an array, we must create an array of desired type. The general form of declaring an one dimensional array is

<data type> <variable name>[ ];

For example consider these arrays declared differently and valid in Java.

```
int month_days[ ];
int[ ] month_days;
```

Declaring an array variable creates only a place holder for the reference to the array, not the memory holding the array of elements. Also, the actual memory used by the array elements is dynamically allocated either by a |new| statement or an array initializer. The memory referenced by the array variable will be automatically garbage - collected (discussed later) when it is no longer referred to. The general form of |new| as it applies to one-dimensional arrays appears as follows:

<variable name>= new <datatype> [size];

For example consider these arrays

```
month_days = new int[ ];
month_days= {31,28,31,30,31,30,31,31,30,31,30,31};
int month_days [] = new int [12];
int month_days [] = {31,28,31,30,31,30,31,31,30,31,30,31};
```

Java strictly checks to make sure that one can not accidently try to store or reference values outside of the range of the array.

Q10. What happens when your program attempts to access an array element with an invalid index ?

ANS : Java follows normal C - style indexing for accessing an array element that is, you attach an integer - valued expression between square brackets after the name of the array. The array index starts with zero.

If the index value is invalid (less than zero or greater than array length), the Java Run Time throws the exception *ArrayIndexOutOfBoundsException*. Which can be handled through the expection handling facility provided in Java for these kind of situations.

Q11. Define Multi-dimensional Arrays. [DEC03,Q2(v)]

ANS : In Java, multidimensional arrays are actually arrays of arrays. These, as you might expect, look and act like regular multidimensionaal arrays. However, as you will see, there are a couple of subtle differences. To declare a multidimensional array variable, specify each additional index using another set of square brackets. For example, the following declares a two-dimensional array variable called twoD.

```
int twoD[ ][ ] = new int [4] [5];
```

This allocates a 4 by 5 array and assigns it to twoD. Internally this matrix is implemented as an array of arrays of int. Conceptually, this array will look like the one shown figure.

a_{00}	a_{01}	a_{02}	a_{03}	a_{04}
a_{10}	a_{11}	a_{12}	a_{13}	a_{14}
a_{20}	a_{21}	a_{22}	a_{23}	a_{24}
a_{30}	a_{31}	a_{32}	a_{33}	a_{34}

To initialize a multi dimensional array without using *new*.

```
int matrix [4][2] = {{1,2}, {3,4}, {5,6}, {7,8}};
```

Q12. Write a Program for Arithmetic Operations IN JAVA.

ANS : class testArith_Operator

```
{
    public static void main(String args[])
    {
      int x=6;
      int y=2;
      System.out.println("The value of x + y is "+ (x + y));
      System.out.println("The value of x - y is "+ (x - y));
/* The parenthesis is neccessary so that compiler treats the + sign as an arithmetic
operator not string concatenate as in the following statement.
      System.out.println("the value of x + y is "+ x + y);
This will print "the value of x + y is 62"
(NOTE: This is Polymorphism) */
      System.out.println("The remainder of x / y is "+ x%y);
      System.out.println("The value of x / y is" + x/y );
      System.out.println("The value of x * y is " + x*y );
    }
}
```

Q13. Write a program for Java supporting two types of data conversion.

ANS : class conv

```
{
        public static void main(String a[])
        {
         int x=128;
         byte b=(byte) x; /*Explict Conversion*/
         long l=x;                    /*Implict Conversion*/
         System.out.println("b = " + b);
        }
}
```

Q14. Write a Program showing use of two dimensional array to store a matrix of 2 × 2.

ANS : class d2array

```
{
    public static void main (String args[])
    {
      int a[][];
      a=new int[2][2];
      a[0][0]=0;
```

```
        a[0][1]=1;
        a[1][0]=2;
        a[1][1]=3;
        System.out.println(a[0][0]);
        System.out.println(a[0][1]);
        System.out.println(a[1][0]);
        System.out.println(a[1][1]);
    }
}
```

CHAPTER 4

JAVA CONTROL STATEMENTS

- SELECTION STATEMENTS
  - IF
  - IF..ELSE..IF
  - NESTED..IF
  - SWITCH
  - NESTED SWITCH
- LOOP STATEMENTS
  - FOR
  - WHILE
  - DO WHILE
- BREAK;
- CONTINUE;

Condition

a. Use of if condition
b. If
c. Nested if
d. Multiple if
e. Switch

Condition control statement

The If statement

The syntax of the if statement is as follows:

```
if(expression)
        statement;
```

The expression must be enclosed in parenthesis. The statement may be a compound statement.

for example:

```
if(y>5)
x=0;
```

The statement will be executed only if the expression is true. The syntax of the if else statement is as follows:

```
if(expression )
        statement-1;
else
```

```
        statement-2;
```

if expression is true statement –1 is executed. If expression is false, statement –2 is executed. So depending on the truth value of expression, either statement-1 or statement 2 is executed,

Nested if statements

The statement sequence of if or else may contain another statement i.e the if else statement can be nested within one another as shown below:

Syntax of nested if statement

```
if (expression-1)
{
    if(expression-2)
{
        statement;
}
    else
        if(expression-3)
        {
        statement;
        }
        else
    {
        statement;
    }
}
```

There may be one problem raised with nested if that is to decide "which if does the else match".

☞ Each else matches to its nearest unmatched preceding if.

For example

```
if(a<10)
{
    if(b>5)
        Sum=Sum + a + b;
    else
        Sum=Sum – a – b ;
```

Multiple if statement

Syntax of multiple if statement.

```
if(expression-1)
        statement –1;
else if (expression –2)
        statement –2;
else if(expression –3)
        statement-3;
..
..
else if(expression –n)
```

```
        statement-n;
else
        default statement;
```

the expressions are evaluated in order and if any condition is true then the statement associated with it is executed and this terminates the whole chain. The last else part is executed as default statement.

The switch statement

If you have a long series of conditions to check, a large block of if...else statements can get tiresome and confusing to write (and read, later on). For this reason, Java provides the switch statement. The general syntax is:

```
switch ( expression)
{
    case value1:
        statements
          [break;]
    case value 2:
        statements
          [break:]
  ....
    default:
        Statements
}
```

An expression is evaluated in the first line of a switch statement, and its value is used to determine the action or actions to take. The value of the expression is compared in turn with each value listed next to a case statement. If a match occurs, the statements following that case statement are executed. The break statement (shown in square brackets to indicate that it is optional; the square brackets are not actually part of the code), if present, causes the switch statement to be terminated after the statements in the current case block are executed, that is, control will pass to the statement immediately after the final brace ending the switch statement without any further case statements being tested, if the break statement is not present, the next case statement will be checked as well. In other words, a switch statement offers greater flexibility than an if.. Else statement.

Iteration Statements

Java's iteration statements are For, while, and do-while. These statements create what we commonly call loops. As you probably know, a loop repeatedly executes the same set of instructions until a termination condition is met.

While

The **while** loop is Java's most fundamental looping statement. It repeats a statement or block while its controlling expression is true. Here is its general form:

```
    While(condition)                    // body of loop
    }
```

The condition can be any Boolean expression. The body of the loop will be executed as long as the conditional expression is true. When condition becomes false, control passes to the next line of code immediately following the loop. The curly braces are unnecessary if only a single statement is being repeated.

Since the **while** loop evaluates its conditional expression at the top of the loop, the body of the loop will not execute even once if the condition is false to begin with. For example, in the following fragment, the call to **println** ( ) is never executed:

```
int a = 10, b = 20;
while (a > b)
System.out.println("This will not be displayed");
```

do-while

As you just saw, if the conditional expression controlling a **while** loop is initially false, then the body of the loop will not be executed at all. Sometimes it is desirable to execute the body of a **while** loop at least once, even if the conditional expression is false to begin with. The **do-while** loop always executes its body at least once, because its conditional expression is at the bottom of the loop. Its general form is

```
do {
        // body of loop
}while (condition);
```

Each iteration of the **do-while** loop first executes the body of the loop and then evaluates the conditional expression. If this expression is true, the loop will repeat. Otherwise, the loop terminates. As with all of Java's loops, condition must be a Boolean expression.

for

The general form of the for statement:

```
for (initialization; condition; iteration) {
        //body
}
```

If only one statement is being repeated, there is no need for the curly braces.

The **for** loop operates as follows. When the loop first starts, the initialization portion of the loop is executed. Generally, this is an expression that sets the value of the loop control variable, which acts as a counter that controls the loop. It is important to understand that the initialization expression is only executed once. Next, condition is evaluated. This must be a Boolean expression. It usually tests the loop control variable against a target value. If this expression is true, then the body of the loop is executed. If it is false, the loop terminates. Next, the iteration portion of the loop is executed. This is usually an expression that increments or decrements the loop control variable. The loop then iterates, first evaluating the conditional expression, then executing the body of the loop, and then executing the iteration expression with each pass. This process repeats until the controlling expression is false.

Nested Loops

Like all other programming languages, Java allows loops to be nested. That is, one loop may be inside another. For example, here is a program that nests for loops:

```
//Loops may be nested.
class Nested {
    public static void main(String args[ ] ) {
        int i, j;
  for(i=0; i<10; i++ ) {
```

```
                for(j=i;j<10;j++)
                System.out.print(".");
                System.out.println( );
        }
    }
}
```

The **output** produced by this program is shown here:

```
..........
.........
........
.......
......
.....
....
...
..
.
```

Break and Labelled Break commands.

By using **break,** you can force immediate termination of a loop, bypassing the conditional expression and any remaining code in the body of the loop. When a **break** statement is encountered inside a loop, the loop is terminated and program control resumes at the next statement following the loop.

Here are two points to remember about **break.** First, more than one **break** statement may appear in a loop. However, be careful. Too many **break** statements have the tendency to destructure your code. Second, the break that terminates a switch statement affects only that **switch** statement and not any enclosing loops.

Labelled Break :

Sometimes you'd like more flexibility, for example the ability to break out two levels. In Java, there's a simpler approach to solving this problem as :

```
  outer_block:
      for (i = 1; i <= 10; i++) {
          for (j = 1; j <= 10; j++) {
              if (some condition)
                  break outer_block;
              // other processing in loop
          }
      }
      // control comes here when break is executed
```

The break statement has a label. When the statement is executed, control transfers out of the enclosed labelled statement. Control is NOT transferred to the label, but to a point past the end of the labelled statement. A labelled continue statement works in a similar way; control is transferred to the end of a labelled loop.

Note that with both break and continue, any finally block will be executed before the labelled statement is exited or the next iteration of a loop takes place. For example:

```
loop:
    while (some condition) {
        try {
            if (some condition)
                continue loop;
            // other processing
        }
        finally {
            // some processing
        }
    }
```

The labelled continue statement will cause the finally block to be executed before going to the bottom of the while loop in preparation for the next iteration of the loop.

Continue

Sometimes it is useful to force an early iteration of a loop. That is, you might want to continue running the loop, but stop processing the remainder of the code in its body for this particular iteration. This is, in effect, a goto pass the body of the loop, to the loop's end. In **while** and **do-while** loops, a **continue** statement causes control to be transferred directly to the conditional expression that controls the loop. In a **for** loop, control goes first to the iteration portion of the for statement and then to the conditional expression. For all three loops, any intermediate code is bypassed.

Here is an example program that uses continue to cause two numbers to be printed on each line:

```
/ / Demonstrate continue.
Class continue {
  public static void main(String args[]) {
    for(int i =0; i<10; i + + ) {
            System.out.print (i + " ");
            if(i % 2 = = 0 ) continue;
            System.out.print In ( " " );
    }
  }
}
```

This code uses the % operator to check if i is even. If it is, the loop continues without printing a newline.

IF Programs

SIMPLE IF ELSE (Single Statement)

```
class simple_if
{
    public static void main(String args[])
    {
      int x=5,y=7;
      if(x<y)
```

```
        System.out.println("y is max.");
      else
        System.out.println("x is max.");
    }
}
/*************************************************************/
```

IF ELSE BLOCKS (Multiple Statements in a if block)

```
class EvenOdd
{
    public static void main(String args[])
    {
    int x=5,y=8;
      if(y%2==0)
      {
        System.out.println("y is even");
        x=y;
      }
      else
      {
        System.out.println("y is odd");
        x=y;
      }
    }
}
/*************************************************************/
```

Nested If Statement

The Statement part of "if" contains another if. This example finds the greatest valued integer in a, b and c.

```
class nested_if
{
    public static void main(String args[])
    {
      int a=34, b=23, c=332;
      if(a > b)
      {
        if (a>c)
                System.out.println("a is greatest");
        else
                System.out.println("c is greatest");
      }
      else
      {
        if (b>c)
                System.out.println("b is greatest");
        else
```

```
                System.out.println("c is greatest");
        }
    }
}
```

Program showing use of switch for welcoming a user.

```
class gender
{
    public static void main(String args[])
    {
      char gender='f';
      String msg;
      switch(gender)
      {
      case 'm':   msg="Hello Mister";
                  break;
      case 'f':   msg="Hello Miss";
                  break;
      default:
                  msg="Hello Alien";
      }
      System.out.print(msg);
    }
}
```

A seasons program (case grouping).

```
class Switch
{
    public static void main(String args[])
    {
      int month=4;
      String season;

      switch(month)
      {
      case 12:
      case 1:
      case 2:     season="winter";
                  break;
      case 3:
      case 4:
      case 5:     season="spring";
                  break;
      case 6:
      case 7:
```

```
    case 8:     season="summer";
                break;
    case 9:
    case 10:
    case 11:    season="autumn";
                break;
    default:
                season="bogus month";
    }
    System.out.println("april is in the " +season+ ".");
  }
}
```

Find my religous book.

```
class holybook
{
    public static void main(String args[])
    {
    String holybook;
    char religion='h';

    switch (religion)
    {
    case 'h': holybook="Srimad Bhagwat Gita";
        break;
    case 'p': holybook="Zenda Avista";
        break;
    case 's': holybook="Sri Guru Granth Sahib Ji";
        break;
    case 'm': holybook="Quran";
        break;
    case 'c': holybook="Bible";

    default: holybook="God Human";
    }
      System.out.print("The holybook chosen is " + holybook);
    }
}
```

A simple for loop demo.

```
class Simple_For
{
    public static void main(String a[])
    {
     int i;
```

```
    //Print the table of 2
    for (i=1;i<=20;i=2*i)
      System.out.print(i);
}
}
```

Program to print first 6 numbers of a fabonacii series.

```
class fabonacii
{
    public static void main(String args[])
    {
      int first=1,second=2;
      int temp;
                                    //Print 1 and 2 as they are the starting values
      System.out.println(first);
  System.out.println(second);
      for(int i=0;i<=6;i++)
      {
        temp=second;
        second=first+second;
        first=temp;
        System.out.println(second);
      }
      System.out.print("\n");
    }
}
```

Program to find binary equivalent of a decimal value.

```
class dec
{
    public static void main(String args[])
    {
      int index=0;
      int dec=132;
      int d[]=new int[8];
      for(int i=dec;i>=1;)
      {
                                    //Store each bit in array
        d[index]=i%2;
        index++;
        i=i/2;
      }
 System.out.print("the binary of" + dec + " is = ");
                                    //Print the array in reverse fashion
      for(int i=index-1;i>=0;i—)
```

```
        {
          System.out.print(d[i]);
        }
        System.out.print("\n");
      }
}
```

Program to find maximum value and its index position in array.

```
class findMAX
{
      public static void main(String args[])
      {
        int a[]={12,32,75,8,182,946,234,234,123,234,76};
        int max=a[0], pos=0;

        for (int i=1;i<=a.length-1;i++)
      {
          if(max > a[i])
          {
                    continue;
          }
          else
          {
                    max=a[i];
                    pos=i;
          }
      }
System.out.print("Max Value is " +max+ " at position "+ pos);
      }
}
```

Program to find Max and Min in an Array.

```
class findMAX_MIN
{
public static void main(String args[])
{
      int
a[]={40,52,75,65,72,75,24,64,73,75,71,52,75,65,72,75,24,64,73,75,71};
      int max=a[0];
      int min=a[0];
      int pmax=0;
      int pmin=0;
      for(int i=1;i<=a.length-1;i++)
      {
        if(max<a[i])
```

```
        {
          max=a[i];
          pmax=i;
        }
        if(min>a[i])
        {
          min=a[i];
          pmin=i;
          }
        }
System.out.println("MAX=( " + max + ","+pmax+") , MIN=(" + min + "," + pmin +")" );

    }
}
```

Program to search an array for a given value.

```
class search_array
{
    public static void main(String gf[])
    {
    int a[]=new int[10];
    int s=24,i;
    boolean found=false;
                                        //fill the array with a table of 3
      for(i=0;i<=9;i++)
      a[i]=i*3;
                                        //Searching the array for s=24
      for(i=0;i<=9;i++)
      {
        if(a[i]==s)
        {
        found=true;
        break;
        }
      }
      if(found)
      {
        System.out.println("The search value " + s + " found at position " + (i+1));
      }
      else
      {
        System.out.println("The search value not found");
      }
    }
}
```

Program to sort an array using Insertion Sort.

```
class INSERTION_SORT
{
    public static void main(String args[])
    {
    int a[]={12,32,75,8,182};                    //,946,234,234,123,234,76};
    int i,j,temp;
    for(i=0;i<=a.length-1;i++)
    {
      for(j=i;j<=a.length-1;j++)
      {
        if(a[i]>a[j])
        {
        temp=a[i];
        a[i]=a[j];
        a[j]=temp;
        }
      }
    }
    System.out.println("Array sorted in decending order");
    for(i=0;i<=a.length-1;i++)
    System.out.println(a[i]);
    }
}
```

Write a Program demonstrating the use of 2-D arrays in matrices calculations. ADDITION or SUBTRACTION

```
class mat_add
{
    public static void main(String args[])
    {
      int a[][]=new int[3][3];
      int b[][]=new int[3][3];
                                                  //Fill Matrix a
      for(int i=0;i<3;i++)
      {
        for(int j=0;j<3;j++)
        {
        a[i][j]=3*(j+1);
        System.out.println(a[i][j]);
      }
      }
                                                  //Fill Matrix b
      for(int i=0;i<3;i++)
      {
```

```
        for(int j=0;j<3;j++)
        {
        b[i][j]=4*(j+1);
        }
      }
                                        //Calculate c=a+b or c=a-b

      for(int i=0;i<3;i++)
      {
        for(int j=0;j<3;j++)
        {
        a[i][j]=a[i][j]+b[i][j];
        }
      }
                                        //Print the resultant matrix

      for(int i=0;i<3;i++)
      {
        for(int j=0;j<3;j++)
        {
        System.out.print("\t" + a[i][j]);
        }
        System.out.print("\n");
      }
    }
}
```

MATRIX MULTIPLICATION

```
class mat_mult
{
    public static void main(String args[])
    {
      int m=2,n=4,p=3;
      int a[][]=new int[m][n];
      int b[][]=new int[n][p];
      int c[][]=new int[m][p];
      a[0][0]=1;
      a[0][1]=1;
      a[0][2]=1;
      a[0][3]=1;
      a[1][0]=1;
      a[1][1]=1;
      a[1][2]=1;
      a[1][3]=1;

      b[0][0]=2;
      b[0][1]=2;
```

```
        b[0][2]=2;
        b[1][0]=2;
        b[1][1]=2;
        b[1][2]=2;
        b[2][0]=2;
        b[2][1]=2;
        b[2][2]=2;
        b[3][0]=2;
        b[3][1]=2;
        b[3][2]=2;

                                                    // Matrix Multiplication
        for(int i=0;i<=m-1;i++)
        {
          for(int j=0;j<=n-1;j++)
          {
                    for(int k=0;k<=p-1;k++)
                    {
                              c[i][k]+=a[i][j]*b[j][k];
                    }
          }
        }

                                                    // Printing Resultant Matrix

        for(int i=0;i<=m-1;i++)
        {
          for(int j=0;j<=p-1;j++)
          {
                    System.out.print("\t"+ c[i][j]);
          }
        System.out.print("\n");
        }
    }
}
```

CHAPTER 5

INTRODUCING CLASSES, CONSTRUCTORS & OBJECTS IN JAVA

- THE GENERAL FORM OF A CLASS
- DECLARING OBJECTS (NEW OPERATOR)
- INTRODUCTION TO METHODS
  - METHODS INSIDE CLASSES
  - RETURNING VALUES (RETURN)
  - PARAMETERIZED METHODS
- CONSTRUCTORS
  - PARAMETERIZED CONSTRUCTORS
- "THIS" KEYWORD
- "FINAL" KEYWORD
- "STATIC" VARIABLES & METHODS
- GARBAGE COLLECTION
- FINALIZERS

Class Fundamentals

A class is a way to bind the data and its associated methods (functions) together. It allows the data & methods to be hidden, if necessary, from external use.

When we define a class, we are creating a new data type that can be treated like any other data type of Java. Once defined, this new type can be used to create object of that type. Thus, a class is a *template* for an object, and an object is an instance of a class.

The general form of a ***class*** definition:

```
class <classname>
{
type <instance_variable1>;
type <instance_variable2>;
type methodname1(parameter_list)
{
// body of Method
}
```

```
    type methodname2 (parameter_list)
    {
                                    //body of Method
    }
}
```

A class can have any number of instance variable or methods. A typical class declaration would look like:

```
class Item
{
    int number;
    float cost;
void getData(int a, float b)
{
    number = a;
    cost = b;
}
void printData( )
{
    System.out.println("Total Items: " + number);
    System.out.println("cost per Item: " + cost);
}
}
```

We usually give a class some meaningful name, such as item. This "item" becomes a new type identifier that can be used to declare *instances* of that class type:
The method "getData( )" can be used to assign values to the instance variables number and cost, and printData( ) for displaying their values.
The figure shows notations used by the OOP analysts to represent a class.

Class : ITEM
DATA number cost ....
METHODS getData( ) putData( ) ....

Figure : Representation of a class

Creating objects

As a class defines a new type of data, we use the class name to declare objects of that class. It is important to note that a class declaration only creates a template; it does not create an object.

To actually create an object, we use the statement like the following.
Item myItem=newItem();
After this statement executes, myItem will be an instance of Item. Thus, it will have physical reality.
We can create as many objects of a class as we like, and each object contains its own copy of instance variables defined by the class.
To access an instance variable, use dot (.) operator. The dot operator links the name of the object with the name of an instance variable.
myItem.Number=100;
Similarly, we can also call the methods of an object
myItem.GetData(5, 13.5);
Since, the getData( ) has a void return type, the above statement works, but if suppose it has an integer return type than we must use an integer type acceptor for method getData( ) and the statement looks like:
int X;
N=myItem.GetData(5,13.5);

Q1. Difference between Constructor and Method. [DEC02,Q2(b)]
ANS : The new operator dynamically allocates memory for an object. It has this gerneral form:

Class-var = new classname();

Here, class-var is a variable of the class type being created. The clasaname is the name of the class that is being instantiated.
The class name followed by parentheses specifies the **constructor** for the class. A constructor defines what occurs when an object of a class is created. Consstructors are an important part of all classes and have many significant attributes. Most real-world classes explicitly define their own constructors within their class definition. However, if no explicit constructor is specified, then Java will automatically supply a default constructor.

Methods
This is the general form of a method:

```
Type name(parameter-list) {
                                  //body of method
}
```

Here, type specifies the type of data returned by the method. This can be any valid type, including class types that you create. If the method does not return a value, its return type must be void. The name of the method is specified by name. This can be any legal identifier other than those already used by other items within the current scope. The parameter-list is a sequence of type and identifier pairs separated by commas. Parameters are essentially variables that receive the value of the arguments passed to the method when it is called. If the method has no paramneters, then the parameter list will be empty.
Methods that have a return type other than **void** return a value to the calling routine using the following form of the **return** statement:
return value;
Here, value is the value returned.

Understanding Return

The implementation of putData( ) simply displays the total number of items and cost of each item. How about having another method itemValue( ), which provides the total value of Item object.

Now, Item class looks like:

```
class Item
{
int number;
float cost;
void getData(int a, float b)
{
number = a;
cost = b;
}
void putData( )
{
System.out.print1n("Total item: " + number + "cost: " + cost);
}
float itemvalue( )
{
return number cost;
}
}
class ItemDemo {
public static void main ( String args [ ] )
{
float value;
Item myItem = newItem();
myItem.getData(10,12.0);
myItem.putData();
Value = myItem.Itemvalue ( ) ;
System.out.print1n( " Total stock held is " + value + " Rs");
}
}
```

Methods that take Parameters

We already have method getData( ) in class Item which has two parameters a and b of type integer & float respectively. Note that whenever in our previous programs we call getData ( ) we always supply the value of matching type as parameters declared.

The values passed in the getData( ) in main( ) method are called the arguments.

Q2. What is constructor ? How can you overload constructor ? Describe with an example. **[DEC03,Q4(i)]**

 # Describe Constructors. **[JUNE03,Q2(e)]**

ANS : It can be tedious to initialize all of the variables in a class each time an instance is created. Even when you add convenience function like getdata ( ), it would be simplest and more concise to have all of the setup done at the time the object is first created. Because the requirement for initialization is so common, Java allows objects to initialize themselves when they are created. This automatic initialization is performed through the use of a constructer.

A constructor initializes an object immediately upon creation. It has the same name as the class, in which it resides and is syntactically similar to a method. Once defined, the constructor is automatically called immediately after the object is created, before the **new** operator completes. Constructors look a little strange because they have not return type, not even **void.** This is because the implicit return type of a class's constructor is the class type itself. It is the constructor's job to initialize the internal state of an object so that the code creating an instance will have a fully initialized, usable object immediately.

Let's how add a constructor in Item template so the values of variable automatically initialized when an object is constructed.

```
Item()
{
    Number = 10;
    Cost = 120;
}
```

The constructor defined above in class Item. Set the instance variable number and cost for each object to the same values. However, there are cases when we want to start an object with different set of values. For this we need to add parameters to the constructor Item

```
Item (int num, cost cost_item)
{
    number = num;
    cost = cost_item;
}
```

Since constructors are also a type of method with some special authorities, so Java allows overloaded constructors.

The program shows three overloaded constructors for class shape.

```
//Overloaded Constructor
class Shape
{
    int x;
    int y;
    int z;

    Shape(int i,int j,int k)
```

```
    {
      x=i;
      y=j;
      z=k;
    }
    Shape(int i)
    {
      x=y=z=i;
    }

    Shape()
    {
      x=y=z=-1;
    }
}

class mainClass
{
    public static void main(String pa[])
    {
    //Unknown shape:: Default Constructor
    Shape b1=new Shape();
    System.out.println(b1.x + " , " + b1.y + " , " + b1.z);

    //Shape is a Cube or Sphere::Constructor with One Parameter
    Shape b2=new Shape(12);
    System.out.println(b2.x + " , " + b2.y + " , " + b2.z);

    //Shape is a Cuboid::Constructor with three Parameter
    Shape b3=new Shape(12,23,2);
    System.out.println(b3.x + " , " + b3.y + " , " + b3.z);
    }
}
```

Q3. Define the Mehods Overloading and Overriding a method.

ANS : Methods Overloading : When an overloaded method is invoked, Java uses the type and /or number of arguments as its guide to determine which version of the overloaded method to actually call. Thus, overloaded methods must differ in the type and / or number of their parameters. While overloaded methods may have different return types, the return type alone is insufficient to distinguish two versions of a method. When Java encounters a call to an overloaded method, it simply executes the version of the method whose parameters match the arguments used in the call.

Since constructors are also a type of method with some special authorities, so Java allows overloaded constructors.

The program shows three overloaded constructors for class shape.

```
//Overloaded Constructor
class Shape
{
    int x;
    int y;
    int z;

    Shape(int i,int j,int k)
    {
      x=i;
      y=j;
      z=k;
    }

    Shape(int i)
    {
      x=y=z=i;
    }

    Shape()
    {
      x=y=z=-1;
    }
}
class mainClass
{
    public static void main(String pa[])
    {
    //Unknown shape:: Default Constructor
    Shape b1=new Shape();
    System.out.println(b1.x + " , " + b1.y + " , " + b1.z);

    //Shape is a Cube or Sphere::Constructor with One Parameter
    Shape b2=new Shape(12);
    System.out.println(b2.x + " , " + b2.y + " , " + b2.z);

    //Shape is a Cuboid::Constructor with three Parameter
    Shape b3=new Shape(12,23,2);
    System.out.println(b3.x + " , " + b3.y + " , " + b3.z);
```

```
    }
}
```

Another program to show overloaded methods are called is given.

```
//Overloaded Constructor
class CalcVolume
{
    int volume()
    {
        return -1;
    }
    int volume(int i)
    {
        return i*i*i;
    }
    long volume(int i,int j,int k)
    {
        return i*j*k;
    } }
class mainClass
{
    public static void main(String pa[])
    {
    int temp;
    CalcVolume myObject=new CalcVolume();

    temp=myObject.volume();
    System.out.println("Volume of Unknown Object is always:" + temp);

    temp=myObject.volume(4);
    System.out.println("Volume of a Cube:" + temp);
    } }
```

Consider, there are three methods with same name but with different parameters. In the main(), depending on number and type of parameters passed the respective method is called.

This is quite a powerful feature of OOP, because in most of situations one want to give the user or programmers, flexibility to choose the type of shape they want.

Q4. Difference between Method Overloading and Overriding a method.

[JUNE03,Q3(i)]

ANS :

Method Overloading	Method Overriding
(i) Overloaded methods **supplement** each other.	(i) An overriding method **replaces** the method it overrides.
(ii) Overloading methods may have **different** argument lists of **different** types.	(ii) An overriding method must have argument lists of **identical** type and order.
(iii) The return type may be **different** for overloaded methods	(iii) The return type must be **same** as that of overridden method.
(iv) Since overloading methods are essentially different methods, there is **no restriction** on exceptions they can throw.	(iv) The overriding method must not throw checked exceptions which cannot be thrown by the original method.

Q5. Define Polymorphism. [DEC03,Q2(i)]

 # What is polymorphism ? How is it implemented ? Show, through an example, the implementation of a polymorphism. [JUNE04,Q6(b)]

ANS : In Java cocept of polymorphism is implemented through Overloading the operators, Overriding a method. Below are the detailed description of both implementations :

OVERLOADING : One of the benefits of objects is that give the programmer a convenient way to construct new data types. Suppose you work with two-dimensional positions (such as X and Y coordinates, or latitude and longitude) in your program. You would like to express operations on these positional values with normal arithmetic operations, such as

Position1 = position2 + origin;

Where the variables position1, position2 and origin each represent a pair of independent numerical quantities. By creating a class that incorporates these two values, and declaring position1, position2 and origin to be objects of this class, we can, in effect, create a new data type. Many features of Java are intended to facilitate the creation of new data types in this manner.

Note that the = (equal) and + (plus) operators, used in the position arithmetic don't act the same way they do in operations on built-in types like int. The object position1 and so on are not predefined in Java, but are programmer-defined objects of class position. How do the = and + operations know how to operate on objects ? The answer is that we can define new operations for these operators. These operators will be member functions of the position class.

Using operators or functions in different ways, depending on what they are operating on , is called **polymorphism**. One thing with several distinct forms. When an existing operator, such as + or = is given the capability to operate on a new data type, it is said to be overloaded. **Overloading** is a kind of polymorphism; it is also an important feature of OOP.

Overriding a method : Java Runtime Polymorphism : Another way objects work together is to define methods that take other objects as parameters. You get even more cooperation and efficiency when the objects are united by a common superclass. All classes in the Java programming language have an inheritance relationship.

For example, if you define a method that takes a java.lang.Object as a parameter, it can accept any object in the entire Java platform. If you define a method that takes a java.awt.Component as a parameter, it can accept any component object. This form of cooperation is called *polymorphism.*

Overriden methods allow Java to support runtime polymorphism. Sometimes, we need to create a new method in a derived class with same signature and name as of its superclass member method. For example, consider a superclass ***AutoMobile*** having a method brake( ) and extended by class ***MotorBike***. Although MotorBike has access of brake( ) of its superclass, but wants to add some new system like disc brakes in front wheel while applying brakes, so MotorBikes declare a method brake() with same return type and parameter list. Now whenever an instance of MotorBike calls the brake( ) method it calls the one implemented in MotorBike, because it overrides the brake( ) of AutoMobile.

```
class AutoMobile
{
      String color;
      int weight;
      double bhp;

      void start()
      {
         System.out.println("Start the engine");
      }

      void brake()
      {
         System.out.println("Apply brakes");
      }
}
class MotorBike extends AutoMobile
{
      //start() is not an Overriden method, b'cos
//signature's of start() in SuperClass is different
      String start(int no_of_kicks)
      {
         return "engine started in " + no_of_kicks + " kicks";
      }
      //Overriden brake()
```

```
    void brake()
    {
      System.out.println("Apply hydrolic brakes in rear and
    disc brakes in front wheel");
    }
}
class mainClass
{
    public static void main(String args[])
    {
      MotorBike myBike=new MotorBike();

      myBike.color="BLUE";
      myBike.weight=120;
      myBike.bhp=9.5;
        String status=myBike.start(2);
                System.out.println(status);
                myBike.brake();
    }
}
      /*
      The output of the program is:
      engine started in 2 kicks
      Apply hydrolic brakes in rear and disc brakes in front wheel
    */
```

Notes

✓ Always use private, public and protected access modifiers, for member declaration.

✓ Attributes of an objects which holds some value at a time should be declared as instance variable, and attributes which has some processing part should be declared as a method.

For example, in class ***Automobile***, attributes such as color, no-of-wheels, weight etc. should be declared as instance variable and attributes such as ignition, acceleration, brake etc. should be declared as methods.

✓ Use final variables for attributes which are constant values and used frequently. For example, value of Pi is fixed to 3.14.

✓ Use the ***println*** statement in the body part of the methods such as brake, ignition etc. where you do not know what to do in a non-real application.

Recursion

Java supports recursion. Recursion is the process of defining something in terms of itself. As it relates to Java programming, recursion is the attribute that allows a method to call itself. A method that calls itself is said to be recursive.

When a method calls itself, new local variables and parameters are allocated storage on the stack, and the method code is executed with these new variables from the start. A recursive call does not make a new copy of the method. Only the arguments are new. As each recursive call returns, the old local variables and parameters are removed from the stack, and execution resumes the point of the call inside the method.

Recursive versions of many routines may execute a bit more slowly than the iterative equivalent because of the added overhead of the additional function calls.

The main advantage to recursive methods is that they can be used to create clearer and simpler versions of several algorithms than can their iterative relatives. For example, the QuickSort sorting algorithm is quite difficult to implement in an iterative way. Some problems, especially AI-related ones, seem to lend themselves to recursive solutions..

Note : *When writing recursive methods, you must have an if statement somewhere to force the method to return without the recursive call being executed. If you don't do this, once you call the method, it will never return. This is a very common error in working with recursion. Use Println( ) statements liberally during development so that you can watch what is going on and abort execution if you see that you have made a mistake.*

Understanding static

There will be times when you will want to define a class member that will be used independently of any object of that class. Normally a class member must be accessed only in conjunction with an object of its class. However, it is possible to create a member that can be used by its class. However, it is possible to create a member that can be used by itself, without reference to a specific instance. To create such a member, precede its declaration with keyword **static.** When a member is declared static, it can be accessed before any objects of its class are created, and without reference to any object. You can declare both methods and variables to be static. The most common example of a **static** member is a **main ( ). Main ( )** is declared as static because it must be called before any objects exist.

Instance variables declared as **static** are, essentially, global variables. When objects of its class are declared, no copy of a **static** variable is made. Instead, all instances of this class share the same **static** variable.

Methods declared as **static** have several restrictions:

✓ They can only call other **static** methods.

✓ They must only access **static** data.

✓ They cannot refer to **this** or **super** in anyway.

If you need to do computation in order to initialize your **static** variables, you can declare a **static** block which gets executed exactly once, when the class is first loaded the following example shows a class that has a static method, some **static** variables, and a **static** initialization block:

```
class Stat_Class
{
 static int counter;
```

```
  Stat_Class()
 {
     counter++;
 }
  //This Block initialized only once during entire life of Stat_Class
 static
 {
  System.out.println("Static block initialized");
  counter=1;
 }
}

class Static_Demo
{
      public static void main(String args[])
      {
        Stat_Class stat1=new Stat_Class();
        System.out.println(stat1.counter);
        // We can also access the static variable counter with
//out using Object name, for example Stat_Class.counter
//which we done next

        Stat_Class stat2=new Stat_Class();
        System.out.println(Stat_Class.counter);
      }
}
```

Outside of the class in which they are defined, **static** methods and variables can be used independently of any object. To do so, you need only to specify the name of their class followed by the dot operator. For example, if you wish to call a **static** method from outside its class, you can do so by using the following, general form:

```
Classname.Method();
```

Here, classname is the name of the class in which the **static** method is declared. As you can see, this format is similar to that used to call non-**static** methods through object-reference variables. A **Static** variable can be accessed in the same way-by use of the dot operator on the name of the class. This is how Java implements a controlled version of global function and global variables.

Garbage Collection

Since objects are dynamically allocated by using the **new** operator, you might be wondering how such objects are destroyed and their memory is released for later reallocation. In some languages, such as C++, dynamically allocated objects must be manually released by use of a **delete** operator. Java takes a different approach; it handles deallocation for you automatically. The technique that accomplishes this is called garbage collection. It works like this: when no references to an object exist, that object is assumed to be no longer needed, and the memory occupied by the object can be reclaimed. There is no explicit need to destroy objects as in C++. Garbage collection only occurs sporadically (if at all) during the execution of your program. It will not occur simply because one or more objects exist that are no longer used. Furthermore, different Java run-time implementation will take varying approached to garbage collection, but for the most part, you should not have to think about it while writing your programs.

The finalize ( ) Method

Sometimes an object will need to perform some action when it is destroyed. For example, if an object is holding some non-Java resource such as a file handle or window character font, then you might want to make sure these resources are freed before an object is destroyed. To handle such situations, Java provides a mechanism called Finalization. By using finalization you can define specific actions that will occur when an object is just about to be reclaimed by the garbage collector.

To add a finalizer to a class, you simply define the **finalize( )** method. The Java run time calls that method whenever it is about to recycle an object of that class. Inside the **finalize( )** method you will specify those actions that must be performed before the object is destroyed. The garbage collector runs periodically, checking for objects that are no longer referenced by any running state or indirectly through other reference objects. Right before an asset is freed, the Java run time calls the **finalize( )** method on the object.

The **finalize( )** method has this general form:

```
Protected void finalize ( )
{
    //finalization code here
}
```

Here, the keyword **protected** is a specifier that prevents access to **finalize( )** by code defined outside its class.

It is important to understand that **finalize( )** is only called just prior to garbage collection. It is not called when an object goes out-of-scope, for example. This means that you cannot know when- or even if-**finalize( )** will be executed. Therefore, your program should provide other means of releasing system resources, etc., used by the object. It must not rely on **finalize( )** for normal program operation.

CHAPTER 6

INHERITENCE

- TYPES OF INHERITENCE
- SUPERCLASSES
- "SUPER" KEYWORD & ITS USES
- EXTENDING CLASSES.
- ABSTRACT CLASSES
- OVERRIDING VS OVERLOADING
- USING FINAL TO PREVENT
  - INHERITENCE
  - OVERRIDING
- WRAPPER CLASSES
- SOME OTHER USEFUL CLASSES [STRINGBUFFER, ARRAYS, MATH]
- INNER CLASSES IN JAVA & AND THEIR IMPORTANCE

Introduction

Reusability is an important feature of OOP. It is always nice if we could reuse something that already exists rather than trying to create the same all over again i.e. "***why to reinvent the wheel.***"

The Java classes can be reused in several ways. Once a class has been written and tested, it can be adapted by other programmers to suit their requirements. This is basically done by creating new classes, reusing the properties of the existing ones. The mechanism of deriving a new class from an old one is called ***Inheritance (or Derivation)***. The old class is referred to as the *base class* and the new one is called the *derived class* or *subclass*. Therefore, a subclass is a specialized version of a super class or base class and adds its own, unique elements.

Q1. Define Extends keyword. **[DEC03,Q2(iii)]**

ANS : To inherit a class, Java uses ***extends*** keyword. To inherit a class, syntax for the derived class declaration is

```
class<derived class name> extends <base class>
{
    //body of the class
}
```

Java doesn't support the multiple inheritance, so a derived class can only inherit one class, but Java fully supprt multilevel inheritance e.g., given three classes called A, B, and C, C can be a subclass of B, which is a subclass of A. Here C inherits all the traits of B, and A classes.

The example shows a short program, here class B inherits class A and all members of class A included in class B. That is, object of the class B can access any member of class A as it access its own member.

```
class A
{
    int i;
    void get_A_Val()
    {
      System.out.println("Value of i is : " + i);
    }
}
class B extends A
{
    int j;
    void get_B_Val()
    {
      get_A_Val(); // get_A_val() is now member of B
      System.out.println("Value of j is : " + j);
    }
}
class mainClass
{
    public static void main(String args[])
    {
      B objB;              //Object of B declared
      objB=new B();  //Object is instantiated

      objB.j=10;

      objB.i=5;     //objB accessing i as its own member

      objB.get_B_Val();
    }
}
```

Even though A is a superclass for B, it is also a completely independent, stand-alone class. Being a superclas for a subclass does not mean that the superclass cannot be used by itself. Further, a subclass can be a superclass for another subclass.

Note *: that not class can be a superclass of itself.*

***Note** : that to include a previously compiled class in a new program, simply put the .class file of that class in the same directory where the new .java file is saved and compiled.*

Member Access and Inheritance

For now, we focus on three types of access specifiers default, private and public.

default : When no specifier is used, default members are accessible within the same class and to other class, provided both are in the same directory, in both ways through inheritance and objects.

private : Accessible only within the class.

public : Accessible in both conditions either inherited or by objects.

Q2. Differentiate between the "This" and "Super". [JUNE03,Q3(iv)]

#. What is 'this' keyword? How is it different from a super keyword ? [JUNE04,Q1(f)]

ANS : The "this" keyword : Sometimes a method will need to refer to the object that invoked it. To allow this, Java defines the **this** keyword. This can be used inside any method to refer to the current object. That is, this is always a reference to the object on which the method was invoked. You can use this anywhere a reference to an object of the current class' type is permitted.

Instance Variable Hiding

As you know, it is illegal in Java to declare two local variables with the same name inside the same or enclosing scopes. Interestingly, you can have local variables, including formal parameters to methods, which overlap with the names of the class' instance variables. However, when a local variable has the same name as an instance variable, the local variable hides the instance variable.

```
class Shape
{
    int x;
    int y;
    int z;
    Shape(int x,int y,int z)
    {
      this.x=i;
      this.y=j;
      this.z=k;
    }
}
class mainClass
{
    public static void main(String pa[])
    {
    Shape myShape=new Shape(12,23,2);
    System.out.println(myShape.x + " , " + myShape.y + " , " + myShape.z);
```

```
    }
}
```

Using super :

super keyword in Java, used to access the methods or data members defined in the superclass. super has two general forms.

super for Constructor Reference

A subclass can call a constructor method defined by its superclass by use of the following form of super:

super (parameter_list);

In a subclass constructor, there is an implied first statement; the superclass constructor with no parameters is automatically called.

```
class A
{
    int i;

    A()
    {
      System.out.println("Default Constructor of A");
    }

    A(int a)
    {
      i=a;
      System.out.println("Parameterised Constructor of A");
    }
}

class B extends A
{
    int i;

    B()
    {
      //Default Constructor of A is automatically called
      System.out.println("Default Constructor of B");
    }

    B(int a,int b)
    {
      super(a);   //Calling the Parameterised constructor of SuperClass A
      i=b;
      System.out.println("Parameterised Constructor of B");
    }
}
```

```
class mainClass
{
    public static void main(String args[])
    {
      B objB1=new B();

      B objB2=new B(2,4);
    }
}
    /*
      The output of the program is:

      Default Constructor of A
      Default Constructor of B
      Parameterised Constructor of A
      Parameterised Constructor of B
    */
```

In the preceding example, super( ) was called with three arguments. Since, constructors can be overloaded, super( ) can be called using any form defined by the superclass. The consructor executed will be the one that mathces the arguments.

Super for Member Access

super finds its use to access a member of the superclass that has been hidden (overloaded) by a member of a subclass. This usage has the following general form:

(i) super. <member variable of superclass>;

(ii)super. <member method of superclass> (parameter_list);

The example shows the second use of super.

```
class A
{
    int i;

    void show_A_val()
    {
      System.out.println("Value of i = " + i);
    }
}
class B extends A
{
    int j;

    void set_B_val(int a,int b)
    {
      super.i=a;            // access instance variable of Super Class
      j=b;
    }
```

```
    void show_B_val()
    {
      super.show_A_val(); //access method of Super Class
      System.out.println("Value of j = " + j);
    }
}
class mainClass
{
    public static void main(String args[])
    {
      B objB=new B();
      objB.set_B_val(12,23);
      objB.show_B_val();
    }
}
      /*
      The output of the program is:
      Value of i = 12
      Value of j = 23
    */
```

Q3. Difference between Final and Abstract. **[DEC02,Q2(c)]**

 # What is final keyword? What happens if we apply keyword in class access specifier? **[DEC03,Q1(ii)]**

 # Describe the modifier abstract. **[JUNE03,Q2(d)]**

ANS : Final

A variable can be declared as **final.** Doing so prevents its content form being modified. This means that you must initialize a **final** variable when it is declared. (In this usage, **final** is similar to **const** in C/C++.) For example:

Final int FILE_NEW = 1;
Final int FILE_OPEN = 2;
Final int FILE_SAVE = 3;
Final int FILE_SAVEAS = 4;
Final int FILE_QUIT = 5;

Subsequent parts of your program can now use **FILE_OPEN**, etc., as if they were constants, without fear that a value has been changed.

It is a common coding convention to choose all uppercase identifiers for final variables. Variable declared as **final** do not occupy memory on a per-instance basis. Thus, a **final** variable is essentially a constant.

The keyword **final** can also be applied to methods but its meaning is substantially different than when it is applied to variables. Keyword ***final*** has its two special uses when applied in inheritance.

(i) ***final*** methods, these methods cannot be overriden, for example:

```
class A
{
```

```
    final void xyz( )
    {
      //body of Method
    }
}
    class B extends A
    {
      /* void xyz( ) overriden xyz( )
    {   }
    ERROR
    */
}
```

(ii) ***final*** classes, these classes cannot inherited by other class, that is, they are just opposite to abstract classes.

A final class can only used to create objects. For example:

```
final class A
{
    //class implementation
}
class B extends A
{
    //ERROR CAN'T SUBCLASS A
}
```

Abstract

When applied to a class, the ***abstract*** modifier indicates that the class has not been fully implemented and that it should not be instantiated like this:

```
    A mgA=new A( ):            //ERROR
```

but they can be used to create object references, because Java's approach to runtime polymorphism is implemented through the use of superclass reference.

```
abstract class A
{
    int i;
    void show()
    {
      System.out.println("Hello! This is A");
    }
}

class B extends A
{
    int j;
    void show()
    {
      System.out.println("Value of j = " + j);
    }
```

```
}
class mainClass
{
      public static void main(String args[])
      {
        B objB=new B();

      /* ERROR: A is abstract,can not be instantiated
        A objA=new A();
      */
        A objA;
        objA=objB;                         // objA references to objB

        objA.i=6;               // objA can now access A's member
        objA.show();                       // show() of B:Run-Time Polymorphism

      /*ERROR : j is not accessible through objA
        objA.j=5;
      */
        objB.j=5;
        objA.show();                       //show() of B:Run-Time Polymorphism
      }
}

      /* Note that when objA calls show(), then Java run_time decides to call show()
of B.
The output of the program is:
        Value of j = 0
        Value of j = 5
      */
```

If applied to a member method declaration, the *abstract* modifier means that the function will be implemented in a subclass. An abstract method has no implementation in class where it is declared. Instead it must be implemented in the subclass.

Note *that any class having an abstract method must be declared abstract.*

An abstract class can have normal method with abstract method.

```
abstract class A
{
     abstract void xyz( );
                                       // No implementation here.
     void abc( )                       // A normal method.
     {
```

```
        //body of the method
    }
}
class B extends A
{
    void xyz()              //This is must
    {
                            //body of the method
    }
}
```

Q4. What is inner class? Give its use. Describe with an example. [DEC03,Q5(ii)]

ANS : Introducing Nested and Inner Classes : It is possible to define a class within another class; such classes are known as nested classes. The scope of a nested class is bounded by the scope of its enclosing class. Thus, if class B is defined within class A, then B is known to A, but not outside of A. A nested class has access to the members, incluuding private members, of the class in which it is nested. However, the enclosing class does not have access to the members of the nested class.

The most important type of nested class is the inner class. It has access to all of the variables and methods of its outer class and may refer to them directly in the same way that other non-static members of the outer class do. Thus, an inner class is fully within the scope of its enclosing class.

The following program illustrates how to define and use an inner class. The class named Outer has one instance variable named outer_x, one instance method named test( ), and defines one inner class called Inner.

```
//Demonstrate an inner class.
class Outer {
int outer_x = 100;

void test( ) {
Inner inner = new Inner( );
inner.display( );
}

//this is an inner class
class Inner {
void display( ) {
System.out.print1n(:display: outer_x = " + outer_x);
}
}
}

class InnerClassDemo {
public static void main(String args[ ]) {
```

```
Outer outer = new Outer( );
outer.test( );
}
}
```

Output from this application is shown here:

display: outer_x = 100

It is important to realize that class Inner is known ony within the scope of class Outer. The Java compiler generates an errror message if any code outside of class Outer attempts to instantiate class Inner. An inner class has access to all of the members of its enclosing class, but the reverse is not true. Members of the inner class are known only within the scope of the inner class and may not be used by the outer class.

CHAPTER 7

EXCEPTION HANDLING

- EXCEPTION HANDLING FUNDAMENTALS
- EXCEPTION TYPES
- USING TRY & CATCH
- MULTIPLE CATCH CLAUSES
- THROW
- THROWS
- FINALLY
- JAVA'S BUILT IN EXCEPTIONS
- USERDEFINED EXCEPTION CLASSES

An *exception* is an abnormal condition that arises in a sequence at run time. In other words, an exception is a run-time error. In computer languages that do not support exception handling, errors must be checked and handled manually-typically through the use of error codes, and so no. This approach is as cumbersome as it is troublesome. Java's exception handling avoids these problems and, in the process, brings run-time error management into the object-oriented world.

Q1. Define Exception handling features in Java. [JUNE02,Q3(d);DEC02,Q3(iv)]
ANS : A Java exception is an object that describes an exceptional (that is, error) condition that has occurred in a piece of code. When an exceptional condition arises, an object representing that exception is created in the method that caused the error. That method may choose to handle the exception itself, or pass it on. Either way, at some point, the exception is *caught* and processed. Exceptions can be generated by the Java run-time system, or they can be manually generated by your code. Exceptions thrown by Java relate to fundamental errors that violate the rules of the Java language or the constraints of the Java execution environment. Manually generated exceptions are typically, used to report some error condition to the caller of a method.

Java exception handling is managed via five keywords: **try, catch, throw, throws,** and **finally**.

This is the general form of an exception-handling block:

```
try {
      // block of code to monitor for errors
    }
```

catch *(Exception Type 2 exOb)* {
// exception handler for Exception Type 1
}
catch (Exception Type2 exOb) {
// exception handler for Exception Type2
}
// ...
finally {
// block of code to be executed before try block ends
}

Here, Exception type is the type of exception that has occurred.

Q2. Describe the following classes : **[JUNE03,Q4(i)]**
*** Exception Class**
*** Runtime Exception class**
*** I/O exception class**

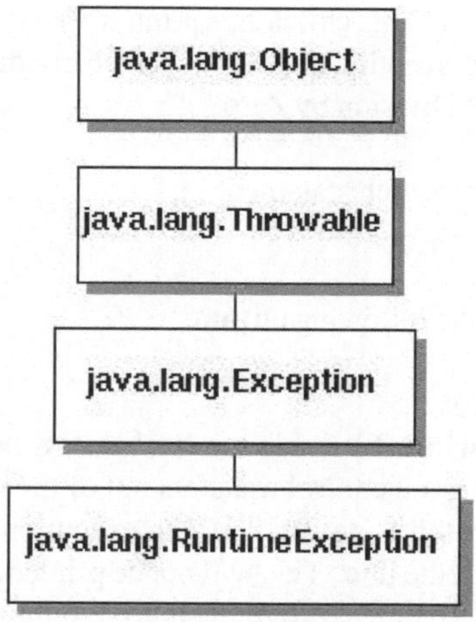

ANS : All exception types are subclasses of the built-in class throwable. Thus, Throwable is at the top of the exception class hierarchy. Immediately below Throwable are two subclasses that partition exceptions into two distinct branches. One branch is headed by **Exception.** This class is used for exceptional conditions that user programs could catch. This is also the class that you will subclass to create your own custom exception types. There is an important subclass of **Exception,** called **Runtime Exception.** Exceptions of this type are automatically defined for the programs that you write and include thing such as "division by zero" and "invalid array indexing".

Q3. Describe in detail Error.

ANS : The other branch is topped by Error, which defines exceptions that are not expected to be caught under normal circumstances by your program. Exceptions of type **Error** are used by the Java run-time system to indicate errors having to do with the run-time environment, itself. "Stack overflow" is an **example** of such an error.

To guard against and handle a run-time error, simply enclose the code that you want to monitor inside a **try** block. Immediately following the **try** block, include a **catch** clause that specifies the exception type that you wish to catch. To illustrate how easily this can be done, the following program includes a **try** block and a **catch** clause which processes the Arithmetic Exception generated by the division-by-zero error:

```
class Exc2 {
    public static void main (String args[ ]) {
    int d, a;
      try {                                   // monitor a block of code.
      d = 0;
      a = 42 / d ;
      System.out.println ("This will not be printed. ");
    } catch (ArithmeticException e) {         //catch divide-by-zero error
    system.out.println ("Division by Zero.");
    }
System.out.println ("After catch statement.");
}
}
```

This program generates the following **output**:

```
Division by zero.
After catch statement.
```

Notice that the call to **println( )** inside the **try** block is never executed. Once an exception is thrown, program control transfers out of the **try** block into the **catch** block. Put differently, **catch** is not "called," so execution never "returns" the try block from a **catch**. Thus, the line "This will not be printed." is not displayed. Once the **catch** statement has executed, program control continues with the next line in the program following the entire **try/catch** mechanism.

A **try** and its **catch** statement form a unit. The scope of the **catch** clause is restricted to those statements specified by the immediately preceding **try** statement.

Multiple catch Clauses

In some cases, more than one exception could be raised by a single piece of code. To handle this type of exception, when an exception is thrown, each **catch** statement is inspected in order, and the first one whose type matches that of the exception is executed. After one **catch** statement executes, the others are bypassed, and execution continues after the **try/catch** block.

```
class multiple_Catch
{
    public static void main(String args[])
```

```
{
  int n=1;
  try
  {
    if(n==1)
    {
              //Expression forces a divede by zero exception
              n=n/(n-n);
    }
    if(n==2)
  {
    int a[]={1};
              //Accessing a non-existing index of Array
              a[42]=99;
  }
}
catch(ArrayIndexOutOfBoundsException e)
{
  // When n=2
  System.out.println("Array Index Out Of Bound Exception" + e);
}
  catch(ArithmeticException e)
  {
    // When n=1
    System.out.println("Arithmetic Exception" + e);
  }
}
}
```

***Note:** when you use multiple **catch** statements, it is important to remember that exception subclasses must come before any of their superclasses. This is because a **catch** statement that uses a superclass will catch exceptions of that type plus any of its subclasses. Thus, a subclass would never be reached if it comes after its superclass.*

Q4. What is the difference between keyword throw and throws?

[JUNE03,Q1(iii)]

#. What is the keyword "throw" used for ? **[DEC02,Q6(i)]**

ANS : So far, you have only been catching exceptions that are thrown by the Java run-time system. However, it is possible for your program to throw an exception explicitly, using the **throw** statement. The general form of throw is shown here;

Throw *Throwableinstance;*

Here, *Throwableinstance* must be an object of type **Throwable** or a subclass, of **Throwable**.

The flow of execution stops immediately after the throw statement; any subsequent statements are not executed. The nearest **try** block is inspected to see if it has a **catch** statement that matches the type of the exception. If it does find a match, control is transferred to that statement. If not, then the next enclosing **try** statement is inspected, and so on. If no matching **catch** is found, then the default exception handler halts the program and prints the stack trace.

```
class exc_throw
{
    public static void main(String args[])
    {
      try
      {
        throw new ArithmeticException("hello");
      }
      catch(ArithmeticException e)
      {
        System.out.println("The exception catched is : " + e);
      }
    }
}

/*********
    Output is:
    The exception catched is : java.lang.ArithmeticException: hello
*********/
```

Here, **new** is used to construct an instance of **NullPointerException**. All of Java's built-in run-time exceptions have two constructors: one with no parameter and one that takes a string parameter.

Throws

If a method is capable of causing an exception that it does not handle, it must specify this behavior so that callers of the method can guard themselves against that exception. You do this by including a throws clause in the method's declaration. A **throws** clause lists the types of exceptions that method might throw.

This is the general *(parameter-list)* throws exception-list

```
{
    // body of method
}
```

Here, *exception-list* is a comma-separated list of the exceptions that a method can throw.

Following is an example of an incorrect program that tries to throw an exception that it does not catch. Because the program does not specify a **throws** clause to declare this fact, the program will not compile.

```
// This program contains an error and will not compile.
class Throws Demo {
    Static void throwOne ( ) {
```

```
        System .out .println ("Inside throwOne");
        Throw new IllegalAccessException ("demo);
    }
    public static void main (String args[ ]) {
        throwOne ( ) ;
    }
}
```

To make this example compile, you need to make two changes. First you need to declare that **throwOne( )** throws **IllegalAccessException.** Second, **main ( )** must define a **try/catch** statement that catches this exception.

The corrected example is shown here:

```
//This is now correct.
class ThrowsDemo {
    Static void throwOne( ) throws IllegalAccessException {
        System.out.println("Inside throwOne.");
        Throw new IllegalegalAccessException("demo);
    }
    public static void main(String args[ ]) {
        try {
            throwOne( );
        } catch(IllegalAccessException e) {
            System.out.println("Caught " + e);
            }
    }
}
```

Here is the **output** generated by running this example program;

Inside throwOne

Caught Java.Lang.IlegalAccessException: demo

Q5. Define keyword 'Finally'.

ANS : Finally creates a block of code that will be executed after a **try/catch** block has completed and before the code following the **try/catch** block. The finally **block** will execute whether or not an exception is thrown. If an exception is thrown, the **finally** block will execute even if no **catch** statement matches the exception. Any time a method is about to return to the caller from inside a **try/catch** block, via an uncaught exception or an explicit return statement, the **finally** clause is also executed just before the method returns. This can be useful for closing file handles and freeing up any other resources that might have been allocated at the beginning of a method with the intent of disposing of them before returning. The **finally** clause is optional. However, each **try** statement requires at least one **catch** or a **finally** clause.

```
class exc_finally
{
    static void methodA()
    {
```

```
        try
        {
          throw new ArithmeticException("hello");
        }
        catch(ArithmeticException e)
        {
          System.out.println("Exception " + e + " is caught");
          throw new NullPointerException("Good Day");
        }
        finally
        {
          System.out.println("methodA's finally");
        }
      }

      public static void main(String args[])
      {
        try
        {
          methodA();
        }
        catch(NullPointerException e)
        {
          System.out.println("Exception " + e + " is caught");
        }
        finally
        {
          System.out.println("main's finally");
        }
      }
}

/*********
      Output is:
      Exception java.lang.ArithmeticException: hello is caught
      methodA's finally
      Exception java.lang.NullPointerException: Good Bye is caught main's finally

*********/
```

Q6. Write an example of user defined exception. [JUNE03,Q4(ii)]
#. Define an exception and discuss how user defined exceptions can be implemented in Java. [DEC03,Q4(ii)]
#. Describe the process of Creating Your Own Exception Subclasses.

ANS : An *exception* is an abnormal condition that arises in a sequence at run time. In other words, an exception is a run-time error. In computer languages that do not support exception handling, errors must be checked and handled manually-typically through the use of error codes, and so no. This approach is as cumbersome as it is troublesome. Java's exception handling avoids these problems and, in the process, brings run-time error management into the object-oriented world.

Although Java's built-in exceptions handle most common errors, you will probably want to create your own exception types to handle situations of **Exception** (which is, of course, a subsclass of **Throwable**). Your subclasses don't need to actually implement anything – it is their existence in the type system that allows you to use them as exceptions.

Method	Description
Throwable fillInStackTrace( )	Returns a Throwable object that contains a completed stack trace. This object can be rethrown.
String getLocalizedMessage( )	Returns a localized description of the exception.
String getMessager( )	Returns a description of the exception.
void printStackTrace( )	Displays the stack trace.
void printStackTrace(PrintStream *stream*)	Sends the stack trace to the specified stream.
void printStackTrace(PrintWriter *stream*)	Sends the stack trace to the specified stream.
String toString( )	Returns a String object containing a description of the exception. This method is called by println( ) when outputting a Throwable object.

Table : The Methods defined by Throwable

The **Exception** class does not define any methods of its own. It does, of course, inherit those methods provided by **Throwable.** Thus, all exceptions, including those that you create, have the methods defined by throwable available to them. They are shown in above Table. You may also wish to override one or more of these methods in exception classes that you create.

The following example declares a new subclass of **Exception** and then uses that subclass to signal an error condition in a method. It overrides the **toString( ) method,** allowing the description of the exception to be displayed using **println ( ).**

```
//This program creates a custom exception types.
Class MyException extends Exception {
    Private int detail;
    MyException(int a) {
```

```
        Detail = a;
    }
    public String toString( ) {
        return "MyException [" + detail + "] " ;
    }
}
class ExceptionDemo {
    static void compute (int a) throws MyException {
        System.out.println(" Called compute) (" + a + ") ");
        If(a > 10)
        Throw new MyException (a);
        System.out.println(" Normal exit") ;
    }
    public static void main(String args [ ] ) {
        try {
            compute(1) ;
            compute(20) ;
        } catch(MyException e) {
        System.out.println(" Caught " + e) ;
        }
    }
}
```

This example defines a subclass of **Exception** called **MyException.** This subclass is quite simple; it has only a constructor plus an overloaded **toString ( )** method that displays the value of the exception. The **ExceptionDemo** class defines a method named **compute ( )** that throws a MyException object. The exception is thrown when **compute( )'s** integer parameter is greater than 10. The **main( )** method sets up an exception handler for **MyException,** then called **compute( )** with a legal value (less than 10) and an illegal one to show both paths through the code.

Here is the **result**:

Called compute (1)
Normal exit
Called compute (20)
Caught MyException [20]

CHAPTER 8

PACKAGES & INTERFACES

- PACKAGES
  - NEED OF PACKAGES
  - DEFINING A PACKAGE
  - UNDERSTANDING CLASS PATH
  - ADDING CLASSES TO EXISTING PACKAGES
  - IMPORTING PACKAGES
- INTERFACES
  - DEFINING AN INTERFACE
  - IMPLEMENTING INTERFACES
  - APPLYING INTERFACES
  - EXTENDING OTHER INTERFACES
  - METHODS IN INTERFACES
  - VARIABLES IN INTERFACES

Q1. What is a package in Java ? How is it created ? How can a package be used in another file ? List two important packages in Java, giving 2 important characteristics of each. [JUNE04,Q4(a)]

 # What are Packages in Java?

ANS : In the preceding chapters, the name of each example class was taken from the same name space. This means that a unique name had to be used for each class to avoid name collision. After a while, without some way to manage the name space, you could run out of convenient, descriptive names for individual classes. You also need some way to be assured that the name you choose for a class will be reasonably unique and not collide with class names chosen by other programmers.

Packages are containers for classes that are used to keep the class name space compartmentalized. Packages are stored in a hierarchical manner and are explicitly imported into new class definitions. You can define classes inside a package that are not accessible by code outside that package. You can also define class members that are only exposed to other members of the same package.

To create a package, Java source file (.java) need to include a **package** statment. The **package** statment has the following syntax:

```
package <packagename>;
```

How to create packages?

Java uses file system directories to store packages. The following statement creates a package called MyPackage.

package MyPackage;

One must remember, while creating package:

· Each Java source file in folder MyPackage must include the statement above.

· package statement is the first statement in Java file.

· Classes you want to be accessible by code outside that package must be declared public.

· package names are case sensitive, so the folder name and name of package sould be same.

· You can create a hierarchy of packages, that is, package within a package. The example of a multileveled package statement is package book.chapter.topic;

Here **book** is the top level package having another package **chapter** inside and **topic** package inside **chapter**.

When we create a package class, we should declare each class member with its access modifier. (private, public, protected).

Access Protection

In the preceding chapters, you learned about various aspects of Java's access control mechanism and its access specifies. For example, you already know that access to a **private** member of a class is granted only to other members of that class. Packages add another dimension to access control. As you will see, Java provides many levels of protection to allow fine-grained control over the visibility of variables and methods within classes, subclasses, and packages.

Classes and packages are both means of encapsulating and containing the name space and scope of variables and methods. Packages act as containers for classes and other subordinate packages. Classes act as containers for data and code. The class is Java's smallest unit of abstraction. Because of the interplay between classes and packages, Java addresses four categories of visibility for class members:

- Subclasses in the same package
- Non-subclasses in the same package
- Subclasses in different packages
- Classes that are neither in the same package nor subclasses

The three access specifies **private, public,** and **protected** provide a variety of ways to produce the many levels of access required by these categories. Following table sums up the interactions.

While Java's access control mechanism may seem complicated, we can simplify it as follows. Anything declared **public** can be accessed from anywhere. Anything declared **private** cannot be seem outside of its class. When a member does not have an explicit access specification, it is visible to subs classes as well as to other classes in the same package. This is the default access. If you want to allow an element to be seen outside your current package, but only to classes that subclass you directly, then declare that element **protected.**

	Private	No modifier	Protected	Public
Same class	☑	☑	☑	☑
Same package subclass	☒	☒	☒	☒
Same package non-subclass	☒	☒	☒	☒
Different package subclass	☒	☒	☒	☒
Different package non-subclass	☒	☒	☒	☒

Table : Class Member Access

Table applies only to members of classes. A has only two possible access levels: default and pubic. When a class is declared as **public**, it is accessible by any other code. If a class has default access, then it can only be accessed by other code within its same package.

The following example shows all combinations of the access control modifiers. This example has two packages and four classes.

```
package p1;
public class X
{
    int def_X=1;
    private int pri_X=2;
    protected int pro_X=3;
    public int pub_X=4;
}
package p1;
// Y is a sub-class of X within the same package
class Y extends X
{
    Y()
    {
      System.out.println("Default member of X = " + def_X);
    // ERROR: Private of X is not accessible
    // System.out.println("Private member of X = " + pri_X);
      System.out.println("Protected member of X = " + pro_X);
      System.out.println("Public member of X = " + pub_X);
        }
}
package p2;
// sub_X is a sub-class of X in a different package
```

```
class sub_X extends p1.X
{
    sub_X()
    {
    // ERROR: Default & Private member of X are not accessible
    // System.out.println("Default member of X = " + def_X);
    // System.out.println("Private member of X = " + pri_X);
       System.out.println("Protected member of X = " + pro_X);
       System.out.println("Public member of X = " + pub_X);
    }
}
package p2;
// non_sub_X is a non sub-class of X in a different package
class non_sub_X
{
    non_sub_X()
    {
       p1.X objX=new p1.X();
    //ERROR: Default, Private and Protected member of X are not accessible
    //System.out.println("Default member of X = " + objX.def_X);
    // System.out.println("Private member of X = " + objX.pri_X);
    // System.out.println("Protected member of X = " + objX.pro_X);
       System.out.println("Public member of X = " + objX.pub_X);
    }
}
```

```
public class X
{
   //body of class
}

class Y extends X
{
   //body of class
}
```

P1

```
class sub_X extends P1.X
{
   //body of class
}

class non_sub_X
{
   //body of class
}
```

P2

Class X has four instance variables, with default, private, protected & public access. Class Y is a subclass of X within the same package. So Y can access default, protected & public variables but not private.

Another package P2 has two classes, one is a subclass of X (subX), and other is a non-subclass of X (non_subX).

The subX can access only public and protected member of X.

The non-subX can access only public member of X.

Importing Packages

Given that packages exist and are a good mechanism for compartmentalizing diverse classes from each other, it is easy to see why all of the built-in Java classes are stored in packages. Since classes within packages must be fully qualified with their package name or names, it could become tedious to type in the long dot-separated package path name for every class you want to use. For this reason, Java includes the **import** statement to bring certain classes, or entire packages, into visibility. Once imported, a class can be referred to directly, using only its name. The **import** statement is a convenience to the programmer and is not technically needed to write a complete Java program. In a Java source file, **import** statements occur immediately following the **package** statement (if it exists) and before any class definitions. This is the general form of the **import** statement:

import *pkg 1 [.pkg 2] (classname | *);*

Here, pkg1 is the name of a top-level package, and pkg 2 is the name of a subordinate package inside the other package separated by a dot (.). There is no practical limit on the depth of a package hierarchy, except that imposed by the file system. Finally, you specify either an explicit *classname* or a star (*), which indicates that the Java compiler should import the entire package.

The example demonstrate, how we can import classes into our program. Here, import the previously created class X of package P1 and see how its member access is possible.

```
import p1.*;
// importing a package p1
class mainClass
{
    public static void main(String args[])
    {
      X objX=new X();
    // ERROR: Default, Private and Protected member of X are not // accessible
    // System.out.println("Default member of X = " + objX.def_X);
    // System.out.println("Private member of X = " + objX.pri_X);
    // System.out.println("Protected member of X = " + objX.pro_X);
      System.out.println("Public member of X = " + objX.pub_X);
    }
}
```

The 7 most commonly used packages in Java :

· package | java.util | : contains languages support classes of a more utilitarian nature. These include Linked List, Stack, Arrays and Hash Table Classes, as well as some useful abstract designs codified by the interfaces ***Enumeration*** and ***Observer***.

· package | java.io | : It provides device_independent file and stream input and output services.

· package | java.awt | : It contains Java's Abstract Windows Toolkil (AWT), the package shouuld really be considered as the heart of entire hierarchy.

· package | java.awt.image | : contains class related to image processing.

· package | java.net | : It combines the classes supporting low-level Internet programming plus World Wide Web/HTML support.

· package | java.applet | : contains a single class with support for HTML embedded Java applets.

Q2. What is a final variable? Can you define a final variable without supplying its value? [JUN02, Q1(ii)(a)]

ANS : A variable can be declared as **final.** Doing so prevents its content form being modified. This means that you must initialize a **final** variable when it is declared. (In this usage, **final** is similar to **const** in C/C++.) For example:

```
Final int FILE_NEW = 1;
Final int FILE_OPEN = 2;
Final int FILE_SAVE = 3;
Final int FILE_SAVEAS = 4;
Final int FILE_QUIT = 5;
```

Subsequent parts of your program can now use **FILE_OPEN**, etc., as if they were constants, without fear that a value has been changed.

It is a common coding convention to choose all uppercase identifiers for final variables. Variable declared as **final** do not occupy memory on a per-instance basis. Thus, a **final** variable is essentially a constant.

Yes, we can define a final variable without supplying its value. We can supply value later on. For example, we can define:

```
Final int quantity;
quantity=50000;
```

Q3. Describe interface. [JUNE03,Q2(vii) ; JUN2001,Q6(i)]

ANS : Interface : Through the use of the interface keyword, Java allows you to fully abstract the interface from its implementation. Using interface, you can specify a set of methods which can be implemented by one or more classes. The interface, itself, does not actually define any implementation. Although they are similar to abstract classes, interfaces have an additional capability: A class can implement more than one interface. By contrast, a class can only inherit a single super class (abstract or otherwise).

Packages and interfaces are two of the basic components of a Java program.

An interface is defined much like a class. This is the general form of an interface.

```
access interface name {
        return-type method-name1(parameter-list);
        return-type method-name2(parameter-list);
        type final-varname1 = value;
        type final-varname2 = value;
        // ...
        return-type method-nameN(parameter-list);
        type final-varnameN = value;
}
```

CHAPTER-9

ABSTRACT WINDOW TOOLKIT

Introduction

The Abstract Windowing Toolkit (AWT) is an API that is responsible for building the Graphical User Interface (GUI). It is a part of the Java Foundation Classes (JFC). AWT includes a rich set of user interface components, a powerful event handling model, graphics and image tools, layout managers and support for data transfer using cut and paste through clipboards. AWT also support javaBeans architecture. Every AWT component is a simple bean. The java.awt contains all classes for creating user interfaces and for painting graphics and images.

The AWT has several subsystems that support the development of Graphical User Interface (GUI programs. The subsystems include :

- Graphics primitives that allow the drawing and rendering of lines and images.
- Components such as Labels, Buttons and TextFields.
- Containers that include Frames, panels and Dialogs.
- Layout managers that control the display in a portable manner.
- Event system, which allows the user to respond to interactions between the user to respond to interactions between the components and containers in the application

The original AWT version 1.0 of the Java Development Kit (JDK) did its work by instantiating peer objects from the native operating system. Starting with JDK 1.1, sun has made substantial changes to the user interface components. The AWT that came with 1.0 is no longer in use, it has been replaced by the AWT in 1.1. The interface in Java 1.1 still does its work through peer objects and these are now know as heavyweight components. These are also lightweight components that do not tie the user to the native operating system.

These instead support the pluggable look and feel. Java makes many details of the graphical user interface (GUI) programming invisible but they are still present. This is possible because of the platform independence of Java.

User Interface Components

A place in which the various drawing needs to be done must be provided and this is called the container. The container is derived from java.awt.container class. The elements of the java.awt.Component class.

The Component class is the abstract superclass of the nonmenu-related Abstract Window Toolkit components. All the user interface components and container classes are derived from this class. This class is responsible for a variety of activities like display event handling and font management.

There are two major sets of classes derived from the component class:

- **Container** classes - They are generic AWT components that can contain other components.
- **User Interface component** classes - these include components like Button, label etc.

Containers

A generic Abstract Window Toolkit (AWT) container object is a component that can contain other AWT components. User interface components added to a container are tracked in a list. The order of the list will define the components' front-to-back stacking order within the container. If no index is specified when adding a component to a container, it will be added to the end of the list. Components have to be necessarily added to a container if they have to be displayed on the screen. Fig. 8.1 shows the class hierarchy of the classes that can act as containers.

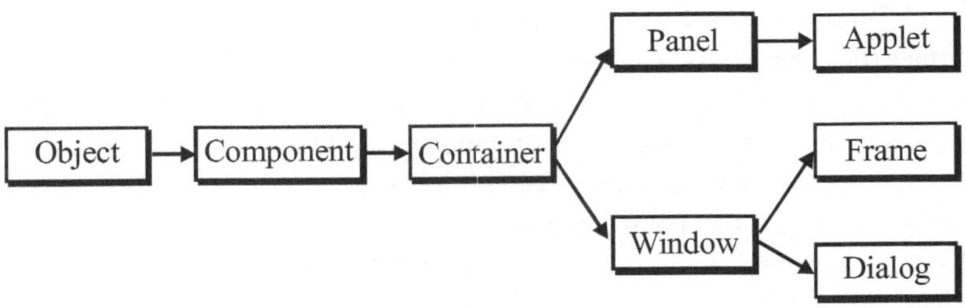

The basic functionalities of containers are encapsulated in an abstract class, Container. This class has methods that allow other components to be nested within it. The panel is a simple non-abstract container that can contain other components. The add( ) method of the Container class can be used to add components to a Panel. The Applet class is derived from the panel class and, hence, can act as a container. This property of the applet shall be exploited by adding user interface components and other containers directly to the applet.

Note

The Applet class, through derived from panel, does not belong to the AWT package.

User Interface Component Classes

The AWT package contains a number of component classes that are typical elements of any interactive user interface. These classes, collectively called UI component classes, are derived from the abstract Component class. Fig. 8.2 shows the class hierarchy of these classes.

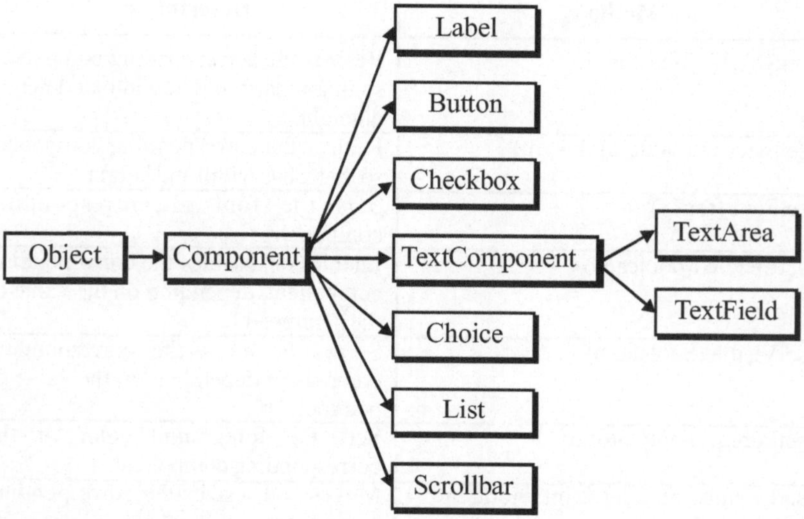

The component class defines a number of methods that can be used on any of the classes that are derived from it. The methods listed below in table 8.1 can be used in all GUI components as well as containers

Method	Description
setSize (Dimension d)	Resizes the corresponding component so that it has width d.width and height d.height.
setSize(int width, int height)	Resizes the corresponding component so that it has width and height.
setFont (font f)	Sets the font of corresponding component.
setEnabled(boolean b)	Enables or disables the corresponding component, depending on the value of the parameter b.
setVisible(boolean b)	Shows or hides the corresponding component depending on the value of parameter b.
setForeground(Color c)	Sets the foreground color of the corresponding component.
setBounds(int x, int y, int width, int height)	Moves and resizes the corresponding component.
setBounds(Rectangle r)	Moves and resizes the corresponding component to conform to the new bounding rectangle r.
setBackground(Color c)	Sets the background color of the corresponding component.
getBackground( )	Gets the background color of the corresponding component.
getBounds( )	Gets the bounds of the corresponding component in the form of a Rectangle object.
getFont( )	Gets the fond of the corresponding component.
getForeground( )	Gets the foreground color of the corresponding component.
getSize( )	Returns the size of the corresponding component in the form of a Dimension object.

The various user interface components have been shown in figure above the following sections will discuss each of these components in detail.

To effectively use these components, the following steps have to be carried out.

- First, the user interface component has to be created using the constructor of the corresponding class. For example, to create a Button object, the following code fragment can be used:

Button mybutton = new Button ("OK");

- Next, the component created is added to a container using the add () method of the Container class. For example, add(but); adds the button created to the container. Since, the Applet itself is derived from the Container class, the add() method can be used on an applet.

▸ Depending on the user interface component, it is necessary to handle the event generated by it. There are two ways of handling events as mentioned in the last chapter. But it is always wise to use listeners rather than letting the component handle its events by itself.

▸ To determine the component in which an event has occurred, it is necessary to use inner classes which was dealt in the fourth chapter. Each object has an inner class defined for it that implements their respective event listeners. The object of this inner class forms a parameter to the XXXListener( ) function in its outer class.

The user interface component classes also have a number of methods that can be used to change the attributes of the component like, the label of a button, text of a text field etc. the user interface component classes, including their events and methods, are discussed next.

Button

Buttons are components that can contain a label. It has an outline. The button is similar to a push button in any other GUI. Pushing a button causes the run time system to generate an event. This event is sent to the program. The program in turn can detect the event and respond to the event. Clicking a button generates an ActionEvent.

However, before a button can be used it has to be created using the new keyboard in association with the constructors that are defined for it. Buttons must be added to the containers before they can be used. This is done using the keyword add. Once the buttons have been created and added they can be used.

When a button is clicked the AWT sends an instance of the ActionEvent to the button, by calling the processEvent on the button. The processEvent method of the button receives all the events of the button. This then passes an action event along by calling its processActionEvent. The processActionEvent then passes the action event to any action listeners that have registered an interest in active events generated by the button in question.

Any application that has to perform an action based on the button has to implement the ActionListener and register the listener to receive the events from the button, by calling its addActionListener method.

Constructor	Description
Button( )	Constructs a button with no label
Button (String label)	Constructs a button with the label specified.

Table lists some of the methods that can be used in relation to a Button component.

Method	Description
addActionListener (ActionListener1)	Adds the specified action listener to receive action events from the corresponding button.
getActionCommand( )	Returns the command name of the action event fired by the corresponding button.
getLabel( )	Returns the label of the corresponding button.
pramString( )	Returns the parameter string representing the state of the corresponding button.
setLabel(Stringlabel)	Sets the label of the button of the value specified.

Example 1 : Write an applet that contains two labels, and two buttons, "OK" and "Cancel". Two labels are used to display the text of the buttons namely - Button1 and Button2. the status bar should indicate about which button was clicked. Enter the following code in a file and save it as Button Test.java.

```
import java.awt.*;
import java.applet.*;
import java.awt.event.*;
public class ButtonTest extends Applet    {
Label 1b1=new Label ("Button1") ;
Button b1 =new Button ("ok");
Label 1b2 =new Label ("Button2");
Button b2 = new Button ("cancel");
public void init () {
setLayout (new FlowLayout () ) ;
b1 . addActionListener (new B1 () );
b2 . addActionListener (new B2 () );
add (1b1);
add (b1);
add (1b2);
add (b2);
}
class B1 implements ActionListener {
public void actionPerformed (ActionEvent e)
getAppletContext ( ).showstatus ("Button1: ok clicked");
}
}
class B2 implements ActionListener {
```

```
24 : public void actionPerformed (ActionEvent e) {
25 : getAppletContext ( ). showStatus ("Button2: cancel clicked");
26 :            }
24 :      }
28 : }
```

▸ Enter the following script in a file and save it as ButtonTest.html.

<APPLET CODE="ButtonTest.class" WIDTH=400 HEIGHT=100> </APPLET>

Two buttons and two labels are added to the applet to the applet in the init ( ) method in lines 13 to 16. Two action listeners are created in the inner classesB1 and B2 and are added to the applet using the addActionlistener ( ) method. Note that these inner casses implement the ActionListener interface. The getAppletContext ( ) method determines this applet's context and uses the showstatus ( ) method to display appropriate messages on the status line when the buttons are clicked. The setLayout() method is dealt in the latter half of this chapter.

CheckBox

Checkbox are user interface components that have state: checked and unchecked. Clicking on it can change the state of the checkbox.

Java supports two types of checkboxes: exclusive and non-exclusive.

▸ In case of exclusive checkbox, only one group of items can be selected at a time. If an item from the group is selected, the checkbox currently checked is deselected and the new selection is highlighted. The exclusive checkboxes are also called **radio buttons.**

▸ The non-exelusive checkboxes are not grouped together and, each chekbox can be selected independent of the other.

The various constructors of checkboxes include:

Constructor	Description
Checkbox( )	Creates a checkbox with no label
Checkbox(String label)	Creates a checkbox with the specified label
Checkbox (String label), boolean state)	Creates a checkbox with the specified label and sets the specified state
Checkbox(String label, boolean state, CheckboxGroup group)	Creates a checkbox with the specified label and sets the specified state and places it in the specified group. The position of the checkbox group and state can be interchanged.

The various method that are supported by checkboxes are listed below :

Method	Description
getCheckboxGroup( )	Determines the group of the corresponding check box
getLabel( )	Gets the name of the corresponding check box
getSelectedObjects( )	Returns an array (length 1) containing the checkbox label or null if the checkbox is not selected.
getState( )	Determines if the checkbox is in the 'on' or 'off' state
setCheckboxGroup(CheckboxGroup g)	Sets the corresponding checkbox's group to the specified one.
setLabel(String label)	Sets the label of the corresponding checkbox to the value specified.
setState(boolean state)	Sets the state of the corresponding checkbox to the value specified.

Choice

The choice classimplements a pop-up menu that allows the user to select an item from that menu. This UI component displays the currently selected item with an arrow to its right. On clicking the arrow, the menu opens and displays options for a user to select.

To create a choice menu, a Choice object is instantiated. Then, various items are added to the Choice by using the addItem( ) method. The various constructors that can be used to create a choice object is given below:

Constructor	Description
Choice( )	Creates a new choice menu

The various methods that can be used along with a choice object are listed below:

Method	Description
add(String item)	Adds an item to the corresponding choice menu
addItem(String item)	Adds an item to the corresponding choice
getItem(int index)	Gets the string at the specified index of the corresponding choice menu
getItemCount( )	Returns the number of items in the corresponding choice menu
getSelectedIndex()	Returns the index of the currently selected item
getSelectedItem( )	Gets a representation of the current choice as a string.
getSelectedObjects( )	Returns an array (length 1) containing the currently selected item.
insert(String item, int index)	Inserts the item into the corresponding choice at the specified position
remove(int position)	Removes an item from the corresponding choice menu at the specified position.
remove(String item)	Remove the first occurrence of item from the corresponding Choice menu.
removeAll( )	Removes all items from the corresponding choice menu.
select (int pos)	Sets the selected item in the corresponding Choice menu to be the item at the specified position
select(String str)	Sets the selected item in the corresponding Choice menu to be the item whose name is equal to the specified string.

Example 2 :

```
import java.awt.*;
import java.awt. event.*;
import java.applet.*;
public class radioTest extends Applet {
public void init( ) {
CheckboxGroup c=new checkboxGroup( );
Checkbox  c1=new checkbox("Colour and White", c, true) ;
Checkbox c2=new checkbox("Colour" ,c, false);
c1.addMouseListener(new check1 ( ));
```

```
c2.addMouseListener(new check2 ( ));
add(c1);
add(c2);
Choice abc= new Choice( );
abc.add("Onida");
abc.add("BPL");
abc.add("Sansung");
abc.add("philips");
abc.add("Videocon");
abc. addItemListener (new ch ( ) );
add(abc);
}
class check1 extends MouseAdapter {
public void mouseClicked (MouseEvent e) {
showStatus("You have selected : Black and white TV");
}
}
class check1 extends mouseAdapter {
public void mouseClicked(MouseEvent e) {
showStatus("You have selected : Colour TV") ;
}
}
class Ch implements Itemlistener {
public void itemStateChanged (itemEvent e) {
String s= (String)e.getItem ( );
showStatus ("You have selected" + s + "brand") ;
                    }
        }
}
```

The radioTest.html file code is as follows:

```
<applet code="RadioTest.class" height =100 width =300>
</applet>
```

SOLVED PAPERS
CS-74

GUESS PAPER-I

Q1. What is a bytecode in Java?

Q2. What is 'this' keyword? How is it different from a super Keyword?

Q3. List the five Java buzzwords, and explain the significance of each.

Q4(a).Implement a class programmer. A programmer has name, company name, working for and basic_salary. Write a default constructor and constructor with parameters to create a programmer object. Further, show the implementation of the constructor method with parameters.

(b)Write the output of the following;

```
Class Demo {
        public static void main (string args[ ])
                {
                        int I;
                int num=0× FFFFFFE;
        for (I=0; I<2; I++)
                {
                        num=num << 1;
                        system.out.println (num);
                }
        }
}
```

Q5(a). Application vs Applet

(b)This vs Super keyword

Q6. Discuss the difference between String and String Buffer class as defined in Java

GUESS PAPER-II

Q1. Write a java program to calculate Fibonacci series recursively.

Q2. Difference between the following :
Method overloading and Overriding a method

Q3(i). Describe the following classes :
Exception class
Runtime exception class
I/O exception class
(ii) Write an example of user defined exception.

Q4(i). What is the relationship between Java and HTML?
(ii) Describe the paint () method. Where is it defined? How is it invoked?

Q5. Differentiate between the following :
(i) Final and Abstract
(ii) Window and Panel
(iii) Thread and Process

Q6(i). Write a recursive program in Java for the greatest common divisor (GCD). Given two position integers, the GCD is the largest integer that divides them both.
(ii) Answer the following questions :
(a) How do you run an applet?
(b) How do you create a button labelled "BCA"? (How do you change a label on a button?)

CS-74 : INTRODUCTION TO INTERNET PROGRAMMING
JUNE - 2001

Note : *Question **one** is **compulsory**. Answer any **three** from the rest.*

Q1(i). Write a Java program to count 1 to 1000 numbers using 10 threads.

ANS : import java.awt.*;

```
class count
{
public static int sum=0;
public static void main(String args[]) throws InterruptedException
{
sub_count t1,t2,t3,t4,t5,t6,t7,t8,t9,t10;
t1=new sub_count(1,100);
t1.start();
t2=new sub_count(101,200);
t2.start();
t3=new sub_count(201,300);
t3.start();
t4=new sub_count(301,400);
t4.start();
t5=new sub_count(401,500);
t5.start();
t6=new sub_count(501,600);
t6.start();
t7=new sub_count(601,700);
t7.start();
t8=new sub_count(701,800);
t8.start();
t9=new sub_count(801,900);
t9.start();
t10=new sub_count(901,1000);
t10.start();
t1.join();
t2.join();
t3.join();
t4.join();
t5.join();
t6.join();
t7.join();
t8.join();
t9.join();
```

```
t10.join();
System.out.println("Sum is:"+sum);
}
}
class sub_count extends Thread
{
int start_no;
int end_no;
sub_count(int start,int end)
{
start_no=start;
end_no=end;
}
public void run()
{
int i,tmp=0;
for(i=start_no;i<=end_no;i++)
{
tmp=tmp+i;
}
count.sum=count.sum+ tmp;
}
}
```

(ii) Write a complete Java program to calculate Fibonacci series non recursively.

ANS : import java.awt.*;

```
class fibonacci
{
public static void main(String args[])
{
int firstno= 1;
int secondno= 1;
int i =0;
int fibono=0;
System.out.println(firstno);
 System.out.println(" ");
System.out.println(secondno);
 System.out.println(" ");
for(i=0;i<30;i++)
{
fibono=firstno+secondno;
System.out.println(fibono);
firstno=secondno;
```

```
secondno=fibono;
}
}
}
```

(iii) Describe main features of Java programming language.

Refer to Study material, Q5, Page no.-14

Q2(i). What is the need of layout manager? Describe a Border Layout. How do you create a Border Layout Container? List the names of five sections in a Border Layout. Can you add multiple components in the same section?

ANS : The need of Layout manager is to automatically arrange the controls within a window. Imagine a window in which we want to put 6 buttons as the size of the window is fixed all the buttons can't be fixed in a single row then layout manager allows to position the controls at an appropriate locations within the window.Compared to the class FlowLayout, which implements the interface java.awt.LayoutManager and sizes each component to be its preferred size, the interface java.awt.LayoutManager allows a constraint to be associated with each component. This constraint is an object that the layout manager uses when determining the size and position of components in a container and is typed as java.lang.Object although each implementer has a specific constraint that it is designed to work with. The class java.awt.BorderLayout implements LayoutManager2 and its constraint is a string that can be one of the values "North", "East", "Center", "South" and "West". Two additional constants are used to support relative positioning based on the container's ComponentOrientation. For example, in a container where Component Orientation is Component Orientation. LEFT_TO_RIGHT, "Before line begins" maps to "West" and "After line ends" maps to "East", respectively. Also, mixing the two types of constants is not recommended. When adding components, you will use these constants with the following form of **add()**, which is defined by **Container :**

void add(Component compObj, Object region) ;

Here, compObj is the component to be added, and region specifies where the component will be added.

Yes, we can add more than one component in the same section.

(ii) How do you create a textfield with a width of 10 characters and the default text "Welcome to Java"?

ANS :

```
import java.awt.*;
import java.applet.*;
/*
<applet code="TextExample" width=200 height=60>
</applet>
*/
public class TextExample extends Applet
```

```
{
TextField txt1;
public void init()
{
txt1=new TextField("Welcome to java", 10);
add(txt1);
}
}
```

(iii) How doyou create a checkbox with three choice items? How do you determine if a box is checked?

ANS : import java.awt.*;

```
import java.awt.event.*;
import java.applet.*;
import java.lang.*;
public class chkbox extends Applet implements ItemListener
{
Checkbox popcorn, icecream, chocolate;
String message;
public void init()
{
popcorn=new Checkbox("popcorn",true);
icecream=new Checkbox("Icecream",false);
chocolate=new Checkbox("Chocolate",false);
add(popcorn);
add(icecream);
add(chocolate);
popcorn.addItemListener(this);
icecream.addItemListener(this);
chocolate.addItemListener(this);
}
public void itemStateChanged(ItemEvent ie)
{
repaint();
}
public void paint(Graphics g)
{
message="popcorn :" + popcorn.getState();
g.drawString(message,10,100);
message="icecream : "+ icecream.getState();
g.drawString(message,10,150);
message= "chocolate :" + chocolate.getState();
g.drawString(message,10,200);
}
}
```

Q3(i). Describe the AWT class hierarchy. Also describe the methods in component, container, frame and panel class.

Refer to JUNE-02, Q6(a), Page no.-158

(ii) Explain the following terms with examples:

- **Panel**
- **Frame**
- **Container**

ANS :

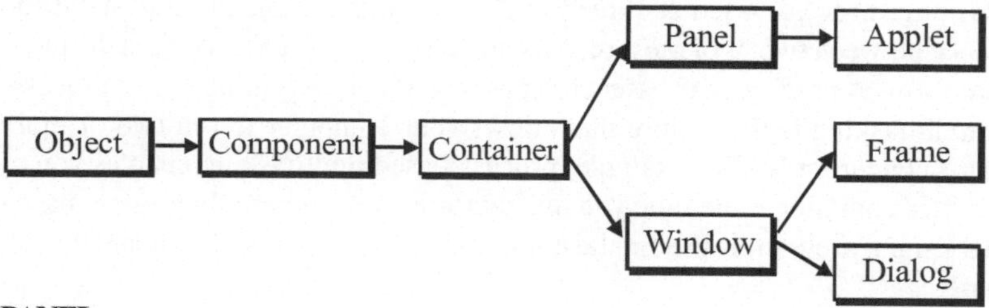

PANEL

The Panel class is a concrete subclass of **Container**. It doesn't add any new methods; it simply implements **Container**. A **Panel** may be thought of as a recursively nestable, concrete screen component. **Panel** is the superclass for **Applet**. When screen output is directed to an applet, it is drawn on the surface of a Panel object. In essence, a **Panel** is a window that does not contain a title bar, menu bar, or border. This is why you don't see these items when an applet is run inside a browser. When you run an applet using an appletviewer, the appletviewer provides the title on border.

Other components can be added to a **Panel** object by its **add()** method (inherited from **Container**). Once these components have been added, you can position and resize them manually using the **setLocation(), setSize(), or setBounds()** methods defined by **Component.**

FRAME

Frame encapsulates what is commonly thought of as a "window." It is a subclass of **Window** and has a title bar, menu bar, borders, and resizing corners. If you create a **Frame** object from within an applet, it will contain a warning message, such as "java Applet Window" to the user that an applet window has been created. This message warns users that the window they see was started by an applet and not by software running on their computer. (An applet that could masquerade as a host-based application could be used to obtain passwords and other sensitive information without the user's knowledge.) When a **Frame** window is created by a program rather than an applet, a normal window is created.

CONTAINER

The **Container** class is a subclass of **Component**. It has additional methods that allow other **Component** objects to be nested within it. Other **Container** objects can be stored inside a **Contianer** (since they are themselves instances of **Component**.) This makes for a multileveled containment system. A container is responsible for laying out (that is, positioning) any components that it contains. It does this through the use of various layout managers .

Q4(a). What is multithreading? What is the difference between a thread and a process? When do you use the thread class and when do you use the Runnable interface? What are the differences? [DEC2002,Q2(e)]

ANS : Unlike most other computer languages, JAVA provides built-in support for multithreading programming. A multithreading program contains two or more parts that can run concurrently. Each point of such program is called thread; specialized form of multitasking.

You are most certainly acquainted with multitasking, because it is supported by virtually all modern Operating Systems. However, there are two district types of multitasking; process-based & thread-based. It is important to understand the difference between two. For most readers, process-based multitasking is the more familiar form. A process is, in essence, a program that is executing. Thus process-based multitasking is the feature that allows your computer to run two or more programs concurrently. For example, process-based multitasking enables you to run the Java compiler at the time you text editor is also running. In process-based multitasking, a program is the smallest unit of code that can be dispatched by the scheduler.

In a thread-based multitasking environment, the thread is the smallest unit of dispatchable code. This means that a single program can perform two or more tasks simultaneously. For instance a text editor can format text at the same time that it is printing, as long as these two actions are being performed by two separate threads. Thus, process-based multitasking deals with the "big-picture", and thread-based multitasking handles the details.

Multitasking threads require less overhead than multitasking process. Processes are heavy weight task that require their own separate address spaces. Inter process communication is expensive and limited. Context switching from one process to another is also costly. Threads, on the other hand, are lightweight. They share the same address space and cooperatively share the same heavyweight process. Inter thread communication is expensive and context switching from one thread to the next is at low cost. While Java programs make use of process-based multitasking environments, process-based multitasking is not under the control of Java. However, multithreaded multitasking is.

Multithreading enables you to write very efficient programs that make maximum use of the CPU, because idle time can be kept to minimum, this is especially important for the interactive, networked environment in which Java operates, because idle time is common. For example, the transmission rate of data over a network is much slower than the rate at which the computer can process it.

If you have programmed for OS such as Windows 98 or Window NT, then you are already familiar with multithreaded programming. However, the fact that Java threads manager makes multithreading especially convenient, because many of the details are handled for you.

You might be wondering why Java has two ways to create child threads, and which approach is better. The answers to these questions turn on the same point. The **Thread** class defines several methods that can be overridden by a derived class. Of these methods, the only one that must be overridden is **run ()**. This is, of course, the same method required when you implement **Runnable**. Many Java programmers feel that classes should be extended only when they are being enhanced or modified in some way. So, if you will not be overriding any of **Thread's** other methods, it is probably the best to simply implement **Runnable** interface. This is up to you, of course.

(b) State true or false :

· **Every element in the array has the same type.**

TRUE

· **Array size is fixed after it is created.**

TRUE

· **You can add a frame to a panel.**

FALSE

· **You can add panel to a frame.**

TRUE

· **You can add a button to a frame.**

TRUE

Q5(a). What is the difference between application and applet? Write an applet to display "I like Java programming" and explain various features of how applet program is written. [DEC03,Q3(i);JUN2003,Q1(iv);JUN2002,Q2(i)]

ANS :

```
import java.awt.*;
import java.applet.*;
public class javaprog extends Applet
{
String s;
public void init()
{
s=getParameter("string");
if(s== null)
s= "I like java programming";
}
public void paint(Graphics g)
{
g.drawString(s, 10,100);
}
}
/*
<applet code= "javaprog" width=300 height=100>
<param name= "string" value="I like java programming">
</applet>
*/
```

(b) Define the init( ), start( ) and destroy( ) method in the Applet class. Is the get parameter( ) method defined in the Applet class? Is the paint( ) method defined in the Applet class? What are these methods originally defined?

ANS : init() : The **init()** method is the first method to be called. This is where you should initialize variables. This method is called only once during the run time of your applet.

start() : The **start()** method is called after **init().** It is also called to restart an applet after it has been stopped. Whereas **init()** is called once- the first time an applet is loaded- **start()** is called each time an applet's HTML document is displayed onscreen. So, if a user leaves a web page and comes back, the applet resumes execution at **start().**

destroy() : The **destroy()** method is called when the environment determines that your applet needs to be removed completely from memory. At this point, you should free up any resources the applet may be using. The **stop()** method is always called before **destroy().**

Yes, getParameter() method defined in the Applet class.

public String getParameter(String name) ;

It allows us to get parameter from within the <APPLET> tag of the HTML file that loaded the applet.

No, the paint() method is not defined in the Applet class.

Paint() method is defined by the AWT component class.

public void paint(Graphics g);

Empty method to be overridden to draw something in the graphics context.

Q6. Describe the following terms with examples :

(i) Interface **[JUN2003,Q2(vii)]**

Refer to Study material, Q3, Page no.-90

(ii) Superclass

Using inheritance, you can create a general class that defines traits common to a set of related items. This class can then be inherited by other, more specific classes, each adding those things that are unique to it. In the terminology of Java, a class that is inherited is called a superclass.

Inheritance Basics

To inherit a class, you simply incorporate the definition of one class into another by using the **extends** keyword. To see how, let's begin with a short example. The following program creates a superclass called **A** and a subclass called **B.** Notice how the keyword extends is used to create subclass of **A.**

```
    // A simple example of inheritance.
    // Create a superclass.
    class A {
    int i, j;
void showij ()        {
```

```
        System.out .println ("i and j: " + i + " " + j) ;
      }
}

// Create a subclass by extending class A.
class B extends A {
  int k;
  void showk () { // creating method.
    System.out.println ("k: " + k) ;
}
 void sum () { //creating a method.
   System.out.println (" i + j + K: " + (i+j+k)) ;
 }
}
class simpleInheritance {
 public static void main (String args []) {
    A superob = new A() ;
B subob = new B() ;
// The superclass may be used by itself.
superob.i = 10;
superob.j = 20;
System.out.println ("contents of superob: ") ;
superob.showij () ;
System.outprintln() ;
// The subclass has access to all public members of its superclass.
subob.i = 7;
subob.j = 8;
subob.k = 9;
System.out.println ("Contents of subob: ");
subob.showij ();
subob.showk ();
System.out.println();
System.out.println("Sum of i, j and k in subob: ") ;
subob.sum () ;
    }
}
```

The output from this program is shown here:

Contents of superob:
i and j: 10 20
Contents of subob:
i and j: 7 8
Sum of i, j and k in subob:
i+j+k+: 24

As you can see, the subclass **B** includes all of the members of its **superclass, A.**

This is why **subOb** can access **i** and **j** and call **showij()**. Also, inside **sum()**, **i** and **j** can be referred to directly, as if they were part of **B.**

Even though **A** is a **superclass** for **B,** it is also a completely independent, stand-alone class. Being a superclass for a subclass does not mean that the superclass cannot be used by itself. Further, a subclass can be a **superclass** for another subclass.

The general from of a **class** declaration that inherits a superclass is shown here.

```
class subclass-name extends superclass-name {
// body of class
}
```

You can only specify one **superclass** for any subclass that you create. Java does not support the inheritance of multiple **superclasses** into single subclass. (This differs from C++, in which you can inherit multiple base classes.) You can, as stated, create a hierarchy of inheritance in which a subclass becomes a **superclass** of another subclass.

However, no class can be a **superclass** of itself.

(iii) Constructors and methods

Refer to Study material, Q1, Page no.-54

(iv) The modifier final

Refer to DEC-03, Q1(ii), Page no.-119

(v) The modifier abstract

Refer to JUNE-03, Q2(iv), Page no.-131

(vi) Private

Refer to JUNE-02, Q2(iv), Page no.-153

(vii) Protected

Refer to JUNE-02, Q2(iv), Page no.-153

CS-74 : INTRODUCTION TO INTERNET PROGRAMMING
DEC2001

Note : *Question* ***one*** *is* ***compulsory****. Answer any* ***three*** *from the rest.*

Q1(i). Describe Unicode and ASCII code. **[JUN2003,Q3(v)]**
Refer to Study material, Q2, Page no.-22

(ii) Java is object-oriented. What are the advantages of object-oriented programming compared to procedural oriented programming?

ANS : JAVA IS OBJECT-ORIENTED :

Although influenced by its predecessors, Java was not designed to be source-code compatible with any other language. This allowed the Java team the freedom to design with a blank state. Once outcome of this was a clean, usable, pragmatic approach to objects. Borrowing liberally from many seminal object-software environment of the last few decades, Java manages to strike a balance between the purist's "everything is an object" paradigm and the pragmatist's "stay out of my way" model. The object model in Java is simple and easy to extend, while simple types, such as integers, are kept as high-performance nonobjects.

Procedural languages are the languages where each statement in the language tells the computer to do something. Get some input add these numbers, divided by 6, display that output. A program in a procedural language is a list of instructions. For very small programs no other organizing principle (often called a paradigm) is needed. The programmer creates the list of instructions, and the computer caries them out. Pascal, C, BASIC, Fortran, and similar languages are procedural languages.

DIVISION INTO FUNCTIONS :

When programs become larger, a single list of instructions becomes unwieldy. Few programmers can comprehend a program of more than a few hundred statements unless it is broken down into smaller units. For this reason the function was adopted as a way to make programs more comprehensible to their human creators. (The term function is used in C++ and C. In other languages the same concept may be referred to as a subroutine, a subprogram, or a procedure)

PROBLEMS WITH STRUCTURED PROGRAMMING

The principal idea behind structured programming was as simple as the idea of "divide and conquer." A computer program could be regarded as consisting of a set of tasks. Any task that was too complex to be simply described would be broken into a set of smaller component tasks, until the tasks were sufficiently small and self-contained to be easily understood. As programs grow ever larger and more complex, even the structured programming approach beings to show signs of strain. You may have heard about, or been involved in, horror stories of program development. The project is too complex, the schedule slips, more programmers are added, complexity increases, cost skyrocket, the schedule slips further, and finally disaster.

Analyzing the reasons for these failures reveals that there are weakness in the procedural paradigm itself. No matter how well the structured programming approach is implemented, large programs become excessively complex.
What are the reason for this failure of procedural languages? One of the most crucial is the role played by data.

DATA IS UNDERVALUED

In a procedural language, the emphasis is on doing things--read the keyboard, add the values, check for error, and so on. The subdivision of a program into functions continues this emphasis. Functions do thing as single program statements do. What they do may be more complex or abstract, but the emphasis is still on the action.

WHAT HAPPENS TO THE DATA IN THIS PARADIGM?

Data is, after all, the reason for a program's existence. Data is given second-class status in the organization of procedural languages.
For example, in an inventory program, the data that makes up the inventory is probably read from a disk file into memory, where it is treated as a global variable. By global we mean that the variables that constitute the data are declared outside of any function, so they are accessible to all functions. These functions perform various operations on the data. They read it, analyze it, update it, rearrange it, display it, write it back to the disk, and so on.
We should note that most languages, such as pascal and C, also support local variables, which are hidden within a single function. But local variables are not useful for important data that must be accessed by many different functions. Figure below shows the relationship between global and local variables.

Global and Local Variables

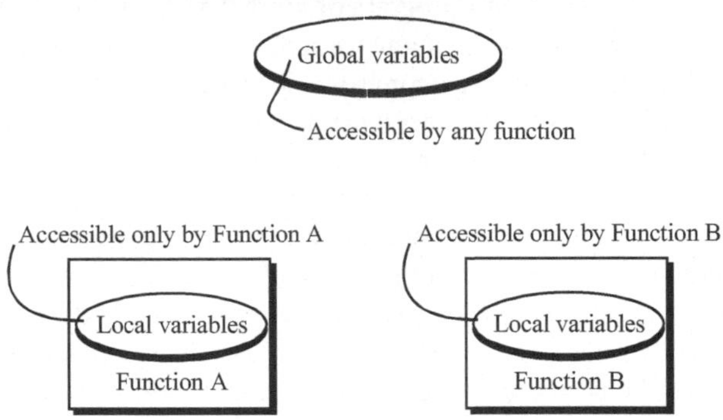

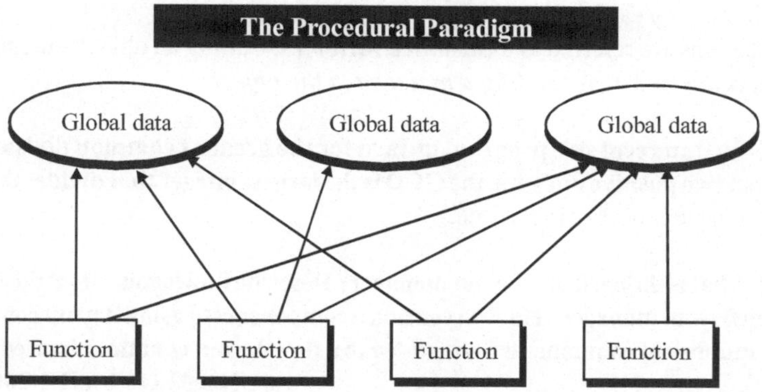

Now suppose a new programmer is hired to write a function to analyze this inventory data in a certain way. Unfamiliar with the subtitles of the program, the programmer creates a function which has complete access to the data. It's like leaving your personal papers in the lobby of your apartment building: Anyone can change or destroy them. In the same way. Global data can be corrupted by functions that have no authorization to change it. What is needed is a way to restrict access to the data, to hide it from all but a few critical functions. This will Protect the data, simplify maintenance, and offer other benefits as well.

TRADITIONAL LANGUAGES DOES NOT PROVIDE EXTENSIBILITY.

One is the difficulty of creating new data types. Computer languages typically have several built-in data types: your own data type? Perhaps you want to work with complex numbers, or two-dimensional coordinates or dates-quantities the built-in-data types don't handle easily. Being able to create your own types is called extensibility; you can extend the capabilities of the language. Traditional languages are not usually extensible. Without unnatural convolutions, you can't bundle together both X and Y coordinates into a single variable called point, and then add subtract values of this type. The result is that traditional programs are more complex to write and maintain.

The object-oriented approach : Solution to all these problems.

The fundamental idea behind object-oriented languages is to combine both data and the functions that operate on that data into a single unit called ***an object***. An object's functions, called member functions in Java typically provide the only way to access its data. If you want to read a data item in an object, you call only way to access its data. If you want to read a data item in an object, you call a member function in the object. It will read the item and return the value to you it can't access the data directly. The data is hidden, so it is safe to accidental alterations. Data and its functions are said to be encapsulated into a single entity, ***data encapsulation and data hiding*** are key terms in the description of object-oriented languages.
No other functions can access the data. This simplifies writing, debugging, and maintaining the program.

A Java program typically consist of a number of objects, which communicates with each other by calling one another's member functions.
Data items are referred to as ***instance variables***. Calling an object's member function is referred to as ***sending a message to the object***.

(iii) Write a recursive program in Java for the greatest common divisor (GCD). Given two positive integers, the GCD is the largest integer that divides them both.
Refer to DEC-02, Q5(i), Page no.-145

(iv) What is the need of a layout manager? Describe flowlayout. How do you create a flowlayout manager? How do you add a componenet to a flow-layout container? Is the number of components to be added to a flow-layout container limited?
[JUN2002,Q6(b);JUN2001,Q2(i)]

ANS : The need of Layout manager is to automatically arrange the controls within a window. Imagine a window in which we want to put 6 buttons as the size of the window is fixed all the buttons can't be fixed in a single row then layout manager allows to position the controls at an appropriate locations within the window.
Flow layout is the default layout manager. Flow layout implements a simple layout style, which is similar to how words flow in a text editor. Components are laid from the upper left corner, left to right and top to bottom. When no more components fit on a line, the next one appears on the next line. A small space is left between each component, above and below, as well as left and right.
A layout manager is an instance of any class that implements the Layout Manager interface. The layout manager is set by the setLayout() method. To set the flow layout manager the following method has to be implemented:
Void setLayout(LayoutManager layoutObj)
In this program we can use :
setLayout(new FlowLayout());

```
                import java.awt.*;
                import java.awt.event.*;
                import java.applet.*;
      public class flowlayout extends Applet implements ItemListener
        {
        String msg="";
                Checkbox popcorn,icecream,chocolate;
      Public void Init()
        {
                setLayout(new FlowLayout(FlowLayout.LEFT));
                popcorn=new Checkbox("Popcorn",true)
                icecream=new Checkbox("Icecream",false)
                chocolate=new Checkbox("Chocolate",false)add(popcorn);
                add(icecream);
                add(chocolate);
      popcorn.addItemListener(this);
      icecream.addItemListener(this);
```

```
chocolate.addItemListener(this);
}
public void itemStateChanged(ItemEvent ie)
  {
        repaint();
  }
public void paint(Graphics g)
  {
g.drawString(popcorn.getState(),10,100);
g.drawString(icecream.getState(),10,150);
g.drawString(icecream.getState(),10,200);
}
```

No there is no limit on the number of components that can be added to the flow layout container.

Q2. Defferentiate between the following :

(a) Methods overloading and overriding a method **[JUN2003,Q3(i)]**

Refer to Study material, Q3, Page no.-57

(b) Constructors and methods

Refer to Study material, Q1, Page no.-54

(c) This and super **[DEC2003,Q3(iii);DEC2002,Q2(a);JUNE03, Q3(iv)]**

Refer to Study material, Q2, Page no.-68

(d) Private and protected

Refer to JUNE-02, Q2(iv), Page no.-154

(e) Extends and interface.

ANS : (i) Extends is used in Inheritance. Interface is keyword used to declare interfaces (whose implementation is not defined).

(ii) Using Extends only one class can be inherited (i.e. Single Inheritance) while through interface we can inherit as many as interfaces (i.e. Multiple Inheritance).

(iii) In using Interface more code has to be written, debugged, and maintained than in using Extends.

(iv) Interfaces are slower than Inheritance through Extends.

To inherit a class, Java uses ***extends*** keyword. To inherit a class, syntax for the derived class declaration is

```
class<derived class name> extends <base class>
{
    //body of the class
}
```

Java doesn't support the multiple inheritance, so a derived class can only inherit one class, but Java fully supprt multilevel inheritance e.g., given three classes called A, B, and C, C can be a subclass of B, which is a subclass of A. Here C inherits all the traits of B, and A classes.

The example shows a short program, here class B inherits class A and all members of class A included in class B. That is, object of the class B can access any member of class A as it access its own member.

```
class A
{
      int i;
      void get_A_Val()
      {
         System.out.println("Value of i is : " + i);
      }
}
class B extends A
{
      int j;
      void get_B_Val()
      {
         get_A_Val(); // get_A_val() is now member of B
         System.out.println("Value of j is : " + j);
      }
}
class mainClass
{
      public static void main(String args[])
      {
         B objB;                  //Object of B declared
         objB=new B();  //Object is instantiated

         objB.j=10;

         objB.i=5;     //objB accessing i as its own member

         objB.get_B_Val();
      }
}
```

Even though A is a superclass for B, it is also a completely independent, stand-alone class. Being a superclas for a subclass does not mean that the superclass cannot be used by itself. Further, a subclass can be a superclass for another subclass. Through the use of the **interface** keyword, Java allows you to fully abstract the interface from its implementation. Using interface, you can specify a set of methods which can be implemented by one or more classes. The interface, itself, does not actually define any implementation. Although they are similar to abstract classes, interfaces have an additional capability: A class can implement more than one interface. By contrast, a class can only inherit a single super class (abstract or otherwise).

Packages and interfaces are two of the basic components of a Java program.

An interface is defined much like a class. This is the general form of an interface.

```
access interface name {
        return-type method-name1(parameter-list);
        return-type method-name2(parameter-list);
        type final-varname1 = value;
        type final-varname2 = value;
        // ...
        return-type method-nameN(parameter-list);
        type final-varnameN = value;
}
```

Q3. Define the following terms and what is their purpose :

(i) Panel

Refer to JUNE-02, Q3(e), Page no.-154

(ii) Frame

Frame encapsulates what is commonly thought of as a "window." It is a subclass of **Window** and has a title bar, menu bar, borders, and resizing corners. If you create a **Frame** object from within an applet, it will contain a warning message, such as "java Applet Window" to the user that an applet window has been created. This message warns users that the window they see was started by an applet and not by software running on their computer. (An applet that could masquerade as a host-based application could be used to obtain passwords and other sensitive information without the user's knowledge.) When a **Frame** window is created by a program rather than an applet, a normal window is created.

(iii) Java is distributed

Refer to JUNE-03, Q2(ii), Page no.-131

(iv) Java is robust

Java is built for creating highly reliable programs. It has extensive compile-time error checking, followed by a second level of checking at run-time. There are no pointers in Java like there are in C++. So Java can't overwrite memory and corrupt data, as could happen in C or C++. Also, Java programs cannot gain unauthorized access to memory, as could happen in C or C++.

(v) Java is interpreted.

Here we're talking about speed. Java has been criticized for slowness because it has to pay for its universality by going through an extra step in interpretation. But in applications when extremely high performance is required, byte-codes can be translated on-the-fly at run-time into machine code for a particular CPU, and Sun claims that the performance of byte-codes thus converted to machine code is almost indistinguishable from that of C or C++. Also, Java developers could compile their programs for the specific processors they want to support. Future versions of the Hypertext Transfer Protocol (http) could let the browser identify its processor type to the server so that the server could download the correct applet type for the user's system.

Q4. Answer the following questions :

(i) Describe the relationship between an object and its defining class. How do you declare a class? How do you declare an object? How do you create an object? How do you declare and create an object in statement?

ANS: Any real world entity is called an object. A class is a group of similar kind of objects. Ram, Ramesh, Rahim all can be considered as objects of class person. So object is an instance of a class.

A class is declared by use of the class keyword.

Declaring a class :

```
class person
{
private int age;
person()
{
age=20
}
void desplay()
{
System.out.println(age);
}
}
class example
{
public static void main(String args[])
{
person p;                  /*Declaring an object*/
p=new person();            /* Creating an object*/
person p1=new person();    /*Declaring and Creating an object in same statement*/
}
}
```

(ii) Describe pass by reference and pass by value through example.

ANS : In general, there are two ways that a computer language can pass an argument to a subroutine. The first way is *call-by-value.* This method copies the *value* of an argument into the formal parameter of the subroutine. Therefore, changes made to the parameter of the subroutine have no effect on the argument used to call it. The second way an argument can be passed is *call-by-reference.* In this method, a reference to an argument (not the value of the argument) is passed to the parameter. Inside the subroutine, this reference is used to access the actual argument specified in the call. This means that changes made to the parameter will affect the argument used to call the subroutine. As you will see, Java uses both methods, depending upon what is passed.

In Java, when you pass a simple type to a method, it is passed by value. Thus, what occurs to the parameter that receives the argument which has no effect outside the mehtod.

For example, consider the following program:

```
// Simple types are passed by value.
class Test {
void meth(int i, int j) {
i *= 2;
j /=2;
}
}
class CallByValue {
public static void main(String args[]) {
Test ob = new Test();
int a = 15, b = 20;
System.out.println("a and b before call:" +a + " " + b);
ob.meth(a, b);
System.out.println("a and b after call: " + a + " "+ b);
}
}
```

The **output** from this program is shown here:

a and b before call: 15 20
a and b after call: 15 20

As you can see, the operations that occur inside **meth()** have no effect on the values of **a** and **b** used in the call; their values here did not change to 30 and 10.
When you pass an object to a method, the situation changes dramatically, because objects are passed by reference. Keep in mind that when you create a variable of a class type, you are only creating a reference to an object. Thus, when you pass this reference to a method, the parameter that receives it will refer to the same object as that referred to by the argument. This effectively means that objects are passed to methods by use of call-by-reference. Changes to the object inside the method do affect the object used as an argument. For example, consider the following program:

```
// Objects are passed by reference.
class that Test {
  int a, b;
  Test(int i, int j) {
    a = i;
    b = j;
  }
// pass an object
void meth(Test o) {
  o.a *= 2;
  o.b /= 2;
}
}
class CallByRef {
 public static void main(String args[]) {
```

```
    Test ob = new Test (15, 20);
    System.out.println("ob.a and ob.b before call: " + ob.a + " " + ob.b);
    ob.meth(ob);
    System.out.println("ob.a and ob.b after call: " + ob.a + " " + ob.b);
  }
}
```

This program generates the following **output**:

```
ob.a and ob.b before call : 15 20
ob.a and ob.b after call  : 30 10
```

As you can see, in this case, the actions inside **meth()** have affected the object used as an argument.

As a point of interest, when an object reference is passed to a method, the reference itself is passed by use of call-by-value. However, since the value being passed refers to an object, the copy of that value will still refer to the same object and its corresponding argument does.

When a simple type is passed to a method, it is done by use of call-by-value. Objects are passed by use of call-by-reference.

Q3. List the modifiers and describe their purposes. [JUN2003,Q5(ii)]

Refer to JUNE-03, Q5(ii), Page no.-135

Q4. Determine *true* or *false* in the following statements :

(a) You can add a component to a button

FALSE

(b) You can add a frame to a panel

FALSE

(c) You can add a button to a frame

TRUE

(d) You can add a panel to a frame.

TRUE

Q5(i). Implement a class employee. An employee a has a name (c string) and a salary (a double). Write a default constructor and constructor with two parameters (name and salary) and two methods :

- **to return the name and salary and**
- **a method that raises the employee's salary. Write a small program that tests your class.**

ANS :

```
import java.awt.*;
class employee
{
String name;
double salary;
employee()
{
name="Anuj";
```

```
salary=10000;
}
employee(String n,double s)
{
name=n;
salary=s;
}
void print()
{
System.out.println(name);
System.out.println(salary);
}
double raise(double d)
{
salary=salary+d;
return(salary);
}
}
class emp
{
public static void main(String args[])
{
employee e=new employee();
e.print();
System.out.println("Now raise equal to 1000");
System.out.println(e.raise(1000));
}
}
```

(ii) What is the purpose of text field? List and explain its constructors and important methods.

ANS : Text field allow the user to enter strings and to edit the text. The **TextField** class implements a single-line text-entry area, usually called an edit control. Text fields allow the user to enter strings and to edit the text using the arrow keys, cut and paste keys, and mouse selections. **TextField** is a subclass of **TextComponent.** **TextField** defines the following constructors:

```
TextField()
TextField(in numChars)
TextField(String str)
TestField(String str, int numChars)
```

The first version creates a default text field. The second form creates a text field that is numChars characters wide. The third form initializes the text field with the string contained in str. The fourth form initializes a text field and sets its width.

TextField (and its superclass **TextComponent)** provides several methods that allow you to utilize a text field. To obtain the string currently contained in the text field, call **getTex()**. To set the text, call **setText()**. These methods are as follows:

```
String getText()
void setText(String str)
```

here, str is the new string.

The user can select a portion of the text in a text filed. Also, you can select a portion of text under program control by using **select()**. Your program can obtain the currently selected text by calling **getSelectedText()**. These methods are shown here:

```
String getSelectedText()
void select(int startIndex, int endIndex)
```

getSelectedText() returns the selected text. The **select()** method selects the characters beginning at startIndex and ending at endIndex-1.

You can control whether the contents of a text field may be modified by the user by calling **setEditable()**. You can determine editability by calling **isEditable()**. These methods are shown here:

```
boolean isEditable()
void setEditable(boolean canEdit)
```

isEditable() returns **true** if the text may be changed and **false** if not. In **setEditable()**, it canEdit is **true**, the text may be changed. If it is **false,** the text cannot be altered.

There may be times when you will want the user to enter text that is not displayed, such as a password. You can disable the echoing of the characters as they are typed by calling **setEchoChar()**. This method specifies a single character that the **TextField** will display when characters are entered thus, the actual character that the **TextField** will display when characters are entered thus, the actual characters typed will not be shown. You can check a text field to see if it is in this mode with the **echoCharSet()** method. You can retrieve the echo character by calling the **getEchoChar()** method. These methods are as follows:

```
void setEchoChar(char ch)
boolean echoCharSet()
char geEchoChar()
```

Here, ch specifies the character to have echoed.

Q6(i). Write is program that let the user enter text from the text field and then append it to the text areas.

ANS : import java.awt.*;

```
import java.awt.event.*;
class test_text extends Frame implements ActionListener
{
static test_text t;
FlowLayout f;
My Window Adapter adapter;
TextField t_field;
TextArea t_area;
Button ok;
public static void main(String args[])
```

```
{
t = new test_text();
t.show();
t.setSize(800,400);
}
test_text()
{

adapter=new MyWindowAdapter(this)
addWindowListener(adapter);
t_field = new TextField(25)
t_area = new TextArea();
ok=new Button("click here");
add(t_field);
add(ok);
f=new FlowLayout();
setLayout(f);
ok.addActionListener(this);

}
public void actionPerformed(ActionEvent ae)
{
        if(ae.getSource()==ok)
        {
        String st1=t_area.getText() + t_field.getText();
        t_area.setText(st1);
        }
}
}

class MyWindowAdapter extends Window Adapter
{
 test_text t;
public MyWindowAdapter(test_text tl)
{
 t=tl;
}
public void windowClosing(WindowEvent we)
{
  t.setVisible(false);
  System.exit(0);
}
{
```

(ii) Answer the following questions :

(1) How do you create a button labelled "YES"? How do you change a label in a button?

ANS : We can create a button labelled "yes" by writing the following code :

Button b1 = new Button('Yes');

And, we can change a label in a button by using setLabel() method.

B1.setLabel("No");

Syntax :

void setLabel(String str) method for a Button object.

(2) Can you specify the size of lists?

ANS : Yes, the constructor is List(int numRows) where numRows denotes the number of entries in the list that will always be visible.

(3) Can you remove a menu item from the menu?

ANS : Yes, Menu items can be removed if they have been created by the constructor Menu(String name, Boolean removable). If removable is true, the menu item can be "torn" from the main menu and place wherever the user desires on the screen.

(4) What is the return value of a main ( ) method?

ANS : "main( )" returns nothing, hence return type is "void". It is the method automatically invoked by Java Run Time Environment.

(5) How do you denote a comment line?

ANS : Comments are of 3 types:

i) "//" used to comment a single line.

ii) "/* */" used to comment out a block of code.

iii) "/** */" used for generation of automatic documentation with Javadoc utility.

CS-74 : INTRODUCTION TO INTERNET PROGRAMMING
JUNE - 2002

Note : *Question **one** is **compulsory**. Answer any **three** from the rest.*

Q1(i). Write a Java program that reads in an integer and breaks it into a sequence of individual digits. for example, the input 16384 is displayed as 1 6 3 8 4.

ANS : import java.io.DataInputStream;

```
class breakno
{
public static void main(String args[])
{
int i=0; int j=0;
int remainder=0;
int number=0;
int store[];
store=new int[10];
DataInputStream in=new DataInputStream(System.in);
try
 {
System.out.println("Please enter the Number:");
number=Integer.parseInt(in.readLine());
}
catch(Exception e)
{}
while(number>0)
{
remainder=number%10;
store[i]=remainder;
System.out.println(remainder);
number=number/10;
i=i+1;
for(j=i-1;j>=0;j--)
System.out.println(" "+sotre[i]);
}
}
```

(ii) Answer the following questions :

(a) What is a final variable? Can you define a final variable without supplying its value?

Refer to Study material, Q2, Page no.-90

(b) What is the Java virtual machine? Explain it.

[JUN2003,Q1(ii);DEC2002,Q6(ii)]

Refer to Study material, Q3, Page no.-13

(c) What is a integrated programming environment?

ANS : If you are new to Java programming, you are probably starting by using notepad. When you want to compile and run a program, you need to open a DOS window and type javac MyProgram.java and java MyProgram. Also, what you type is what you get: notepad does not help you any way with Java syntax or design. This is fine if you are just starting, and even experts sometimes use command-line Java options. However, a good Java-savvy editor or Integrated Programming Environment (IPE) will make the job of creating Java code a lot easier. **Editors are simpler :** they generally highlight the Java syntax, indent for you, balance your parentheses and braces, and let you compile from within the editor. But that's about it: they don't write code, integrate tightly with the compiler or app server, or have graphical Java development tools. Provides you Integrated Programming Environment (IPE), which makes the programming easier by saving time in formatting commands, syntax etc. An integrated programming environment is open if it is able to grow up according to the user needs. In other words, it should take into account the possibility of integrating new tools, and to be dynamically configured by a user.

(d) Describe the paint( ) method. Where is it defined? How is it invoked?

Refer to DEC-02, Q1(d), Page no.-140

(e) What method do you use to obtain an input character from a keyboard?

ANS : To input a character from a keyboard following procedure has to be followed:
Create an object of DataInputStream class.
Here,
DataInputStream in=new DataInputStream(System.in);
Now,
We can read a string or character:
String a=in.readLine();

OR

We use read() method to obtain an input character from keyboard. It reads a character from the input stream and return it as an integer value. We used read() method of 'System class' which is defined in 'java.lang' package via a predefined stream variable called 'in' to obtain an input from the keyboard i.e., System.in.read( ).

Example:-

```
Char ch;
Ch = (Char) System.in.read( );
```

(f) Describe important mehtods in a container and in a panel.

Methods in container :

ANS : A container is a subclass of component. Container allows us to create grouping of objects on the screen.

(i) protected container()

(ii) public int getComponentCount()

(iii) public int countComponents()

Methods in Panel :-

The panel class provides a generic container within an existing display area. It is the simplest of all the container.

(i) public Panel ( )

Creates a panel with a layout manager of flowlayout.

(ii) public Panel (LayoutManager layout)

(iii) public void addNotify( )

Q2. Differentiate between the following :

(i) Applet and Application **[DEC2003,Q3(i);JUN2001,Q5(a)]**

Refer to JUNE-03, Q1(iv), Page no.-130

(ii) Inheritance and Interface

ANS : The idea of classes leads to the idea of inheritance. In our daily lives, we use the concept of classes being divided into subclasses. We know that the class of animals is divided into mammals, amphibians, insects, bird, and so on. The class of vehicles is divided into cars, truck, buses, and motorcycles.

The principle in this sort of division is that each subclass shares common characteristics with the class from which it's derived. Cars, truck, buses, and motorcycles all have wheels and a motor; these are the defining characteristics of vehicles. In addition to the characteristics: buses, for instance, have seats for many people, while trucks have space for hauling loads.

As functions do in a procedural program, inheritance shortens an object-oriented program and clarifies the relationship among program elements.

While, using the keyword interface, you can fully abstract a class interface from its implementation. That is, using interface, you can specify what a class must do, but not how it does it. Interfaces are syntactically similar to classes, but they lack instance variables, and their methods are declared without anybody. In practice, this means that you can define interfaces which don't make assumptions about how they are implemented. Once it is defined, any number of classes can implement an interface. Also, one class can implement any number of interfaces.

To implement an interface, a class must create the complete set of methods defined by the interface. However, each class is free to determine the details of its own implementation. By providing the interface keyword, Java allows you to fully utilize the "one interface, multiple methods" aspect of polymorphism.

Interfaces are designed to support dynamic method resolution at run time. Normally, in order for a method to be called from one class to another, both classes need to be present at compile time so the Java compiler can check to ensure that the method signatures are compatible. This requirement by itself makes for a static and non-extensible classing environment. Inevitably in a system like this, functionality gets pushed by higher and higher in the class hierarchy so that the mechanisms will be available to more and more subclasses. Interfaces are designed to avoid this problem. They disconnect the definition of a method or set of methods from the inheritance hierarchy. Since interfaces are in a different hierarchy from classes, it is possible for classes that are unrelated in terms of the class hierarchy to implement the same interface. This is where the real power of interfaces is realized.

(iii) Browser and Applet viewer

there are two ways in which you can run an applet:

* Executing the applet within a Java-compatible Web browser, such as Netscape Navigator.
* Using an appletviewer utility, such as the standard JDK tool, appletviewer. An appletviewer executes your applet in a window. This is generally the fastest and easiest way to test your applet.

Each of these methods is described below :

To execute an applet in a Web browser, you need to write a short HTML text file that contains the appropriate APPLET tag. Here is the HTML file that executes SimpleApplet:

```
<applet code="FirstApplet" width=200 height=60>
</applet>
```

The width and height statements specify the diamensions of the display area used by the applet. After you create this file, you can execute your browser and then load this file, which causes FirstApplet to be executed.

To execute FirstApplet with an appletviewer, you may also execute the HTML file shown earlier. For example, if the preceding HTML file is called RunApp.html, then the following command line will run FirstApplet:

```
C:\>appletviewer RunApp.html
```

Run the Applet

To see the applet in action, you need an HTML file with the Applet tag as follows:

```
<HTML>
<BODY>
<APPLET CODE=FirstApplet.class WIDTH=200 HEIGHT=100>
</APPLET>
</BODY>
</HTML>
```

The easiest way to run the applet is with appletviewer shown below where FirstApplet.html is a file that contains the above HTML code:

```
appletviewer FirstApplet.html
```

Note: To run an applet written with Java 2 APIs in a browser, the browser must be enabled for the Java 2 Platform. If your browser is not enabled for the Java 2 Platform, you have to use appletviewer to run the applet or install Java Plug-in. Java Plug-in lets you run applets on web pages under the 1.2 version of the Java VM instead of the web browser's default Java VM.

(iv) Private and Protected

Private

It is narrowly visible and the highest level of protection that can possibly be obtained. Private methods and variables cannot be seen by any class other than the one in which they are defined. They are extremely restrictive but are most commonly used. Any representation unique to the implementation is declared private. An object's primary job is to encapsulate its data and limit manipulation. This is achieved by declaring data as private.

Protected

This specifier is a relationship between a class and its present and future subclasses. The subclasses are closer to the parent class than any other class. This level gives more protection and narrows visibility.

(v) This and Super **[DEC2003,Q3(iii);DECD202,Q2(a)]**

Refer to Study material, Q2, Page no.-68

Q3. Define the following terms in detail :

(a) Java is multi-threaded

Refer to Study material, Q5, Page no.-14

(b) Java is secure **[JUN2003,Q2(vi)]**

ANS : As you are likely aware, every time that you download a "normal" program, you are risking a viral infection. Prior to Java, most users did not download executable programs frequently, and those who did scanned them for viruses prior to execution. Even so, most users still worried about the possibility of infecting their systems with a virus. In addition to viruses, another type of malicious program exists that must be guarded against. This type of program can gather private information, such as credit card numbers, bank account balances, and passwords, by searching the contents of your computer's local file system.

When you use a Java-compatible Web browser, you can safety download Java applets without fear of viral infection or malicious intent. Java achieves this protection by confining a Java program to the Java execution environment and not allowing it access to other parts of the computer. The ability to download applets with confidence that no harm will be done and that no security will be breached is considered by many to be the single most important aspect of Java.

(c) Operator overloading

Refer to Study material, Q10, Page no.-10

(d) Exception handling **[DEC2002,Q3(iv)]**

Refer to Study material, Q1, Page no.-76

(e) Panel **[DEC2001,Q3(i)]**

ANS : The Panel class is a non-abstract, recursively nestable, container. The panel can contain UI components and other containers.

A panel object can be constructed using the following code:

Panel p1=new Panel();

The add() method of the Container class can be used to add a component to the panel.

pl.add(myButton);

Like all containers, the layout of the Panel can be set using the setLayout() method.

Q4(i). Write a program in Java to find out whether a given string is a palindrome or not.

ANS :
```
import java.io.*;
public class Palindrome
{
public static void main(String args[]) throws IOException
{
BufferedReader br=new BufferedReader(new InputStreamReader(System.in));
System.out.println("Enter a string :");
StringBuffer str=new StringBuffer(br.readLine());
int len=str.length();
for(int i=0;i<len/2+1;i++)
{
if(str.charAt(i)!=str.charAt(len-i-1))
{
System.out.println("The string is not a palindrome");
System.exit(0);
}
}
System.out.println("The string is a palindrome");
}
}
```

(ii) Draw an inheritance diagram for the following classes:

Person
Employee
Student
Instructor
Classroom

List the important methods and variables in the classes .

ANS :

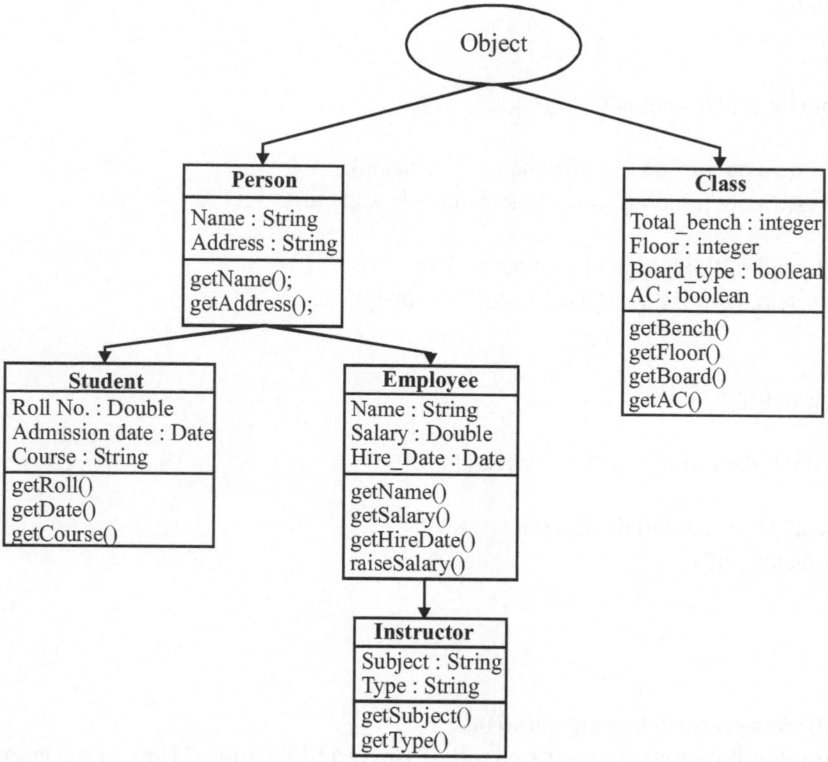

Q5(i). Implement a class student. A student has a name and stipend (double data type). Write a default constructor and constructor with two parameters (name and stipend) and two mehtods:

*** to return the name and stipend and**

*** a method that raises the employee's salary. Write a small program that tests your class.**

ANS : import java.io.*;

```
class student
{
String name;
float stipend;
student()
{
name = " ";
stipend = 0.00;
}7
student (String n,float s)
{
```

```
name = n;
stipend = s;
}
public void displaysal()
{
System.out.println ("student name = " + name) ;
System.out.println ("student's stipend = "+ stipend);

stipend = (float) stipend + (stipend* 10);
System.out.println ("Raised salary" + stipend);
}
}
class  test
{
public static void main (String args[] )
{
student s = new student ("Anand", 8000f);
s.displaysal() ;

}
}
```

(ii) Answer the following questions :

(a) How do you create a text area with 10 rows and 20 columns? How do you insert 2 lines into the text area?

ANS :

```
import java.awt.*;
import java.awt.event.*;
class test_textarea extends Frame implements ActionListener
{
static test_textarea t;
FlowLayout f;
MyWindowAdapter1  adapter;
TextArea t_area;
Button ok;
public static void main(String args[])
{
t=new test_textarea();
t.show();
t.setSize(800,400);
}
test_textarea()
{
adapter=new MyWindowAdapter1(this);
```

```
addWindowListener(adapter);
t_area = new TextArea(10,20);
ok=new Button("Click here");
add(t_area);
add(ok);
f=new FlowLayout();
setLayout(f);
ok.addActionListener(this);
}
public void actionPerformed(ActionEvent ae)
{
if(ae.getSource()==ok)
{
String st1="hello!\nhow r u?\n";
t_area.setText(st1);
}
}
}
class MyWindowAdapter1 extends WindowAdapter
{
test_textarea t;
public MyWindowAdapter1(test_textarea t1)
{
t=t1;
}
public void windowClosing(WindowEvent we)
{
t.setVisible(false);
System.exit(0);
}
}
```

(b) How do you create a checkbox group with three items? How do you determine if a box is checked?

ANS : import java.awt.*;

```
import java.awt.event.*;
import java.applet.*;
import java.lang.*;
public class chkbox extends Applet implements ItemListener
{
Checkbox popcorn, icecream, chocolate;
String message;
public void init()
```

```
{
popcorn=new Checkbox("popcorn",true);
icecream=new Checkbox("Icecream",false);
chocolate=new Checkbox("Chocolate",false);
add(popcorn);
add(icecream);
add(chocolate);
popcorn.addItemListener(this);
icecream.addItemListener(this);
chocolate.addItemListener(this);
}
public void itemStateChanged(ItemEvent ie)
{
repaint();
}
public void paint(Graphics g)
{
message="popcorn :" + popcorn.getState();
g.drawString(message,10,100);
message="icecream : "+ icecream.getState();
g.drawString(message,10,150);
message= "chocolate :" + chocolate.getState();
g.drawString(message,10,200);
}
}
```

Q6(a). Draw the AWT class hierarchy and discuss important classes and its methods.

ANS : The Abstract Windowing Toolkit (AWT) is an API that is responsible for building the Graphical User Interface (GUI). It is a part of the Java Foundation Classes (JFC). AWT includes a rich set of user interface components, a powerful event handling model, graphics and image tools, layout managers and support for data transfer using cut and paste through clipboards. AWT also support javaBeans architecture. Every AWT component is a simple bean. The java.awt contains all classes for creating user interfaces and for painting graphics and images.

AWT Class hierarchy

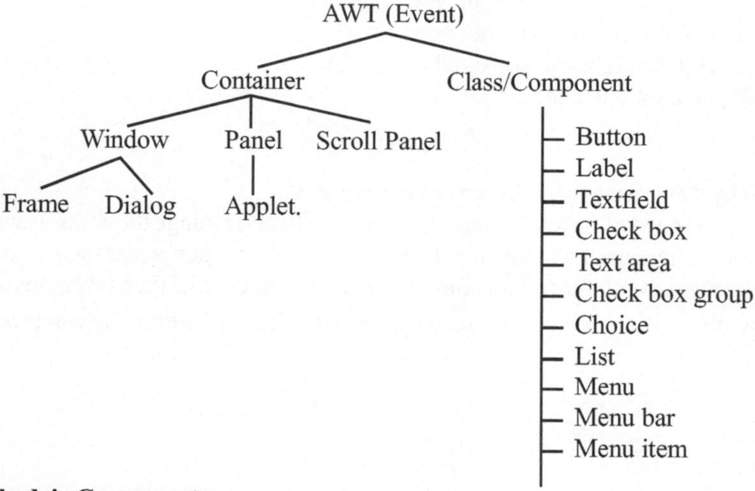

Methods in Component :

(i) Public static final float BOTTOM_ALLIGNMENT

The BOTTOM_ALIGANMENT indicates that the component should align itself to the bottom of its available space.

(ii) Public static final float CENTER_ALIGNMENT constant indicates that the component should align itself to the middle of its available apace. This constant represent both the horizontal and vertical center.

(iii) Public static final float LEFT_ALIGNMENT

(iv) Public static final float RIGHT_ALIGNMENT

(v) Public static final float TOP_ALIGNMENT

Methods in Container :

A container is a subclass of component. Container allows us to create grouping of object on the screen.

(i) Protected Container( )

(ii) Public int getComponents( )

(iii) Public int countComponents( )

Methods in Panel :

The Panel class provides a generic container within an existing display area. It is the simplest of all the container.

(i) Public Panel( )

Creates a panel with a layout manager of type flowlayout

(ii) Public Panel (layoutmanager layout)

public void addNotify ( )

Methods in Frame :

Frame encapsulates what is commonly thought of as a "window". It is a subclass of Window and has a title bar, menu bar, borders, and resizing corners.

(i) Frame()

Frame(String title)

These are Frame's constructors.

(ii) viod setSize(int newWidth, int newHeight)

To setting the Window's Diamensions.

(iii) void setVisible(boolean visibleFlag)

To hide or show a window.

(b) Why do we need to use the layout manager?

ANS : The need of Layout manager is to automatically arrange the controls within a window. Imagine a window in which we want to put 6 buttons as the size of the window is fixed all the buttons can't be fixed in a single row then layout manager allows to position the controls at an appropriate locations within the window.

CS-74 : INTRODUCTION TO INTERNET PROGRAMMING
DEC - 2002

Note : *Question one is compulsory. Answer any* ***three*** *from the rest.*

Q1(i). Write a complete Java program to find out whether the string t_1 is contained in the string t. If so, it returns the offset of the first match. If not, it returns -1.

ANS :
```
import java.awt.*;
class abc
{
public static void main (String args[])
{
try {
String t = "Hello world" ;
String t1  = "Hello" ;
if(t1. indexOf(t) < 0)
{

System.out.println ("string not found") ;
}
else
{
System.out.println ("String match") ;
}
}
catch (Exception e)
{
System.out.println ("Some error has found");
}
}
}
```

(ii) Answer the following questions :

(a) What is the relationship between Java and HTML?

Refer to Study material, Q6, Page no.-17

(b) What happens when your program attempts to access an array element with an invalid index ?

ANS : If we attempt to go out of valid indexes it will create a runtime error to be prompted. It will generate ArrayIndexOutOfBoundException. So it is advisable to handle such an error in the program otherwise it can lead to an inefficient programming style/code.

(c) How do you set colours and fonts in a graphics context? How do you find the current colour and font style?

ANS : We can set fonts by using setFont() method in a Graphics class.

```
Public void paint(Graphics g) {
        Font f=new font("Times New Roman"' font.Plain, 36);
        g.setFont();
        g.drawString("This is a big font:' 10, 100);
            }
```

To set a colour, we use setColor() method.

To find the current colours and font style we use :

getColor() and getStyle() method.

(d) Describe the paint( ) method. Where is it defined? How is it invoked?

ANS : The paint() method is called each time your applet's output must be redrawn. This situation can occur for several reasons. For example, the window in which the applet is running may be overwritten by another window and then uncovered. Or the applet window may be minimized and then restored. paint() is also called when the applet begins execution. Whatever the cause, whenever the applet must redraw the output, paint() is called. The paint() method has one parameter of type Graphics. This parameter will contain the graphics context, which describes the graphics environment in which the applet is running. This context is used whenever output to the applet is required. paint() is defined by the AWT(Abstract Window Toolkit) Component class. To use this method, it is necessary to import the Graphics class as *import java.awt.Graphics;*. It is invoked by overriding paint() method in the class and using repaint() method to call it when needed.

(e) Comment on "Java is a robust programming language".

ANS : The multiplatformed environment of the Web places extraordinary demands on a program, because the program must execute reliably in a variety of systems. Thus, the ability to create robust programs was given a high priority in the design of Java. Because Java is a strictly typed language, it checks your code at compile time.

To understand how Java is robust, consider two of the main reasons for program failure: memory management mistakes and mishandled exceptional conditions (that is, run-time errors). Memory management can be a difficult, tedious task in traditional programming environments. For example, in C/C++, the programmer must manually allocate and free all dynamic memory. This sometimes leads to problems, because programmer will either forget to free memory that has been previously allocated or, worse, try to free some memory that another part of their code is still using. Java virtually eliminates these problems by managing memory allocation and deallocation for you. (In fact, deallocation is completely automatic, because Java provides garbage collection for unused objects.) Exceptional conditions in traditional environment often arise in situation such a division by zero or "file not found," and they must be managed with clumsy and hard-to-read constructs. Java helps in this area by providing object-oriented exception handling. In a well-written Java program, all run-time errors can-and should-be managed by your program.

Q2. Differentiate between the following :

(a) This and Super **[DEC2003,Q3(ii) ; DEC2001,Q2(c)]**

Refer to Study material, Q2, Page no.-68

(b) Constructor and Methods

Refer to Study material, Q1, Page no.-54

(c) Final and Abstract

Refer to Study material, Q3, Page no.-71

(d) Window and Panel

ANS : The Window class creates a top-level window. A top-level window is not contained within any other object; it sits directly on the desktop. Generally, you won't create Window objects directly. Instead, you will use a subclass of Window called Frame, described next.

While the Panel class is a concrete subclass of Container. It doesn't add any new methods; it simply implements Container. A **Panel** may be thought of as a recursively nestable, concrete screen component. **Panel** is the superclass for Applet. When screen output is directed to an applet, it is drawn on the surface of a Panel object. In essence, a **Panel** is a window that does not contain a title bar, menu bar, or border. This is why you don't see these items when an applet is run inside a browser. When you run an applet using an applet viewer, the applet viewer provides the title and border.

Other components can be added to a **Panel** object by its **add()** method (inherited from Container). Once these components have been added, you can position and resize them manually using the **setLocation(), setSize(), or setBounds()** methods defined by Component.

(e) Thread and Process **[JUN2001,Q4(a)]**

ANS : Unlike most other computer languages, JAVA provides built-in support for multithreading programming. A multithreading program contains two or more parts that can run concurrently. Each point of such program is called thread; specialized form of multitasking.

You are most certainly acquainted with multitasking, because it is supported by virtually all modern Operating Systems. However, there are two distinct types of multitasking; process-based & thread-based. It is important to understand the difference between two. For most readers, process-based multitasking is the more familiar form. A process is, in essence, a program that is executing. Thus process-based multitasking is the feature that allows your computer to run two or more programs concurrently. For example, process-based multitasking enables you to run the Java compiler at the time your text editor is also running. In process-based multitasking, a program is the smallest unit of code that can be dispatched by the scheduler.

In a thread-based multitasking environment, the thread is the smallest unit of dispatchable code. This means that a single program can perform two or more tasks simultaneously. For instance a text editor can format text at the same time that it is printing, as long as these two actions are being performed by two separate threads. Thus, process-based multitasking deals with the "big-picture", and thread-based multitasking handles the details.

Multitasking threads require less overhead than multitasking process. Processes are heavy weight task that require their own separate address spaces. Inter process communication is expensive and limited. Context switching from one process to another is also costly. Threads, on the other hand, are lightweight. They share the same address space and cooperatively share the same heavyweight process. Inter thread communication is less expensive and context switching from one thread to the next is at low cost. While Java programs make use of process-based multitasking environments, process-based multitasking is not under the control of Java. However, multithreaded multitasking is.

Multithreading enables you to write very efficient programs that make maximum use of the CPU, because idle time can be kept to minimum, this is especially important for the interactive, networked environment in which Java operates, because idle time is common. For example, the transmission rate of data over a network is much slower than the rate at which the CPU can process it.

If you have programmed for OS such as Windows 98 or Window NT, then you are already familiar with multithreaded programming. However, the fact that Java threads manager makes multithreading especially convenient, because many of the details are handled for you.

Q3. Define the following terms :

(i) Data encapsulation

Refer to Study material, Q5, Page no.-7

(ii) Methods overloading and overriding a method **[JUN2003,Q3(i)]**

Refer to Study material, Q3, Page no.-57

(iii) Border Layout Manager

ANS : Compared to the class FlowLayout, which implements the interface java.awt.LayoutManager and sizes each component to be its preferred size, the interface java.awt.LayoutManager allows a constraint to be associated with each component. This constraint is an object that the layout manager uses when determining the size and position of components in a container and is typed as java.lang.Object although each implementer has a specific constraint that it is designed to work with. The class java.awt.BorderLayout implements LayoutManager2 and its constraint is a string that can be one of the values "North",

"East", "Center", "South" and "West". Two additional constants are used to support relative positioning based on the container's ComponentOrientation. For example, in a container where Component Orientation is Component Orientation. LEFT_TO_RIGHT, "Before line begins" maps to "West" and "After line ends" maps to "East", respectively. Also, mixing the two types of constants is not recommended. When adding components, you will use these constants with the following form of **add()**, which is defined by **Container :**

void add(Component compObj, Object region) ;

Here, compObj is the component to be added, and region specifies where the component will be added.

(iv) Exception handling features in Java **[JUN2002,Q3(d)]**

Refer to Study material, Q1, Page no.-76

(v) Security feature in Java programming

ANS : As you are likely aware, every time that you download a "normal" program, you are risking a viral infection. Prior to Java, most users did not download executable programs frequently, and those who did scanned them for viruses prior to execution. Even so, most users still worried about the possibility of infecting their systems with a virus. In addition to viruses, another type of malicious program exists that must be guarded against. This type of program can gather private information, such as credit card numbers, bank account balances, and passwords, by searching the contents of your computer's local file system.

When you use a Java-compatible Web browser, you can safety download Java applets without fear of viral infection or malicious intent. Java achieves this protection by confining a Java program to the Java execution environment and not allowing it access to other parts of the computer. The ability to download applets with confidence that no harm will be done and that no security will be breached is considered by many to be the single most important aspect of Java.

Q4(i). In an object oriented taffic simulation system, we have the following classes :

- **Vehicle**
- **Car**
- **Truck**
- **Pick up truck**
- **Sport utility vehicle**
- **Mini van**
- **Bicycle**
- **Motorcycle**

Draw an inheritance diagram that shows the relationship between these classes. Identify methods, variables in each class.

ANS :

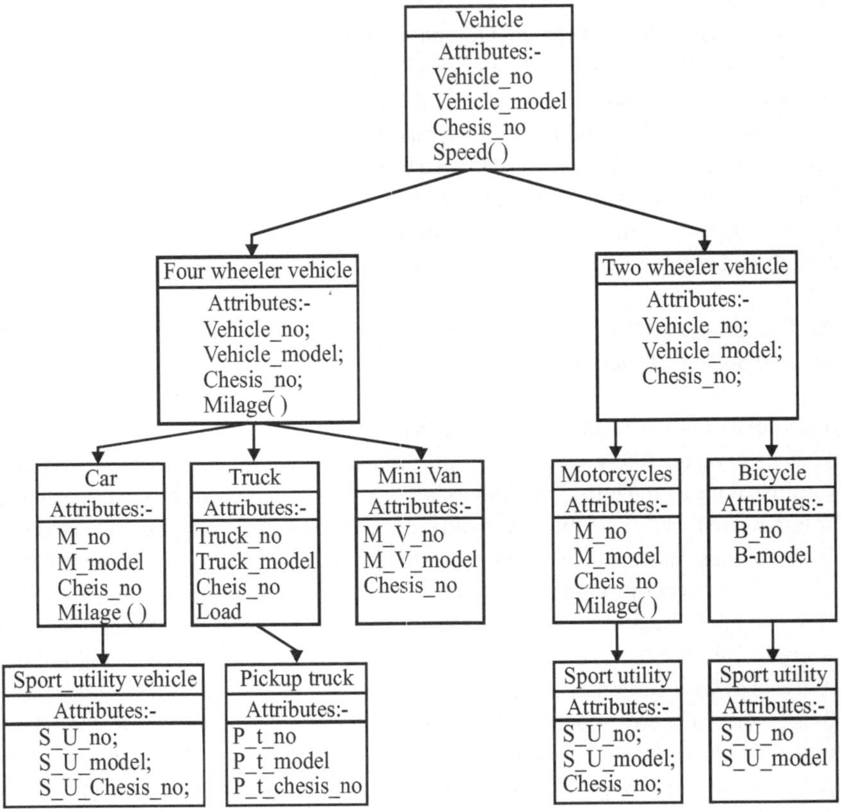

(ii) Describe the init( ), start( ), stop( ) and destroy( ) methods in the applet class.

ANS : init() : The **init()** method is the first method to be called. This is where you should initialize variables. This method is called only once during the run time of your applet.

start() : The **start()** method is called after **init().** It is also called to restart an applet after it has been stopped. Whereas **init()** is called once- the first time an applet is loaded- **start()** is called each time an applet's HTML document is displayed onscreen. So, if a user leaves a web page and comes back, the applet resumes execution at **start().**

destroy() : The **destroy()** method is called when the environment determines that your applet needs to be removed completely from memory. At this point, you should free up any resources the applet may be using. The **stop()** method is always called before **destroy().**

Yes, getParameter() method defined in the Applet class.

public String getParameter(String name) ;

It allows us to get parameter from within the <APPLET> tag of the HTML file that loaded the applet.

No, the paint() method is not defined in the Applet class.
Paint() method is defined by the AWT component class.
public void paint(Graphics g);
Empty method to be overridden to draw something in the graphics context.

Q5(i). Write a recursive program in Java for the greatest common divisor(GCD). Given two position integers, the GCD is the largest integer that divides them both. [DEC2001,Q1(iii)]

ANS :
```
import java.io.*;
public class gcd
{
public static void main(String args[]) throws IOException
{
BufferedReader br=new BufferedReader(new InputStreamReader(System.in));
System.out.println("Enter the first number :");
int m=Integer.parseInt(br.readLine());
System.out.println("Enter the second number :");
int n=Integer.parseInt(br.readLine());
GCD(m,n);
}
private static void GCD(int m, int n)
{
if(n<=m && m%n==0)
System.out.println("GCD is "+n);
else
if(m<n)
GCD(n,m);
else
GCD(n,m%n);
}
}
```

(ii) Answer the following questions :

(a) How do you run an applet?

ANS : Applets don't have a **main()** method. Instead, an applet begins execution when the name of its class is passed to an appletviewer or to a network browser. After you enter the source code for say program FirstApplet, compile in the same way that you have been compiling programs. However, running FirstApplet involves a different process. In fact, there are two ways in which you can run an applet:

* Executing the applet within a Java-compatible Web browser, such as Netscape Navigator.

* Using an appletviewer utility, such as the standard JDK tool, appletviewer. An appletviewer executes your applet in a window. This is generally the fastest and easiest way to test your applet.

Each of these methods is described below :

To execute an applet in a Web browser, you need to write a short HTML text file that contains the appropriate APPLET tag. Here is the HTML file that executes SimpleApplet:

```
<applet code="FirstApplet" width=200 height=60>
</applet>
```

The width and height statements specify the diamensions of the display area used by the applet. After you create this file, you can execute your browser and then load this file, which causes FirstApplet to be executed.

To execute FirstApplet with an appletviewer, you may also execute the HTML file shown earlier. For example, if the preceding HTML file is called RunApp.html, then the following command line will run FirstApplet:

```
C:\>appletviewer RunApp.html
```

Run the Applet

To see the applet in action, you need an HTML file with the Applet tag as follows:

```
<HTML>
<BODY>
<APPLET CODE=FirstApplet.class WIDTH=200 HEIGHT=100>
</APPLET>
</BODY>
</HTML>
```

The easiest way to run the applet is with appletviewer shown below where FirstApplet.html is a file that contains the above HTML code:

```
appletviewer FirstApplet.html
```

Note: To run an applet written with Java 2 APIs in a browser, the browser must be enabled for the Java 2 Platform. If your browser is not enabled for the Java 2 Platform, you have to use appletviewer to run the applet or install Java Plug-in. Java Plug-in lets you run applets on web pages under the 1.2 version of the Java VM instead of the web browser's default Java VM.

(b) How do you create a button labelled "BCA"? (How do you change a label on a button?)

ANS : We create a button labelled 'BCA' by writing the following code:

```
Button b1=new Button('BCA');
```

and, we can change a label in a button by use of setLabel() method.

```
b1.setLabel("new name");
```

Q6. Answer the following questions :

(i) What is the keyword "throw" used for?

Refer to Study material, Q4, Page no.-79

(ii) What is the Java virtual machine? **[JUN2003,Q1(ii);JUN2002,Q1(b)]**

Refer to Study material, Q3, Page no.-13

(iii) What is the difference between radio buttons and check boxes?

ANS : We can create a set of mutually exclusive check boxes in which one and only one check box in the group can be checked at any one time. These check boxes are often called radio buttons, because they act like the station selector on a car radio-only one station can be selected at any one time. To create a set of mutually exclusive check boxes, you must first define the group to which they will belong and then specify that group when you construct the check boxes. Check box groups are objects of type CheckboxGroup. Only the default constructor is defined, which creates an empty group.

You can determine which check box in a group is currently selected by calling getSelectedCheckbox(). You can set a check box by calling setSelectedCheckbox(). These methods are as follows:

Checkbox getSelectedCheckbox();
void setSelectedCheckbox(Checkbox which);

Here, which is the check box that you want to be selected. The previously selected check box will be turned off.
While a check box is a control that is used to turn an option on or off. It cosists of a small box that can either contain check mark or not. There is a label associated with each check box that describes what option the box represents. You change the state of a check box by clicking on it. Check boxes can be used individually or as part of a group. Check boxes are objects of the Checkbox class.
When a group of check boxes are made then it is called Radio Buttons. And as individually it can be used to select or deselec an option.

(iv) What is the difference between a menu, menu bar and menu item?

ANS : A top-level window can have a menu bar associated with it. A menu bar displays a list of top-level menu choices. Each choice is associated with a drop-down menu. This concept is implemented in Java by the following classes: Menu, MenuBar, and MenuItem. In general, a menu bar contains one or more Menu objects. Each Menu object contains a list of MenuItem objects. Each MenuItem object represents something that can be selected by the user. Since Menu is a subclass of MenuItem, a hierarchy of nested submenus can be created. It is also possible to include checkable menu items. These are menu options of type CheckboxMenuItem and will have a check mark next to them when they are selected.
To create a menu bar, first create an instance of MenuBar. This class only defines the default constructor. Next, create instances of Menu that will define the selections desplayed on the bar. Following are the constructors for Menu:
Menu();
Menu(String optionName);
Menu(String optionName, boolean removable);

Here, optionName specifies the name of the menu selection. If removable is true, the pop-up menu can be removed and allowed to float free. Otherwise, it will remain attached to the menu bar. (Removable menus are implementation-dependent.) The first form creates an empty menu.

Individual menu items are of type MenuItem. It defines these constructors:

MenuItem();

MenuItem(String itemName);

MenuItem(String itemName, MenuShortcut keyAccel);

Here, itemName is the name shown in the menu, and keyAccel is the menu shortcut for this item.

Once you have added all items to a Menu object, you can add that object to the menu bar by using this version of add() defined by MenuBar:

Menu add(Menu menu);

Here, menu is the menu being added. The menu is returned.

Menus only generate events when a item of type MenuItem or CheckboxMenuItem is selected.

CS-74 : INTRODUCTION TO INTERNET PROGRAMMING
JUNE - 2003

Note : *Question* ***one*** *is* ***compulsory****. Answer any* ***three*** *from the rest.*

Q1(i). Write a java program to calculate Fibonacci series recursively. **[10]**

ANS :
```
import java.awt.*;
import java.io.*;
class fibo
{
public static void main(String args[]) throws IOException
{
int n=0;
BufferedReader br=new BufferedReader(new InputStreamReader(System.in));
String str;
System.out.println("Enter how many no:s");
str=br.readLine();
try{
n=Integer.parseInt(str);
}catch(NumberFormatException e)
{
System.out.println("Invalid format");
}
System.out.print("0 1 ");

fib(n-2,0,1);
}
static void  fib(int n,int d1,int d2)
{
 if(n==0)
 return;
 else
 {
int sum=d1+d2;
System.out.print(sum+" ");
d1=d2;
d2=sum;
fib(n-1,d1,d2);
}
}
}
```

(ii) What is a Java virtual machine? **[DEC2002,Q6(ii);JUN2002,Q1(b)] [5]**

Refer to Study material, Q3, Page no.-13

(iii) What is the difference between keyword throw and throws? **[5]**

Refer to Study material, Q4, Page no.-79

(iv) What is the difference between an application and an applet? **[5]**

Java Application	Java Applet
1. GUI (Graphical User Interface)	
Optional	Inherently graphical
2. Memory Requirements	
Minimal Java Application requirements	Java Application requirements plus web browser requirements
3. Distribution	
Loaded from the file system or by a custom class loading process.	Linked via HTML and transported via HTTP.
4. Environmental Input	
Command-Line Parameters	Browser client location and size; parameters embedded in the host HTML document.
5. Method Expected by Virtual Machine	
"main( )"- startup method.	int( ) - initialize method. start( ) - startup method stop( ) - pause/deactivate method destroy( ) - termination method paint( ) - drawing method.
6. Typical Applications	
Network server; multimedia kiosks,	public-access order-entry system for the developer tools; appliance and consumer web; online multimedia presentations; electronics control. web based animations and navigations.

(v) List all primitive data types, size and range of values they accept. **[5]**

Refer to Study material, Q1, Page no.-22

.

Q2. Describe the following terms: **[15]**

ANS :

(i) Multithreading

Java was designed to meet the real-world requirement of creating interactive, networked programs. To accomplish this, Java supports multithreaded programming, which allows you to write programs that do many things simultaneously. The Java run-time system comes with an elegant yet sophisticated solution for multiprocess synchronization that enables you to construct smoothly running interactive systems. Java's easy-to-use approach to multithreading allows you to think about the specific behavior of your program, not the multitasking subsystem

(ii) Distributed **[DEC2001,Q3(iii)]**

Java is designed for the distributed environment of the Internet, because it handles TCP/IP protocols. In fact, accessing a resource using a URL is not much different from accessing a file. The original version of Java (Oak) included features for intra-address-spaces messaging. This allowed objects on two different computers to execute procedure remotely. Java has recently revived these interfaces in a package called *Remote Method Invocation* (*RMI*). This feature brings an unparalleled level of abstraction to client/server programming.

(iii) Object oriented

Although influenced by its predecessors, Java was not designed to be source-code compatible with any other language. This allowed the Java team the freedom to design with a blank state. Once outcome of this was a clean, usable, pragmatic approach to objects. Borrowing liberally from many seminal object-software environment of the last few decades, Java manages to strike a balance between the purist's "everything is an object" paradigm and the pragmatist's "stay out of my way" model. The object model in Java is simple and easy to extend, while simple types, such as integers, are kept as high-performance nonobjects.

(iv) The modifier abstract **[JUN2001,Q6(v)]**

When applied to a class, the ***abstract*** modifier indicates that the class has not been fully implemented and that it should not be instantiated like this:

```
A mgA=new A( ):                //ERROR
```

but they can be used to create object references, because Java's approach to runtime polymorphism is implemented through the use of superclass reference.

```
abstract class A
{
    int i;
    void show()
    {
      System.out.println("Hello! This is A");
    }
}

class B extends A
{
    int j;
    void show()
    {
      System.out.println("Value of j = " + j);
    }
```

```
}
class mainClass
{
    public static void main(String args[])
    {
      B objB=new B();

    /* ERROR: A is abstract,can not be instantiated
      A objA=new A();
    */
      A objA;
      objA=objB;                    // objA references to objB

      objA.i=6;          // objA can now access A's member
      objA.show();                  // show() of B:Run-Time Polymorphism

    /*ERROR : j is not accessible through objA
      objA.j=5;
    */
      objB.j=5;
      objA.show();                  //show() of B:Run-Time Polymorphism
    }
}

    /* Note that when objA calls show(), then Java run_time decides to call show()
of B.
The output of the program is:
       Value of j = 0
       Value of j = 5
    */
```

If applied to a member method declaration, the *abstract* modifier means that the function will be implemented in a subclass. An abstract method has no implementation in class where it is declared. Instead it must be implemented in the subclass.

***Note** that any class having an abstract method must be declared abstract.*

An abstract class can have normal method with abstract method.

```
abstract class A
{
    abstract void xyz( );
                                    // No implementation here.
    void abc( )                     // A normal method.
    {
      //body of the method
```

```
    }
}
class B extends A
{
    void xyz()              //This is must
    {
                            //body of the method
    }
}
```

(v) Constructors

Refer to Study material, Q2, Page no.-56

(vi) Secure **[JUN2002,Q3(b)]**

As you are likely aware, every time that you download a "normal" program, you are risking a viral infection. Prior to Java, most users did not download executable programs frequently, and those who did scanned them for viruses prior to execution. Even so, most users still worried about the possibility of infecting their systems with a virus. In addition to viruses, another type of malicious program exists that must be guarded against. This type of program can gather private information, such as credit card numbers, bank account balances, and passwords, by searching the contents of your computer's local file system.

When you use a Java-compatible Web browser, you can safety download Java applets without fear of viral infection or malicious intent. Java achieves this protection by confining a Java program to the Java execution environment and not allowing it access to other parts of the computer. The ability to download applets with confidence that no harm will be done and that no security will be breached is considered by many to be the single most important aspect of Java.

(vii) Interface **[JUN2001,Q6(i)]**

Refer to Study material, Q3, Page no.-90

Q3. Difference between the following: **[15]**

(i) Method overloading and Overriding a method **[DEC2002,Q3(ii)]**

ANS :

Method Overloading	Method Overriding
(i) Overloaded methods **supplement** each other.	(i) An overriding method **replaces** the method it overrides.
(ii) Overloading methods may have **different** argument lists of **different** types.	(ii) An overriding method must have argument lists of **identical** type and order.
(iii) The return type may be **different** for overloaded methods	(iii) The return type must be **same** as that of overridden method.
(iv) Since overloading methods are essentially different methods, there is **no restriction** on exceptions they can throw.	(iv) The overriding method must not throw checked exceptions which cannot be thrown by the original method.

(ii) Interpreter and Compiler
Refer to Study material, Q2, Page no.-13

(iii) Class and Object
Refer to Study material, Q2, Page no.-4

(iv) This and Super **[DEC2003,Q3(ii);DEC2002,Q2(c)]**
Refer to Study material, Q2, Page no.-68

(v) Unicode and ASCII code **[DEC2001,Q1(i)]**
Refer to Study material, Q2, Page no.-22

Q4(i). Describe the following classes: **[9]**

- **Exception class**
- **Runtime exception class**
- **I/O exception class**

Refer to Study material, Q2, Page no.-77

(ii) Write an example of user defined exception. **[JUN2003,Q4(ii)]** **[6]**
Refer to Study material, Q6, Page no.-82

Q5(i). List the Java core libraries and describe their functionalities. **[10]**
ANS : Java core libraries permit flexibility in interface design and programming. We have following libraries :

1. Java.lang : It has classes
this package permits data conversion, threading, string handling etc.

2. Java.util : It has classes
We can work on arrays, collections, linked list, trees, stacks, vectors, with this package.
3. Java.io : It has classes that are used for I/O at byte and character level. We can serialize classes withit. We can use networking also.
4. Java.awt : It has classes for designing and managing windows. It helps in making buttons, menus, checkboxes, adding images etc.

(ii) List the modifiers and describe their purpose. [DEC2001,Q4(3)] [5]

ANS : Default modifier : *In the absence of any modifiers fields are associated with objects and are visible to all classes in a package, and accessible by a subclass in the same package only.*
public modifier : *A public variable or function can be accessed in any other class.*
private modifier : *A private variable or function can only be accessed its own class.*
protected modifier : *A degree of hiding lie between public and private, subclasses and classes in the same package have access to these items.* — deprecated since any class can claim to be a member of the same package! Note for C++ programming, the C++ protected is the Java 1.0 *private_protected.*
private protected : 'A private protected field or function can be accessed by any subclass, but can not be used otherwise', — in Java 1.0 only, and equivalent to the C++ protected.
static : *A variable or functions associated with a class rather than with the objects of the class.*
Note for C programmers. In C a static variable declared in a functions is the same variable each time you call it. This is not available in Java. In C a static variable declared outside a function is shared by the set of functions in the same file and following the declaration an hidden from other functions. In Java a static variable is shared by all functions in that class. Whether other classes can access it depend on whether it is private, public, and/or protected. A Java variable that is nonstatic is something that is not found in C. Each object in the class has its own variable, and all functions refer to that particular variable. The variable is created as part of the object and deleted with it.
In Java instance variables are the same each time you call them. A variable or function is declared to be static when it is associated with the class of objects rather than a particular object in that class. This means that a static function can not refer any data in an object - because it has no object. It also means that static data is essentially shared in common by every object but only stored in a single place. If you are in doubt about whether some data should be static or not - ask yourself how many times it occurs: once per class(static) or once per object(not static) or many time per object (its in a different class!).
final : *once initialized it can not be changed.* A variable(a field of a class or object) is declared *final* when you want it to keep its initial value for ever. It makes it a constant variable. A class is declared as *final* if it can not be extended.
native : *Preprogrammed in another language and running as machine code.*

synchronized : *Only one thread can execute this at a time.* A method or block of code is marked as *synchronized* if only one thread of control can be in it at a time. Other threads are locked out. The code is reentrant. It protects resources from interference by multiple access at one time.

abstract method : *A method that must exist for objects in a class but is fully defined only in subclasses*, abstract::class=*A class with one or more abstract methods.* abstract::=*not concrete, not yet implemented, deferred, prototypical.* An abstract method is one that is defined in classes derived from this class. All subclasses have a version as defined in the base class or also declare it as abstract. Certain methods can not be abstract: constructors, static, private, final, native, synchronized, plus those that override superclass methods. An abstract method makes the whole class *abstract.* A class that inherits an abstract method and does not override it is also an abstract class. An abstract class can not be used to construct new objects. You can only call an abstract method via an object in a class that has extended the abstract class and defined all the abstract methods.

threadsafe : *If another thread excuting this code at the same time can not change the value of a variable then the variable is* threadsafe *and the compiler may do clever things with it to make the code faster or smaller..*

transient : *something that does last longer than a function call.* If an object can exist longer than a given applet....is persistent.... then its transient data does not have to be preserved when a function exits.

Q6(i). Implement a student class. A student has a name, stipend, enrolment number. Write a default constructor and a constructor with two parameters (name and enrolment number) and two methods.

(a) To return the name and enrolment number.

(b) A method that increases the student's stipend.

Write a small program that tests your class. **[10]**

ANS : java.awt.*;

```
class student1
{
 String name;
 int enrol_no=0;
 double stipend;
 student1()
 {
  name="Dhaval";
  stipend=1000;
 }
student1(String n,double s)
 {
  name=n;
  stipend=s;
```

```
 }
 void print()
 {
 System.out.println(name);
 System.out.println(enrol_no);
 }
 double raise(double d)
 {
   stipend=stipend+d;
   return(stipend);
  }
}
class stud
 {
 public static void main(String args[])
 {
   student1 e=new student1();
  e.print();
  System.out.println("Now raise equal to 1000");
  System.out.println(e.raise(1000));
 }
}
```

(ii) State true or false with reasons: **[5]**

Every element in the array has the same type.

TRUE

Reason : by definition array is a collection of data of same type only.

Array size is fixed after it is created.

TRUE

Reason : A runtime error occurs if we try to

Java supports multiple inheritance.

FALSE

Every java class has a default constructor.

TRUE

Reason : Java uses default constructor to initialize the object at runtime.

The static keyword is used to access a program code without instantiating the class to which that code belongs.

TRUE

Reason : If you need to do computation in order to initialize your **static** variables, you can declare a **static** block which gets executed exactly once, when the class is first loaded the following example shows a class that has a static method, some **static** variables, and a **static** initialization block:

```
class Stat_Class
```

```
{
 static int counter;
  Stat_Class()
 {
     counter++;
 }
 //This Block initialized only once during entire life of Stat_Class
 static
 {
  System.out.println("Static block initialized");
  counter=1;
 }
}

class Static_Demo
{
     public static void main(String args[])
     {
        Stat_Class stat1=new Stat_Class();
        System.out.println(stat1.counter);
        // We can also access the static variable counter with
        //out using Object name, for example Stat_Class.counter
        //which we done next

        Stat_Class stat2=new Stat_Class();
        System.out.println(Stat_Class.counter);
     }
}
```

Outside of the class in which they are defined, **static** methods and variables can be used independently of any object. To do so, you need only to specify the name of their class followed by the dot operator. For example, if you wish to call a **static** method from outside its class, you can do so by using the following, general form:

Classname.Method();

Here, classname is the name of the class in which the **static** method is declared. As you can see, this format is similar to that used to call non-**static** methods through object-reference variables. A **Static** variable can be accessed in the same way-by use of the dot operator on the name of the class. This is how Java implements a controlled version of global function and global variables.This whole concept permits us to call the main() function from outside Java classes.

CS-74 : INTRODUCTION TO INTERNET PROGRAMMING
DEC- 2003

Note : *Question **one** is **compulsory**. Answer any **three** from the rest.*

Q1(i). Write a Java program to calculate $^{n}C_{r}$,

where $^{n}C_{r} = \dfrac{n!}{(n-r)!\,(r!)}$.

The input of n and r should be accepted from command line. **[10]**

ANS :
```
import java.awt.*;
class combination
{
public static void main(String args[])
{
float f1=1, f2=1, f3=1;
int i=0;
int n=Integer.parseInt(args[0]);
int r=Integer.parseInt(args[1]);
float result=0;
for( i=2;i<=n;i++)
f1=f1*i;
for(i=2;i<=n-r;i++)
f2=f2*i;
for(i=2;i<=r;i++)
f3=f3*i;
System.out.println("k"+f1+"l"+f2+"n"+f3);
result=f1/(f2*f3);
System.out.println("The combinations are"+result);
}
}
```

(ii) What is final keyword? What happens if we apply keyword in class access specifier? **[5]**

ANS : Final: A variable can be declared as final. Doing so prevents its content form being modified. This means that you must initialize a final variable when it is declared. (In this usage, final is similar to const in C/C++.) For example:

```
Final int FILE_NEW = 1;
Final int FILE_OPEN = 2;
Final int FILE_SAVE = 3;
Final int FILE_SAVEAS = 4;
Final int FILE_QUIT = 5;
```

Subsequent parts of your program can now use **FILE_OPEN**, etc., as if they were constants, without fear that a value has been changed.

It is a common coding convention to choose all uppercase identifiers for final variables. Variable declared as **final** do not occupy memory on a per-instance basis. Thus, a **final** variable is essentially a constant.

The keyword **final** can also be applied to methods but its meaning is substantially different than when it is applied to variables. Keyword ***final*** has its two special uses when applied in inheritance.

(i) ***final*** methods, these methods cannot be overriden, for example:

```
class A
{
    final void xyz( )
    {
      //body of Method
    }
}
    class B extends A
    {
      /* void xyz( ) overriden xyz( )
    {    }
    ERROR
    */
}
```

(ii) ***final*** classes, these classes cannot inherited by other class, that is, they are just opposite to abstract classes.

A final class can only used to create objects. For example:

```
final class A
{
    //class implementation
}
class B extends A
{
    //ERROR CAN'T SUBCLASS A
}
```

Abstract

When applied to a class, the ***abstract*** modifier indicates that the class has not been fully implemented and that it should not be instantiated like this:

```
        A mgA=new A( ):                    //ERROR
```

but they can be used to create object references, because Java's approach to runtime polymorphism is implemented through the use of superclass reference.

```
abstract class A
{
    int i;
    void show()
    {
      System.out.println("Hello! This is A");
```

```
    }
}

class B extends A
{
    int j;
    void show()
    {
        System.out.println("Value of j = " + j);
    }
}
class mainClass
{
    public static void main(String args[])
    {
        B objB=new B();

    /* ERROR: A is abstract,can not be instantiated
        A objA=new A();
    */
        A objA;
        objA=objB;                    // objA references to objB

        objA.i=6;            // objA can now access A's member
        objA.show();                  // show() of B:Run-Time Polymorphism

    /*ERROR : j is not accessible through objA
        objA.j=5;
    */
        objB.j=5;
        objA.show();                  //show() of B:Run-Time Polymorphism
    }
}
```

/* Note that when objA calls show(), then Java run_time decides to call show() of B.

The **output** of the program is:

Value of j = 0
Value of j = 5

*/

If applied to a member method declaration, the *abstract* modifier means that the function will be implemented in a subclass. An abstract method has no implementation in class where it is declared. Instead it must be implemented in the subclass.

***Note** that any class having an abstract method must be declared abstract.*

An abstract class can have normal method with abstract method.

```
abstract class A
{
    abstract void xyz( );
                                  // No implementation here.
    void abc( )                   // A normal method.
    {
      //body of the method
    }
}
class B extends A
{
    void xyz( )             //This is must
    {
                            //body of the method
    }
}
```

(iii) List all the primitive data types with their sizes as defined in Java. [5]

ANS : Java defines eight simple (or elemental) types of data: byte, short, int, long, char, float, double and boolean. these can be put in four groups :

✓ ***Integers :*** This group includes byte, short, int and long, which are for whole-valued signed number.

✓ ***Floating-point numbers :*** This group includes float and double, which represent numbers with fractional precision.

✓ ***Characters :*** This group includes char, which represents symbols in a character set, like letters and numbers.

✓ ***Boolean :*** This group includes boolean, which is a special type for representing true/false values.

Integers : Java defines four integer types: byte, short, int and long. All of these are signed, positive and negative values. The width and ranges of these integer types vary widely, as shown in this table:

Name	Width	Range
long	64	-9,223,372,036,854,775,808 to 9,223,372,036,854,775,807
int	32	-2,147,483,648 to 2,147,483,647
short	16	-32,768 to 32,767
byte	8	-128 to 127

Floating-Point Types : Floating-point numbers, also known as real numbers, are used when evaluating expressions that require fractional precision.

Name	Width in Bits	Range
double	64	1.7e-308 to 1.7e+308
float	32	3.4e-038 to 3.4e+038

(iv) Explain the action of break and labelled break commands. [5]

ANS : By using **break,** you can force immediate termination of a loop, bypassing the conditional expression and any remaining code in the body of the loop. When a **break** statement is encountered inside a loop, the loop is terminated and program control resumes at the next statement following the loop.

Here are two points to remember about **break.** First, more than one **break** statement may appear in a loop. However, be careful. Too many **break** statements have the tendency to destructure your code. Second, the break that terminates a switch statement affects only that **switch** statement and not any enclosing loops.

Labelled Break :

Sometimes you'd like more flexibility, for example the ability to break out two levels. In Java, there's a simpler approach to solving this problem as :

```
outer_block:
    for (i = 1; i <= 10; i++) {
        for (j = 1; j <= 10; j++) {
            if (some condition)
                break outer_block;
            // other processing in loop
        }
    }
    // control comes here when break is executed
```

The break statement has a label. When the statement is executed, control transfers out of the enclosed labelled statement. Control is NOT transferred to the label, but to a point past the end of the labelled statement. A labelled continue statement works in a similar way; control is transferred to the end of a labelled loop.

(v) What are reference type variables? How many types of reference variables are available in Java? [5]

ANS : Java is an object-oriented language. An object is a collection of variables and associated methods that is described by a class. The name of a class can be used as a type, so you can declare an object-type variable or specify that a method returns an object. If you declare a variable using the name of a class for its type, that variable can contain a reference to an object of that class. Such a variable does not contain an actual object, but rather a reference to the class instance, or object, the variable refers to. Because using a class name as a type declares a reference to an object, such types are called reference types. Java also allows the use of an interface name to specify a reference type. In addition, array types in Java are reference types because Java treats arrays as objects.

It is possible to cause a reference variable to contain a reference to nothing by assigning the special value represented by the keyword null to the variable. The value null can be assigned to any reference variable without a type cast.
There are three types of reference variables: array, class, and interface.

Q2. Define the following terms : **[15]**

(i) Polymorphism

Refer to Study material, Q5, Page no.-60

(ii) Abstraction

Refer to Study material, Q8, Page no.-9

(iii) Extends keyword

Refer to Study material, Q1, Page no.-66

(iv) Class variable

Refer to Study material, Q4, Page no.-6

(v) Multi-dimension arrays

Refer to Study material, Q11, Page no.-34

Q3. Differentiate between the following: **[15]**

(i) Application vs Applet

[JUN2003,Q1(iv) ; JUN002, Q2(i) ; JUN2001,Q5(a)]

ANS : Java can be used to create two types of programs: applications and applets. An *application* is a program that runs on your computer, under the operating system of that computer. When used to create applications, Java is not much different from any other computer language. Rather, it is Java's ability to create applets that makes it important. An *applet* is an application designed to be transmitted over the Internet and executed by a Java-compatible Web browser. An applet is actually a tiny Java program, dynamically downloaded across the network, just like an image, sound file, or video clip. The important difference is that an applet is an *intelligent program*, not just an animation or media file. In other words, an applet is a program that can react to user input and dynamically change-not just run the same animation or sound over and over.
As exciting as applets are, they would be nothing more than wishful thinking if Java were not able to address the two fundamental problems associated with them: security and portability. Let us define difference between them.

Java Application	Java Applet
1. GUI (Graphical User Interface)	
Optional	Inherently graphical
2. Memory Requirements	
Minimal Java Application requirements	Java Application requirements plus

	web browser requirements
3. Distribution	
Loaded from the file system or by a custom class loading process.	Linked via HTML and transported via HTTP.
4. Environmental Input	
Command-Line Parameters	Browser client location and size; parameters embedded in the host HTML document.
5. Method Expected by Virtual Machine	
"main( )"- startup method.	int( ) - initialize method. start( ) - startup method stop( ) - pause/deactivate method destroy( ) - termination method paint( ) - drawing method.
6. Typical Applications	
Network server; multimedia kiosks,	public-access order-entry system for the developer tools; appliance and consumer web; online multimedia presentations; electronics control. web based animations and navigations.

(ii) This vs Super keyword [JUN2003,Q3(iv) ; DEC2002,Q2(a) ; DEC2001,Q2(iii)]
Refer to Study material, Q2, Page no.-68

(iii) Interface vs Class
ANS : Using the keyword interface, you can fully abstract a class interface from its implementation. That is, using interface, you can specify what a class must do, but not how it does it. Interfaces are syntactically similar to classes, but they lack instance variables, and their methods are declared without anybody. In practice, this means that you can define interfaces which don't make assumptions about how they are implemented. Once it is defined, any number of classes can implement an interface. Also, one class can implement any number of interfaces.
To implement an interface, a class must create the complete set of methods defined by the interface. However, each class is free to determine the details of its own implementation. By providing the interface keyword, Java allows you to fully utilize the "one interface, multiple methods" aspect of polymorphism.
Interfaces are designed to support dynamic method resolution at run time. Normally, in order for a method to be called from one class to another, both classes need to be present at compile time so the Java compiler can check to ensure that the method signatures are compatible. This requirement by itself makes for a static and non-extensible classing environment. Inevitably in a system like this, functionality gets pushed by higher and higher in the class hierarchy so that the mechanisms will be available to more and more subclasses. Interfaces are designed to avoid this

problem. They disconnect the definition of a method or set of methods from the inheritance hierarchy. Since interfaces are in a different hierarchy from classes, *it is possible for classes that are unrelated in terms of the class hierarchy to implement the same interface. This is where the real power of interfaces is realized.*
Interfaces add most of the functionality that is required for many applications which would normally resort to using multiple inheritance in a language such as C++.

Q4(i). What is constructor? How can you overload constructor? Describe with an example. [7]

ANS : It can be tedious to initialize all of the variables in a class each time an instance is created. Even when you add convenience function like getdata ( ), it would be simplest and more concise to have all of the setup done at the time the object is first created. Because the requirement for initialization is so common, Java allows objects to initialize themselves when they are created. This automatic initialization is performed through the use of a constructer.

A constructor initializes an object immediately upon creation. It has the same name as the class, in which it resides and is syntactically similar to a method. Once defined, the constructor is automatically called immediately after the object is created, before the **new** operator completes. Constructors look a little strange because they have not return type, not even **void.** This is because the implicit return type of a class's constructor is the class type itself. It is the constructor's job to initialize the internal state of an object so that the code creating an instance will have a fully initialized, usable object immediately.

Let's how add a constructor in Item template so the values of variable automatically initialized when an object is constructed.

```
Item()
{
    Number=10;
    Cost=120;
}
```

The constructor defined above in class Item. Set the instance variable number and cost for each object to the same values. However, there are cases when we want to start an object with different set of values. For this we need to add parameters to the constructor Item

```
Item (int num, cost cost_item)
{
    number=num;
    cost = cost_item;
}
```

Since constructors are also a type of method with some special authorities, so Java allows overloaded constructors.

The program shows three overloaded constructors for class shape.

//Overloaded Constructor

```
class Shape
{
    int x;
    int y;
    int z;

    Shape(int i,int j,int k)
    {
      x=i;
      y=j;
      z=k;
    }
    Shape(int i)
    {
      x=y=z=i;
    }

    Shape()
    {
      x=y=z=-1;
    }
}

class mainClass
{
    public static void main(String pa[])
    {
    //Unknown shape:: Default Constructor
    Shape b1=new Shape();
    System.out.println(b1.x + " , " + b1.y + " , " + b1.z);

    //Shape is a Cube or Sphere::Constructor with One Parameter
    Shape b2=new Shape(12);
    System.out.println(b2.x + " , " + b2.y + " , " + b2.z);

    //Shape is a Cuboid::Constructor with three Parameter
    Shape b3=new Shape(12,23,2);
    System.out.println(b3.x + " , " + b3.y + " , " + b3.z);
    }
}
```

(ii) Define an exception and discuss how user defined exceptions can be implemented in Java. **[JUN2003,Q4(ii)]** **[8]**

Refer to Study material, Q6, Page no.-82

Q5(i). What is an access specifier? Discuss the available access specifier in Java. [7]

ANS : Access control is controlling visibility of a variable or method. When a method or variable is visible to another class, its methods can reference the method or variable. There are four levels of visibility that are used. Each level is more restrictive than the other and provides more protection than the one preceding it.

Public

Any method or variable is visible to the class in which it is defined. If the method or variable must be visible to all classes, then it must be declared as public. A variable or method with public access has the widest possible visibility. Any class can use it.

Package

Package is indicated by the lack of any access modifier in a declaration. It has an increased protection and narrowed visibility and is the default protection when none has been specified.

Protection

This specifier is a relationship between a class and its present and future sub-classes. The subclasses are closer to the parent class than any other class. This level gives more protection and narrows visibility.

Private

It is narrowly visible and the highest level of protection that can possibly be obtained. Private methods and variables cannot be seen by any class other than the one in which they are defined. They are extremely restrictive but are most commonly used. Any representation unique to the implementation is declared private. An object's primary job is to encapsulate its data and limit manipulation. This is achieved by declaring data as private.

(ii) What is inner class? Give its use. Describe with an example. [5]

Refer to Study material, Q4, Page no.-74

Q6(a). Implement a class Programmer. A Programmer has name, company, working_for and bas_salary. Write a default constructor and constructor with parameters to create Programmer object. Implement two methods: [10]

(i) to return the company name,

(ii) to return the gross salary after calculating from its basic salary. Make necessary assumption.

Refer to JUNE-04, Q5, Page no.-114

(b) Discuss the difference between String and StringBuffer class as defined in Java. [5]

Refer to Study material, Q4, Page no.-23

CS-74 : INTRODUCTION TO INTERNET PROGRAMMING
JUNE - 2004

Note : *Question **one** is **compulsory**. Answer any **three** from the rest.*

Q1(a). What is a bytecode in Java?

ANS : As with many other programming languages, Java uses a compiler to convert human-readable source code (.java) files into executable code (.class) files. Traditional compilers produce code that can be executed by specific hardware; for example, and Windows 98, C++ compiler creates executable program that works with Intel x^{86} compatible processors. In contrast the Java compiler (javac.exe) generates architecture - independent "bytecodes".

This bytecode can be executed by only a Java Virtual Machine (JVM), which is an idealized Java processor chip usually implemented in software rather than hardware.

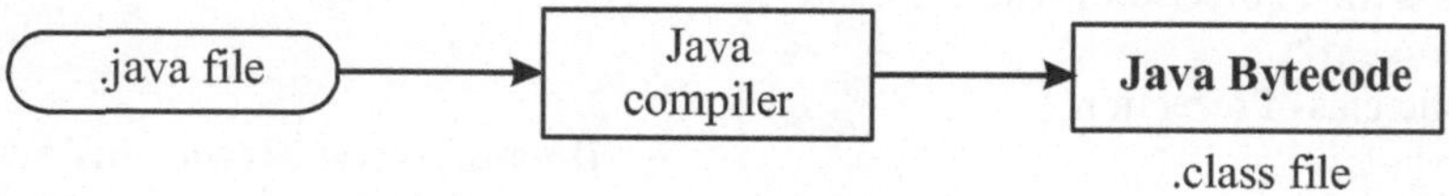

A Java source code file that can contain more than one class, on compilation will produce different ".class" file for each class in the source code.

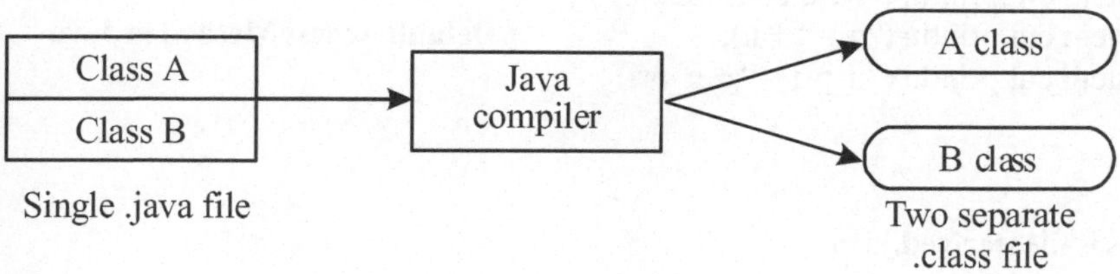

Remember, although the details of the JVM will differ from platform to platform, all interpret the same Java bytecode. So bytecode(.class file) created on Windows platform can be executed by UNIX platform without any problem.

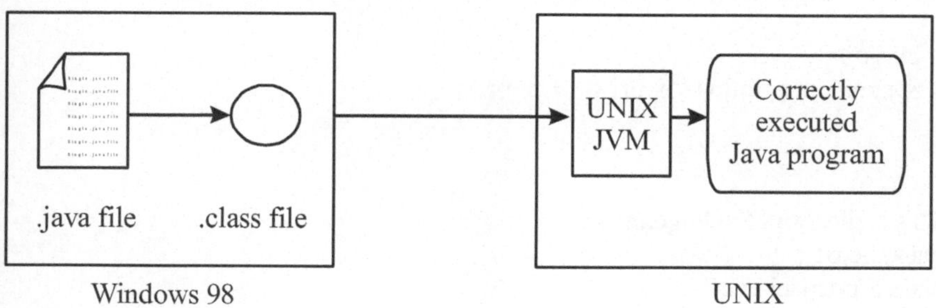

The execution unit of the VM carries out the instructions specified in the bytecodes. The simplex execution unit is an "interpreter", which is a program that reads the bytecodes, interprets their meaning, and then performs the associated function.

(b) What is the default access method in Java? Explain this with the help of a suitable example.

ANS : When a member does not have an explicit access specification, it is visible to subclass as well as to other classes in the same package. This is default access.
The following example shows default access control :
The Protection.java defines two **int** variables. The variable **n** is declared with the default protection, **n_pri** is **private**.
The second class, **Derived**, is a subclass of **Protection** in the same package, **p1**. This grants **Derived** access to every variable in **Protection** except for **n_pri,** the **private** one.
The third class, **SamePackage**, is not a subclass of **protection,** but is in the same package and also has access to all but **n_pri**.

This is file **Protection.java :**

```
package p1;
public class Protection {
int n = 1;                                    //Default Access Method in Java
private int n_pri = 2;

public Protection ( ) {
System.out.println ("base constructor" ) ;
System.out.println ("n = " + n);              //Default Access Method in Java
System.out.println ("n_pri = " + n_pri) ;
}
}
```

This is file **Derived.java :**

```
package p1;
class Derived extends Protection {
Derived ( ) {
System.out.println ("derived constructor") ;
System.out.println ("n = " +  n) ;            //Default Access Method in Java

// class only
// System.out.println ( "n_pri = " + n_pri) ;
}
}
```

This is file **SamePackage.java :**

```
package p1 ;
class Samepackage {
SamePackage ( ) {
```

```
Protection p = new Protection ( ) ;
System.out.println ( “Same Package Constructor”) ;
System.out.println ( “n = “ + p.n) ;   //Default Access Method in Java

// class only
// System.out.println ( “n_pri = “  + p.n_pri ) ;
}
}
```

(c) Can an abstract method be declared as final? Justify your answer.

ANS : No, an abstract method can not be declared as final. It is a compile time error for a final method to be declared abstract.

Justification : Abstract means *not concrete, not yet implemented, deferred. Final means ready to use, which can not be changed. An abstract method must exist for objects in a class but is fully defined only in subclasses.* An abstract method is one that is defined in classes derived from this class otherwise compile time error may occur. While final method can not be overriden. And it is implemented at the time of declaring. So, both are opposite to each other and can not be used together in any way.

(d) Write a program in Java to print the following pattern for a given input n = 5:

```
    1
   222
  33333
 4444444
555555555
```

ANS :

```
import java.awt.*;
class  series
{
public static void main(String args[])
{
int i;
int j;
System.out.println("The series is:");
for(i=1;i<=5;i++)
{
for(j=1;j<=5-i;j++)
System.out.print(" ");
for(j=1;j<=2*i-1;j++)
System.out.print(i);
System.out.println("");
}
}
}
```

(e) Find the error(s), if any, in the following blocks. Also correct the error(s).

(i) Class Demo {

```
Static void f( )
{ system.out.println ("Inside f( )");
throw new Illegal Access Exception ("demo");
}
public static void main (string args[ ])
{
f( );
}
}
```

ANS : class Demo {

```
static void f()
{
try {
System.out.println("Inside f()");
throw new.IllegalException("demo");
} catch(IllegalAccessException e) { }
public static void main(String args[])
{
f();
}
}
```

(ii) Abstract Class A {

```
Abstract void f( );
Abstract void g( );
Void display ( ) {
System.out.println ("Inside A");
}
}
Class B extends A
{
void f( ) {
system.out.println ("Version of B");
}
Void display( ) {system.out.println ("Inside B");
}
}
Class Demo {
Public static void main (string args [])
{
B        b = new B( );
         b.display( );
}
```

```
}
```

ANS :
```
abstract class A {
abstract void f( );
abstract void g( );
void display( ) {
System.out.println("Inside A");
}
}
class B extends A
{
void f( ) {
System.out.println ("Version of B");
}
void display( ) {System.out.println ("Inside B");
}
}
class Demo {
public static void main (String args[])
{
B b = new B( );
b.display( );
}
}
```

(f) What is 'this' keyword? How is it different from a super Keyword?

ANS : The "this" keyword : Sometimes a method will need to refer to the object that invoked it. To allow this, Java defines the **this** keyword. This can be used inside any method to refer to the current object. That is, this is always a reference to the object on which the method was invoked. You can use this anywhere a reference to an object of the current class' type is permitted.

Instance Variable Hiding

As you know, it is illegal in Java to declare two local variables with the same name inside the same or enclosing scopes. Interestingly, you can have local variables, including formal parameters to methods, which overlap with the names of the class' instance variables. However, when a local variable has the same name as an instance variable, the local variable hides the instance variable.

```
class Shape
{
    int x;
    int y;
    int z;
    Shape(int x,int y,int z)
    {
      this.x=i;
      this.y=j;
```

```
        this.z=k;
    }
}
class mainClass
{
    public static void main(String pa[])
    {
    Shape myShape=new Shape(12,23,2);
    System.out.println(myShape.x + " , " + myShape.y + " , " + myShape.z);
    }
}
```

this Different from super : ***super*** keyword in Java is used to access the methods or data members defined in the superclass. super has two general forms.

super for Constructor Reference

A subclass can call a constructor method defined by its superclass by use of the following form of super:

super (parameter_list);

In a subclass constructor, there is an implied first statement; the superclass constructor with no parameters is automatically called.

super for Member Access

super finds its use to access a member of the superclass that has been hidden (overloaded) by a member of a subclass. This usage has the following general form:

(i) super. <member variable of superclass>;

(ii) super. <member method of superclass> (parameter_list);

While, this is used, when a method will need to refer to the object that invoked it.

(g) Write a Java program to calculate the sum of the digits of a number. The sum should be calculated recursively to get a singledigit sum. (For example, if input is 189, then the result will be 9).

The input should be accepted from the command line.

ANS :
```
import java.awt.*;
import java.io.*;
class digit
{
public static void main(String args[])
{
int sum;
int n=Integer.parseInt(args[0]);
sum=calcsum(n);
System.out.println("The sum is"+sum);
}
static int calcsum(int n)

{
int s;
```

```
if(n==0)
return 0;
else
s=n%10+calcsum(n/10);

return s;

}
}
```

Q2(a). List the five Java buzzwords, and explain the significance of each.

ANS : There are many Java buzzwords, but five among them are listed below with significance of each :

Java is robust : Java is built for creating highly reliable programs. It has extensive compile-time error checking, followed by a second level of checking at run-time. There are no pointers in Java like there are in C++. So Java can't overwrite memory and corrupt data, as could happen in C or C++. Also, Java programs cannot gain unauthorized access to memory, as could happen in C or C++.

Java is secure : It is intended for use on networks which are distributed environments. Java is as virus-free and tamper-free as any system developed so far. Its applications are safe from intrusion from the outside by unauthorized code which might create viruses or invade file systems.

Java is architecture-neutral : Java applications will run anywhere on the network on just about any kind of platform. I think this is one of the greatest strengths of Java. The Java compiler generates "byte-codes" from the source file, which are not processor-specific. Rather, these byte-codes run on the Java Virtual Machine which converts the code to the ones and zeros which a specific processor, like an Intel or a Motorola, understands. Thus Java programs can run on any processor and code does not need to be re-written for different processors. Hence, Sun's Java slogan: "write once, run anywhere." But when Microsoft starts tampering with the Java classes so they can only run on Windows, then the universality of the Java standard is compromised.

Java is portable : To achieve portability across platforms, it is very strict in the definition of its basic, or "primitive" data types. It is also strict about the behavior of its arithmetic operators. Thus, Java programs are the same on every platform, with no data-type incompatibilities across hardware and software architectures.

Java is an interpreted and high performance language : Here we're talking about speed. Java has been criticized for slowness because it has to pay for its universality by going through an extra step in interpretation. But in applications when extremely high performance is required, byte-codes can be translated on-the-fly at run-time into machine code for a particular CPU, and Sun claims that the performance of byte-codes thus converted to machine code is almost indistinguishable from that of C or C++. Also, Java developers could compile their programs for the specific processors they want to support. Future versions of the Hypertext Transfer Protocol (http) could let the browser identify its processor type to the server so that the server could download the correct applet type for the user's system.

(b) What is finalize method in java? Explain this through an example.

ANS : In Java memory is managed automatically for you by the Java Virtual Machine (JVM). You do not therefore have to destroy any objects nor do you have to reclaim the memory they use. However, there is a Java facility which allows you to execute a special method (referred to as a finalize method) when the JVM reclaims (or garbage collects) an object. These methods are typically used for application specific house keeping and are not intended as destructor methods (that you may have seen in other languages).

It should therefore only be used to perform house keeping operations which can be left until the object is destroyed. That is, house keeping operations which should be performed as soon as all references to the object are removed should not be placed in the finalize method (for example, closing a file). This is because you cannot guarantee when the object will actually be garbage collected. One approach to their use is to ensure that any housekeeping which should already have been performed, has been performed.

For example :

```
protected void finalize () throws Throwable {
super.finalize();
if (fileWriter != null) {
fileWriter.close();
fileWriter = null;
}
}
```

This can be useful as a final check to ensure that subclasses of this class will clean up themselves in an appropriate manner.

Q3(a). Write a program in Java that enters a string at the command line. If the string is not equal to "BCA" then a user-defined exception is thrown called "No match". Also do a proper documentation of the program.

ANS :

```
import java.awt.*;
import java.io.*;
class MyException extends Exception{
private String a;
MyException(String s){
a=s;}
public String toString()
{
return "MyException:String should be BCA"+a;
}
}
class except
{
static void reply(String s)
{
if(s.compareTo("BCA")!=0)
```

```
throw new MyException("No Match");
System.out.println("Alright");
}
public static void main(String args[]) throws IOException
{
BufferedReader br=new BufferedReader(new InputStreamReader(System.in));
String str;
System.out.println("Enter the string");
str=br.readLine();
try{
reply(str);
}
catch(MyException e){
System.out.println(e);
}
}
}
```

(b) Write the output of the following program and justify your answer:

```
class Demo {
static void f( ) {
Try {
System.out.println ("Inside f( )");
throw new RuntimeException ("demo");
}
finally { System.out.println ("f( ) finally");
}
}
Static void g( ) { try
{ System.out.println ("Inside g( )");
return;
}
finally {System.out.println ("g( ) finally")
}
}
public static void main(String args[])
{
try {
f();
}
catch (Exception e)
{ System.out.println ("Exception caught");
}
g( );
}
```

}

ANS : OUTPUT :

inside f()

f() finally

Exception caught

inside g()

The control first goes to main(), where in try/catch block funcion f() is called. In function f() try/finally block having output statement "Inside f()". Then an exception is thrown that is caught by finally block having output statement "f() finally" we then return to the function main(), where its catch block prints the output statement "Exception Caught" function g() is called at last in void main. This function has output statement "Inside g()", which is then printed.

Q4(a). What is a package in Java? How is it created? How can a package be used in another file? List two important packages in Java, giving 2 important characteristics of each.

ANS : A package is a collection of classes. Packages are simply a convenient place for developers to put classes of a common purpose. The Java developers at Sun Microsystems have organized the many hundreds of classes in the Java API into just over 50 core packages. Within these, hundreds of classes and thousands of methods are defined.

Creating package : To create a package, Java source file (.java) need to include a **package** statement. The **package** statement has the following syntax:

```
package <packagename>;
```

Java uses file system directories to store packages. The following statement creates a package called MyPackage.

```
package MyPackage;
```

One must remember, while creating package:

· Each Java source file in folder MyPackage must include the statement above.

· package statement is the first statement in Java file.

· Classes you want to be accessible by code outside that package must be declared public.

· package names are case sensitive, so the folder name and name of package should be same.

· You can create a hierarchy of packages, that is, package within a package. The example of a multilevel package statement is : package book.chapter.topic;

Here **book** is the top level package having another package **chapter** inside and **topic** package inside **chapter**.

When we create a package class, we should declare each class member with its access modifier. (private, public, protected).

Two important package in Java with their characteristics : The **java.lang package** is special. It provides classes that are fundamental to the design of the Java language. The most important class is Object, which is the root of the class hierarchy, and Class, instances of which represent classes at run time. In most cases, we are not aware of the presence or use of these classes, as they operate "behind the

scenes" in a program. As well, the java.lang package provides the wrapper classes, the String class, and the System class.
Since the java.lang package is so fundamental to the language, the following statement is implied for all Java programs:

```
import java.lang.*;          // Implied! Not necessary
```

The AWT classes are contained in the **java.awt package**. It is one of the largest packages. The Abstract Windowing Toolkit (AWT) is an API that is responsible for building the Graphical User Interface (GUI). It is a part of the Java Foundation Classes (JFC). AWT includes a rich set of user interface components, a powerful event handling model, graphics and image tools, layout managers and support for data transfer using cut and paste through clipboards. AWT also support javaBeans architecture. Every AWT component is a simple bean. The java.awt contains all classes for creating user interfaces and for painting graphics and images.

```
import java.awt.*;          // Must when to create any GUI
```

(b) What is typecasting? Give two examples of typecasting in Java.

ANS : It is fairly common to assign a value of one type to a variable of another type. If the two types are compatible then Java will perform the conversion automatically. For example, it is always possible to assign an int value to a long variable. However, not all types are compatible, and thus, not all type conversions are implicitly allowed. For instance, there is no conversion defined from double to byte. Fortunately, it is still possible to obtain a conversion between incompatible types. To do so, you must use a cast, which perform an explicit conversion between incompatible types. This phenomenon is called typecasting.

Casting Incompatible Types :

Although the automatic type conversions are helpful, they will not fulfill all needs. For example, what if you want to assign an int value to a byte variable? This conversion will not be performed automatically, because a byte is smaller than an int. This kind of conversion is sometimes called a narrowing conversion, since you are explicitly making the value narrower so that it will fit into the target type.
To create a conversion between two incompatible types, you must use a cast. A cast is simply an explicit type conversion. It has this general form:

```
(target-type) value
```

Here, target-type specifies the desired type to convert the specified value to. For example, the following fragment casts an int to a byte. If the integer's value is larger than the range of a byte, it will be reduced modulo (the remainder of an integer division by) the byte's range.

```
int a;
byte b;
// ...
b = (byte)a;
```

A different type of conversion will occur when a floating-point value is assigned to an integer type: truncation. As you know, integers do not have fractional component. For example, if the value 1.23 is assigned to an integer, the resulting value will simply be 1. The 0.23 will have been truncated. Of course, if the size of the whole number component is large to fit in the target integer type, then that value will be reduced modulo to the target type's range.

The following program demonstrates some type conversions that require casts:

```
// Demonstrate casts.
class Conversion {
    public static void main(String args[] ){
    byte b;
    int i=257;
    double d=323.142;
    System.out.println("\nConversion of int to byte.");
      b = (byte)i;
    System.out.println("i and b " + i + " " + b);
    System.out.println("\nConversion of double to int.");
      i=(int)d;
    System.out.println("d and i " + d + " " + i);
    System.out.println("\nConversion of double to byte.");
      b = (byte)d;
    System.out.println("d and b " + d + " " + b);
    }
}
```

```
Conversion of int to byte.
        i and b 257          1
Conversion of double to int.
        d and i 323.142      323
Conversion of double to byte.
        d and b 323.142      67
```

Let's look at each conversion. When the value 257 is cast into a byte variable, the result is the remainder of the division of 257 by 256 (the range of a byte), which is 1 in this case. When the d is converted to an int, its fractional component is lost. When d is converted to a byte, its fractional component is lost, and the value is reduced modulo 256, which in this case is 67.

Q5(a). Implement a class programmer. A programmer has name, company name, working for and basic_salary. Write a default constructor and constructor with parameters to create a programmer object. Further, show the implementation of the constructor method with parameters.

ANS :

```
import java.awt.*;
class programmer
{
String name;
String working_for;
double bas_salary;
programmer()
{
name="GullyBaba";
```

```
working_for="MEWS";
bas_salary=10000;
}
programmer(String nam, String company, double s)
{
name=nam;
working_for=company;
bas_salary=s;
}
void print_company()
{
System.out.println("Working for Company"+working_for);
}

double gross()
{
double gs=0;
gs=bas_salary*.1+bas_salary*.2+bas_salary*.3;
return(gs);
}
}
class prog
{
public static void main(String args[])
{
programmer p=new programmer();
p.print_company();
System.out.print("Gross Salary is");
System.out.print(p.gross());
}
}
```

(b) Write the output of the following;

```
class Demo {
public static void main(String args[ ])
{
int I;
int num = 0xFFFFFFE;
for (I = 0; I < 2; I + +)
{
num = num << 1;
System.out.println(num);
}
}
}
```

ANS : 1073741816
-32

Q6(a). Write a recursive function in Java to print the contents of an array of integers.

ANS :
```
import java.awt.*;
class print1
{
int val[];
print1(int i)
{
val=new int[i];
}
void printarray(int i)
{
if(i==0)
return;
else
printarray(i-1);
System.out.println("["+(i-1)+"] "+val[i-1]);
}
}
class print{
public static void main(String args[])
{
print1 ob=new print1(10);
int i;

for(i=0;i<10;i++)
ob.val[i]=i+2;
ob.printarray(10);
}
}
```

(b) What is a polymorphism. How is it implemented? Show, through an example, the implementation of a polymorphism.

 # Polymorphism. **[DEC03, Q2(i)]**

ANS : In Java concept of polymorphism is implemented through overloading of operators, Overriding a method. Below are the detailed description of both implementations :

Overloading : One of the benefits of objects is that give the programmer a convenient way to construct new data types. Suppose you work with two-dimensional positions (such as X and Y coordinates, or latitude and longitude) in your program. You would like to express operations on these positional values with normal arithmetic operations, such as

Position1 = position2 + origin;

Where the variables position1, position2 and origin each represent a pair of independent numerical quantities. By creating a class that incorporates these two values, and declaring position1, position2 and origin to be objects of this class, we can, in effect, create a new data type. Many features of Java are intended to facilitate the creation of new data types in this manner.

Note that the = (equal) and + (plus) operators, used in the position arithmetic don't act the same way they do in operations on built-in types like int. The object position1 and so on are not predefined in Java, but are programmer-defined objects of class position. How do the = and + operations know how to operate on objects ? The answer is that we can define new operations for these operators. These operators will be member functions of the position class.

Using operators or functions in different ways, depending on what they are operating on , is called **polymorphism**. One thing with several distinct forms. When an existing operator, such as + or = is given the capability to operate on a new data type, it is said to be overloaded. **Overloading** is a kind of polymorphism; it is also an important feature of OOP.

Overriding a method : Java Runtime Polymorphism : Another way objects work together is to define methods that take other objects as parameters. You get even more cooperation and efficiency when the objects are united by a common superclass. All classes in the Java programming language have an inheritance relationship.

For example, if you define a method that takes a java.lang.Object as a parameter, it can accept any object in the entire Java platform. If you define a method that takes a java.awt.Component as a parameter, it can accept any component object. This form of cooperation is called *polymorphism*.

Overriden methods allow Java to support runtime polymorphism. Sometimes, we need to create a new method in a derived class with same signature and name as of its superclass member method. For example, consider a superclass ***AutoMobile*** having a method brake( ) and extended by class ***MotorBike***. Although MotorBike has access of brake( ) of its superclass, but wants to add some new system like disc brakes in front wheel while applying brakes, so MotorBikes declare a method brake( ) with same return type and parameter list. Now whenever an instance of MotorBike calls the brake( ) method it calls the one implemented in MotorBike, because it overrides the brake( ) of AutoMobile.

```
class AutoMobile
{   String color;
    int weight;
    double bhp;
    void start()
    {   System.out.println("Start the engine");        }
    void brake()
    {   System.out.println("Apply brakes");            }}
class MotorBike extends AutoMobile
{
    //start() is not an Overriden method, b'cos
    //signature's of start() in SuperClass is different
    String start(int no_of_kicks)
```

```
    {    return "Engine started in " + no_of_kicks + " kicks";  }
    //Overriden brake()
void brake()
{
System.out.println("Apply hydrolic brakes in rear and disc brakes in front wheel");
}
}
class mainClass
{
    public static void main(String args[])
    {
      MotorBike myBike=new MotorBike();
      myBike.color="BLUE";
      myBike.weight=120;
      myBike.bhp=9.5;
      String status=myBike.start(2);
      System.out.println(status);
      myBike.brake();
    }
}
    /*The output of the program is:
      engine started in 2 kicks
      Apply hydrolic brakes in rear and disc brakes in front wheel*/
```

Notes

✓ Always use private, public and protected access modifiers, for member declaration.

✓ Attributes of an objects which holds some value at a time should be declared as instance variable, and attributes which has some processing part should be declared as a method.

For example, in class ***Automobile***, attributes such as color, no-of-wheels, weight etc. should be declared as instance variable and attributes such as ignition, acceleration, brake etc. should be declared as methods.

✓ Use final variables for attributes which are constant values and used frequently. For example, value of Pi is fixed to 3.14.

✓ Use the ***println*** statement in the body part of the methods such as brake, ignition etc. where you do not know what to do in a non-real application.

CS-74 INTRODUCTION TO INTERNET PROGRAMMING
DEC 2004

Note : *Question number 1 is* ***compulsory*** *. Attempt any* ***three*** *questions from the rest.*

1(a) Why is Java platform independent ? Explain two advantages of Java independency. [6]

Java is platform independent as it is not dependent upon a particular architecture for execution of its networked programs. Java compiler converts the source code into highly optimized set of instructions called byte code. This is different from normally formed executable code by a compiler.

The specification of bytecode remains the same for any environment (architecture). This bytecode can be run at any machine having Java runtime system called JVM (Java Virtual Machine). It is an interpreter that executes the bytecode. Details of JVM may vary from system to system but bytecode remains same.

Two advantages of Java platform independency:-
(1) It is secure to deploy reworked programs (Applets) across internet as execution of these applets is limited to Java exe Environment & not other parts of computer.
(2) Java programs are portable as they are not dependant upon a particular architecture due to uniform structure of bytecode.

(b) Explain why main method of any Java program is always static. Your explanation should include all the properties of any static method. [5]

The keyword static allows main() to be called without having to instantiate a particular instance of the class. This is important as main() is called by the Java interpreter before any objects are made. Normally any function, made static can be called without making object of a class but that process itself has to be applied by the user. Method main() is not called by the user. It is called by operating system, so main() is made static in view of the concept of calling main() by operating system.

Methods declared as **static** have several restrictions:
- ✓ They can only call other **static** methods.
- ✓ They must only access **static** data.
- ✓ They cannot refer to **this** or **super** in anyway.

(c) Write a program in Java to print the following pattern for a given input n = 5. **[5]**

Number = 1 Sum = 1
Number = 2 Sum = 3
Number = 3 Sum = 6
Number = 4 Sum = 10
Number = 5 Sum = 15

```
import java.io.*;
class pattern{
public static void main(String args[]) throws IOException
{
System.out.print("Enter the no:");
BufferedReader br=new BufferedReader(new InputStreamReader(System.in));

String str;
int i,s=0;

str=br.readLine();
i=Integer.parseInt(str);

for(int k=1;k<=i;k++)
{
s+=k;
System.out.println("Number="+k+" Sum="+s);
}
}
}
```

(d) Explain three uses of final keyword with the help of suitable example for each. **[6]**

A variable can be declared as **final.** Doing so prevents its content from being modified. This means that you must initialize a **final** variable when it is declared. (In this usage**, final** is similar to **const** in C/C+ +.) For example:

```
Final int FILE_NEW = 1;
Final int FILE_OPEN = 2;
Final int FILE_SAVE = 3;
Final int FILE_SAVEAS = 4;
Final int FILE_QUIT = 5;
```

Subsequent parts of your program can now use **FILE_OPEN**, etc., as if they were constants, without fear that a value has been changed.

It is a common coding convention to choose all uppercase identifiers for final variables. Variable declared as **final** do not occupy memory on a per-instance basis. Thus, a **final** variable is essentially a constant.

The keyword **final** can also be applied to methods but its meaning is substantially different than when it is applied to variables. Keyword ***final*** has its two special uses when applied in inheritance.

(i) ***final*** methods, these methods cannot be overridden, for example:

```
class A
{
    final void xyz( )
    {
      //body of Method
    }
}
    class B extends A
    {
      /* void xyz( ) overriden xyz( )
    {   }
    ERROR
    */
}
```

(ii) ***final*** classes, these classes cannot be inherited by other class, that is, they are just opposite to abstract classes.

A final class can only be used to create objects. For example:

```
final class A
{
    //class implementation
}
class B extends A
{
    //ERROR CAN'T SUBCLASS A
}
```

(e) What are the different data types available in Java ? Explain the need of various data types. [7]

Java defines eight simple (or elemental) types of data: byte, short, int, long, char, float, double and boolean. These can be put in four groups :

✓ ***Integers :*** This group includes byte, short, int and long, which are for whole-valued signed number.

✓ ***Floating-point numbers :*** This group includes float and double, which represent numbers with fractional precision.

✓ ***Characters :*** This group includes char, which represents symbols in a character set, like letters and numbers.

✓ ***Boolean :*** This group includes boolean, which is a special type for representing true/false values.

✓ ***Integers :*** Java defines four integer types: byte, short, int and long. All of these are signed, positive and negative values. The width and ranges of these integer types vary widely, as shown in this table:

Name	Width	Range
long	64	-9,223,372,036,854,775,808 to 9,223,372,036,854,775,807
int	32	-2,147,483,648 to 2,147,483,647
short	16	-32,768 to 32,767
byte	8	128 to 127

Floating-Point Types : Floating-point numbers, also known as real numbers, are used when evaluating expressions that require fractional precision.

Name	Width in Bits	Range
double	64	1.7e-308 to 1.7e+308
float	32	3.4e-038 to 3.4e+038

2(a) What is Class ? How do you define a Class in Java ? When will you declare a member of a class as private ? Explain with an example. [8]

A class is a way to bind the data and its associated methods (functions) together. It allows the data & methods to be hidden, if necessary, from external use. When we define a class, we are creating a new data type that can be treated like any other data type of Java. Once defined, this new type can be used to create object of that type. Thus, a class is a *template* for an object, and an object is an instance of a class.

The general form of a ***class*** definition:

```
class <classname>
{
type <instance_variable1>;
type <instance_variable2>;
type methodname1(parameter_list)
{
// body of Method
}
        type methodname2 (parameter_list)
    {
                                    // body of Method
    }
}
```

Add : We define member of a class as private by using the keyboard private which essentially implies that the member would be accessed only by methods of that class.

e.g.

```
class Test {
        int a; // default access or implicitly public
        public int a; // public access
        private int c; // private access
void set c(int i).
{
c = i;}
int getc() { return c; }}
```

(b) What is inheritance ? Explain how you can inherit a class into another class in Java with the help of a program. [7]

The Java classes can be reused in several ways. Once a class has been written and tested, it can be adapted by other programmers to suit their requirements. This is basically done by creating new classes, reusing the properties of the existing ones. The mechanism of deriving a new class from an old one is called ***Inheritance (or Derivation)***. The old class is referred to as the *base class* and the new one is called the *derived class* or *subclass*. Therefore, a subclass is a specialized version of a super class or base class and adds its own, unique elements.

To inherit a class, Java uses ***extends*** keyword. To inherit a class, syntax for the derived class declaration is

```
class<derived class name> extends <base class>
{
   //body of the class
}
```

Java doesn't support the multiple inheritance, so a derived class can only inherit one class, but Java fully support multilevel inheritance e.g., given three classes called A, B, and C, C can be a subclass of B, which is a subclass of A. Here C inherits all the traits of B, and A classes.

The example shows a short program, here class B inherits class A and all members of class A included in class B. That is, object of the class B can access any member of class A as it access its own member.

```
class A
{
   int i;
   void get_A_Val()
   {
     System.out.println("Value of i is : " + i);
   }
}
```

```
class B extends A
{
    int j;
    void get_B_Val()
    {
      get_A_Val(); // get_A_val() is now member of B
      System.out.println("Value of j is : " + j);
    }
}
class mainClass
{
    public static void main(String args[])
    {
      B objB;               //Object of B declared
      objB=new B();  //Object is instantiated

      objB.j=10;

      objB.i=5;      //objB accessing i as its own member

      objB.get_B_Val();
    }
}
```

Even though A is a superclass for B, it is also a completely independent, stand-alone class. Being a superclass for a subclass does not mean that the superclass cannot be used by itself. Further, a subclass can be a superclass for another subclass.

3(a) Find the error(s), if any, in the following codes. Also correct the error(s). **[8]**

```
class Find_Error
        private static void main [string args]
{

        int check = 10;
        system.out.println ("Hi" + check);
```

program is ok

Correct program

```
class Find_Error{
```

```
public static void main (String args[ ])
{
    int check = 10;
    System.out.println ("Hi" + check );
    // program is OK
}
```

(b) What is the need of exception handling ? Explain the use of try-catch block in exception handling with the help of a program. [7]

An *exception* is an abnormal condition that arises in a sequence at run time. In other words, an exception is a run-time error. In computer languages that do not support exception handling, errors must be checked and handled manually-typically through the use of error codes, and so no. This approach is as cumbersome as it is troublesome. Java's exception handling avoids these problems and, in the process, brings run-time error management into the object-oriented world.

To guard against and handle a run-time error, simply enclose the code that you want to monitor inside a **try** block. Immediately following the **try** block, include a **catch** clause that specifies the exception type that you wish to catch. To illustrate how easily this can be done, the following program includes a **try** block and a **catch** clause which processes the Arithmetic Exception generated by the division-by-zero error:

```
class Exc2 {
    public static void main (String args[ ]) {
    int d, a;
      try {                              // monitor a block of code.
      d = 0;
      a = 42 / d ;
      System.out.println ("This will not be printed. ");
    } catch (ArithmeticException e) {    //catch divide-by-zero error
    system.out.println ("Division by Zero.");
    }
System.out.println ("After catch statement.");
}
}
```

This program generates the following **output**:

```
    Division by zero.
    After catch statement.
```

Notice that the call to **println( )** inside the **try** block is never executed. Once an exception is thrown, program control transfers out of the **try** block into the **catch** block. Put differently, **catch** is not "called," so execution never "returns" the try block from a **catch**. Thus, the line "This will not be printed." is not displayed. Once the **catch** statement has executed, program control continues with the next line in the program following the entire **try/catch** mechanism.

4(a) Give the value of int a = 24 after following : [6]
(i) a = a + a>>2;
(ii) a = a + a<<2;

(i) a = a + a>>2; → 12
(ii) a = a + a<<2; → 192

(b) What s a constructor ? Why is constructor overloading how constructor of a superclass is called in a subclass. [9]

It can be tedious to initialize all of the variables in a class each time an instance is created. Even when you add convenience function like getdata ( ), it would be simplest and more concise to have all of the setup done at the time the object is first created. Because the requirement for initialization is so common, Java allows objects to initialize themselves when they are created. This automatic initialization is performed through the use of a constructor.

Since constructors are also a type of method with some special authorities, so Java allows overloaded constructors. This is done for flexible initialization of class variable

The program shows three overloaded constructors for class shape.

```
//Overloaded Constructor
class Shape
{
    int x;
    int y;
    int z;

    Shape(int i,int j,int k)
    {
      x=i;
      y=j;
      z=k;
    }
    Shape(int i)
    {
      x=y=z=i;
    }
    Shape()
    {
```

```
        x=y=z=-1;
    }
}

class mainClass
{
    public static void main(String pa[])
    {
    //Unknown shape:: Default Constructor
    Shape b1=new Shape();
    System.out.println(b1.x + " , " + b1.y + " , " + b1.z);

    //Shape is a Cube or Sphere::Constructor with One Parameter
    Shape b2=new Shape(12);
    System.out.println(b2.x + " , " + b2.y + " , " + b2.z);

    //Shape is a Cuboid::Constructor with three Parameter
    Shape b3=new Shape(12,23,2);
    System.out.println(b3.x + " , " + b3.y + " , " + b3.z);
    }
}
```

A subclass can call a constructor method defined by its superclass by use of the following form of super:

super (parameter_list);

In a subclass constructor, there is an implied first statement; the superclass constructor with no parameters is automatically called.

```
class A
{
    int i;

    A()
    {
      System.out.println("Default Constructor of A");
    }

    A(int a)
    {
      i=a;
      System.out.println("Parameterised Constructor of A");
    }
}
```

```
class B extends A
{
    int i;

    B()
    {
      //Default Constructor of A is automatically called
      System.out.println("Default Constructor of B");
    }

    B(int a,int b)
    {
      super(a);    //Calling the Parameterised constructor of SuperClass A
      i=b;
      System.out.println("Parameterised Constructor of B");
    }
}

class mainClass
{
    public static void main(String args[])
    {
      B objB1=new B();

      B objB2=new B(2,4);
    }
}
    /*
      The output of the program is:

      Default Constructor of A
      Default Constructor of B
      Parameterised Constructor of A
      Parameterised Constructor of B
    */
```

In the preceding example, super( ) was called with three arguments. Since, constructors can be overloaded, super( ) can be called using any form defined by the superclass. The constructor executed will be the one that matches the arguments.

5(a) What is a String class ? Explain any three constructors of String class. [8]

Java implements strings as objects of type String which is a class.
String objects can be by a number of ways, making it easy to operate a string as needed.
String class makes an objects such that String cannot be changed.

Implementing strings as built-in objects allows Java to provide full complement of features that make string handling convenient. Java has methods to compare strings, search for a substring, concatenate two strings & change case of letters with in a string.

String constructors

(1) To create an empty String, you call the default constructor

String S = new String();

will create an instance of String with no characters in it.

(2) To create a string initialized by a
no. of characters, use the constructor :
String (char char[])
e.g.

```
char chars[] = {'a', 'b', 'c'];
String S = new String (chars);
```

(3) You can specify a subrange of a character array as an initialization using the following constructor:

String (char chars[ ], int startindex, int numbers}
e.g. char chars[ ] = {'a', 'b', 'c', 'd', 'e', 'f',};
String S = new String (chars, 2, 3);
This initializes S to the characters 'bcd'

(b) Write the output of the following program and explain the processing of program. **[7]**

```
Class X {
Public static void main (string args [ ] )
{    int i=50;
   while (i >=0)
  {

       System.out.println("i;"+i);
       If (i%2==0) break;
       i - - ;
```

```
System.out.println("Nothing will be printed");
        }
    System.out.println("loop Terminated");
    }}
```

Output

L : 50
Loop Terminated

Reason

When we enter void main L is set to 50
Because 50 $\geq$ 0, we enter while Loop & print

L : 50
Now, 50% L = 0, so while loop breaks, & we come out of loop & the following statement is printed that is "Loop terminated."

6(a) Write a program for addition of two matrices in Java. [5]
(b) What is access modifier ? Explain the access modifiers in Java. [5]
(c) What is interface in Java ? Explain the need of it. [5]

(a) import java.io.*;

```
class array{
public static void main(String args[])throws IOException
{

   int arr1[][]=new int[5][5];
   int arr2[][]=new int[5][5];
   int arr3[][]=new int[5][5];

BufferedReader br=new BufferedReader(new InputStreamReader(System.in));
   String str;
  int i=0,j=0;
  System.out.println("Enter the first matrix elements");
  for(;i<5;i++)
  for(j=0;j<5;j++)
  {
  str=br.readLine();
   arr1[i][j]=Integer.parseInt(str);
  }
  System.out.println("Enter the second matrix elements");
  for(i=0;i<5;i++)
```

```
for(j=0;j<5;j++)
{
str=br.readLine();
arr2[i][j]=Integer.parseInt(str);
}

for(i=0;i<5;i++)
for(j=0;j<5;j++)
arr3[i][j]=arr1[i][j]+arr2[i][j];

System.out.println("Sum of matrices is:");

for(i=0;i<5;i++)
{
for(j=0;j<5;j++)
System.out.print(arr3[i][j]+" ");
System.out.println();
}

}}
```

(b) Access control is controlling visibility of a variable or method. When a method or variable is visible to another class, its methods can reference the method or variable. There are four levels of visibility that are used. Each level is more restrictive than the other and provides more protection than the one preceding it.

Public ⇒ Any method or variable is visible to the class in which it is defined. If the method or variable must be visible to all classes, then it must be declared as public. A variable or method with public access has the widest possible visibility. Any class can use it.

Package ⇒ Package is indicated by the lack of any access modifier in a declaration. It has an increased protection and narrowed visibility and is the default protection when none has been specified.

Protected ⇒ This specifier is a relationship between a class and its present and future subclasses. The subclasses are closer to the parent class than any other class. This level gives more protection and narrows visibility.

Private ⇒ It is narrowly visible and the highest level of protection that can possibly be obtained. Private methods and variables cannot be seen by any class other than the one in which they are defined. They are extremely restrictive but are most commonly used. Any representation unique to the implementation is declared private. An object's primary job is to encapsulate its data and limit manipulation. This is achieved by declaring data as private.

(c) Through the use of the interface keyword, Java allows you to fully abstract the interface from its implementation. Using interface, you can specify a set of methods which can be implemented by one or more classes. The interface, itself, does not actually define any implementation. Although they are similar to abstract classes, interfaces have an additional capability: A class can implement more than one interface. By contrast, a class can only inherit a single super class (abstract or otherwise).

Packages and interfaces are two of the basic components of a Java program. An interface is defined much like a class. This is the general form of an interface.

```
access interface name {
        return-type method-name1(parameter-list);
        return-type method-name2(parameter-list);
        type final-varname1 = value;
        type final-varname2 = value;
        // ...
        return-type method-nameN(parameter-list);
        type final-varnameN = value;
}
```

CS-74 INTRODUCTION TO INTERNET PROGRAMMING
JUNE 2005

Note : *Question no. 1 is* ***compulsory.*** *Attempt any* ***three*** *from the rest.*

1(a) Write a program in Java to find the largest and smallest of n numbers stored in an array, where n is a positive integer. [5+1]

Program to find Max and Min in an Array.

```
class findMAX_MIN
{
public static void main(String args[])
{
int a[]={40,52,75,65,72,75,24,64,73,75,71,52,75,65,72,75,24,64,73,75,71};
    int max=a[0];
    int min=a[0];
    int pmax=0;
    int pmin=0;
    for(int i=1;i<=a.length-1;i++)
    {
      if(max<a[i])
      {
        max=a[i];
        pmax=i;
      }
      if(min>a[i])
      {
        min=a[i];
        pmin=i;
        }
      }
System.out.println("MAX=( " + max + ","+pmax+") , MIN=(" + min + "," +
pmin +")" );

    }
}
```

(b) What happens if final is applied to method in a class ? Explain with the help of suitable example. [3]

If final is applied to a method in a class, that portion for method cannot be overridden.

eg
```
class first {
        final void func ( ) {
        System.out.print("final method");
class second extends first
    {
    void func  ( ) { // ERROR! Can't overload
        System.out.print ("Illegal !");
      }
    }
```

Here, method func( ) is declared as final in class first, so it cannot be overridden in class second.

(c) Write the output of the following statements where int a = - 10; b =2; [2+2]

(i) a + 1 << 2;
(ii) a >> b + 1;

(i) a + 1 << 2; → - 36
(ii) a >> b + 1; → - 2

(d) What is method overloading in Java ? Overload a method swap( ) to swap values of two variables x, y. Write a program that swaps two integer values as well as two char values. [6]

Method overloading : We can define in JAVA two or more methods with same name, in the class, as long as their parameter declaration is different This is called method over loading. Java implements polymorphism by this way.

```
class OverLoadeg
{
void swap(int a,int b)
{
int temp;
temp=a;
a=b;
b=temp;

System.out.println("Values are"+a+" and "+b);
}

void swap(char a,char b)
{
```

```
char ch;

ch=a;
a=b;
b=ch;
System.out.println("Values are"+a+" and "+b);
}

}
class OverLoad{
public static void main(String args[])
{
OverLoadeg o=new OverLoadeg();
int a=2,b=3;
char c='a',d='b';
o.swap(a,b);
o.swap(c,d);
}

 }
```

(e) What are the inner classes in Java ? Explain with example. [3]

An inner class is a non static nested class. It has access to all of the variables & methods of its outer class and may refer to them directly in the same way that other non static member of outer class do.

e.g.

Class outer has an inner class Inner

```
class outer {
        int outer_X = 10;
        void testit ( )
              {
                Inner inner = new Inner ( );
                inner.display ( );
              }
        class Inner {
              void display ( ) {
                System.out.println("display : outer_X = " + outer_X);
               }}}
class ClassDemo{
                  public static void main (String args[ ])
                  {
```

```
            Outer outer = new Outer ();
            outer.testit ();
            }
    }
```

In this program, an inner class named Inner is defined within the space of class Outer.
Thus any code in class Inner can directly access the variable outer_X..

(f) What is 'this' pointer ? Explain with example. [3]

The "this" keyword ⇒ Sometimes a method will need to refer to the object that invoked it. To allow this, Java defines the **this** keyword. This can be used inside any method to refer to the current object. That is, this is always a reference to the object on which the method was invoked. You can use this anywhere a reference to an object of the current class' type is permitted.

Instance Variable Hiding ⇒ As you know, it is illegal in Java to declare two local variables with the same name inside the same or enclosing scopes. Interestingly, you can have local variables, including formal parameters to methods, which overlap with the names of the class' instance variables. However, when a local variable has the same name as an instance variable, the local variable hides the instance variable.

```
class Shape
{
    int x;
    int y;
    int z;
    Shape(int x,int y,int z)
    {
      this.x=i;
      this.y=j;
      this.z=k;
    }
}
class mainClass
{
    public static void main(String pa[])
    {
    Shape myShape=new Shape(12,23,2);
    System.out.println(myShape.x + " , " + myShape.y + " , " + myShape.z);
    }
}
```

(g) The commission paid to a salesperson is calculated as follows :

- **If sales < 50, no commission**
- **If 50 < = sales ,< = 500, then 10% commission**
- **If sales > 500 then commission = Rs. 50 + 8%**

Write a Java program and test it with five samples of data. [5]

```
import java.io.*;

class sales{

public static void main(String args[]) throws IOException
{
String str;
int sale;
double com;
BufferedReader br=new BufferedReader(new InputStreamReader(System.in));

for(int i=0;i<=4;i++)
{
System.out.println("Enter no: of items sold");
str=br.readLine();
sale=Integer.parseInt(str);

System.out.println(sale);
if(sale<50)
System.out.println("No Commission");
else
if(sale<=500)
{
com=.1*sale;
System.out.println("Commission="+com);
}
else
{
//com=50+.8*sale;
System.out.println("Commission="+(50+.8*sale));
}
}

}
}
```

2(a) How do interfaces and abstract classes differ in Java ? Give an example of each type. [5]

INTERFACES	ABSTRACT CLASSES
(1) Using interface you can specify,. what a class must do, but not how it does. Interface is a standalone structure.	(1) Abstract classes also specify what must be done but not how it does but it is used with inheritance i.e. Abstract class is super class of the subclass in which abstract methods will be overridden. It is not a standalone structure.
(2) Method overridden in the class that implements interface must be preceeded by keyword public.	(2) Method overridden does n't require public to be preceeded.
(3) They are designed to support dynamic method resolution at runtime without. complexion of extensibility	(3) They are also for dynamic method resolution but complexion of extensibility is there.

eg <u>Interface</u>

```
interface Callback {
                    void callback (int param);
                            }
class client implements Callback{
          public void callback (int p)
          {
          System.out.println ("Callback called with " + p);
    }
}
```

<u>Abstract class</u>

```
abstract class A {
                    abstract void callme ();
                    }

class B extends A {
          void call me ( )
                 {
          System.out.pinrtln ("B's implementation of callme");
```

```
}}.
class AbstractDemo {
        public static void main (String args [ ])
        {
        B b = new B():
        b.callme ( );
        }
```

(b) Write the output of the following program segments. Also explain step by step processing. [6]

```
for (int i = 1; i<10; i++) {
for (int j=1; j<4; j++) {
    if (j = = 2)
        break;
    System.out.println(i +","+j);
  }
}
```

What is the difference between 'throw' and 'throws' ? Explain with proper examples.

1,1
2,1
3,1
4,1
5,1
6,1
7,1
8,1
9,1

So far, you have only been catching exceptions that are thrown by the Java run-time system. However, it is possible for your program to throw an exception explicitly, using the **throw** statement. The general form of throw is shown here;

Throw *Throwableinstance;*

Here, *Throwableinstance* must be an object of type **Throwable** or a subclass, of **Throwable**.

The flow of execution stops immediately after the throw statement; any subsequent statements are not executed. The nearest **try** block is inspected to see if it has a **catch** statement that matches the type of the exception. If it does find a match, control is transferred to that statement. If not, then the next enclosing **try** statement is inspected, and so on. If no matching **catch** is found, then the default exception handler halts the program and prints the stack trace.

```
class exc_throw
{
    public static void main(String args[])
    {
      try
      {
        throw new ArithmeticException("hello");
      }
      catch(ArithmeticException e)
      {
        System.out.println("The exception catched is : " + e);
      }
    }
}

/*********
    Output is:
    The exception catched is : java.lang.ArithmeticException: hello
*********/
```

Here, **new** is used to construct an instance of **NullPointerException**. All of Java's built-in run-time exceptions have two constructors: one with no parameter and one that takes a string parameter.

Throws

If a method is capable of causing an exception that it does not handle, it must specify this behavior so that callers of the method can guard themselves against that exception. You do this by including a throws clause in the method's declaration. A **throws** clause lists the types of exceptions that method might throw.

This is the general *(parameter-list)* throws exception-list

```
{
    // body of method
}
```

Here, *exception-list* is a comma-separated list of the exceptions that a method can throw.

Following is an example of an incorrect program that tries to throw an exception that it does not catch. Because the program does not specify a **throws** clause to declare this fact, the program will not compile.

```
// This program contains an error and will not compile.
class Throws Demo {
    Static void throwOne ( ) {
      System .out .println ("Inside throwOne");
      Throw new IllegalAccessException ("demo);
```

```
    }
    public static void main (String args[ ]) {
      throwOne ( ) ;
    }
}
```

To make this example compile, you need to make two changes. First you need to declare that **throwOne( )** throws **IllegalAccessException.** Second, **main ( )** must define a **try/catch** statement that catches this exception.
The corrected example is shown here:

```
//This is now correct.
class ThrowsDemo {
    Static void throwOne( ) throws IllegalAccessException {
      System.out.println("Inside throwOne.");
      Throw new IllegalegalAccessException("demo);
    }
    public static void main(String args[ ] ) {
      try {
        throwOne( );
      } catch(IllegalAccessException e) {
        System.out.println("Caught " + e);
        }
    }
}
```

Here is the **output** generated by running this example program;
Inside throwOne
Caught Java.Lang.IlegalAccessException: demo

(c) "A java file can have only one public class." Explain. [4]
Javafile can have onlyone public class i.e. there can only be one origin of entrance in the program by means of Java interpreter which is an absolutely logical implementation.
Java interpreter searches for main() function in the class which has same name as that of program. The class containing main() function is the public class. You cannot have two main() functions in the program in two different classes as then both class names will be same as program name which is impossible. Moreover, there can't be two entrances to the program for purpose of executing it, that will be illogical.
eg. employee.Java

```
    class figure {
          void getdata ( )
```

```
                        {}
            }
class employee {                        ;   class name same as program
                                            name, only one class can have this
                                            name i.e. "employee"
        public static void main (String args [ ])
        {
            figure f = new figure ( );
            f.getdata ();
            }
        }
```

3(a) What is Java Virtual Machine (JVM) ? Explain.
[JUN02,1(b)][JUN03,1(ii)][3]

The core of Java technology, the Java Virtual Machine(JVM) is an abstract computing machine that enables the Java platform to host applications on any computer or operating system without rewriting or recompiling. Anyone interested in designing a language or writing a compiler for the Java Virtual Machine must have an in-depth understanding of its binary class format and instruction set. If you are programming with the Java programming language, knowledge of the Java virtual machine will give you valuable insight into the Java platform's security capabilities and cross-platform portability. It will increase your understanding of the Java programming language, enabling you to improve the security and performance of your programs.

(b) What is default access for class members in Java ? Explain with the help of suitable example. [3]

When a member does not have an explicit access specification, it is visible to subclass as well as to other classes in the same package. This is default access.
The following example shows default access control :
The Protection.java defines two **int** variables. The variable **n** is declared with the default protection, **n_pri** is **private**.
The second class, **Derived**, is a subclass of **Protection** in the same package, **p1**. This grants **Derived** access to every variable in **Protection** except for **n_pri,** the **private** one.
The third class, **SamePackage**, is not a subclass of **protection,** but is in the same package and also has access to all but **n_pri**.

This is file **Protection.java :**

```
package p1;
public class Protection {
```

```
int n = 1;                                    //Default Access Method in Java
private int n_pri = 2;

public Protection ( ) {
System.out.println ("base constructor" ) ;
System.out.println ("n = " + n);              //Default Access Method in Java
System.out.println ("n_pri = " + n_pri) ;
}
}
```

This is file **Derived.java :**

```
package p1;
class Derived extends Protection {
Derived ( ) {
System.out.println ("derived constructor") ;
System.out.println ("n = " + n) ;             //Default Access Method in Java

// class only
// System.out.println ( "n_pri = " + n_pri) ;
}
}
```

This is file **SamePackage.java :**

```
package p1 ;
class Samepackage {
SamePackage ( ) {
Protection p = new Protection ( ) ;
System.out.println ( "Same Package Constructor") ;
System.out.println ( "n = " + p.n) ;          //Default Access Method in Java

// class only
// System.out.println ( "n_pri = "  + p.n_pri ) ;
}
}
```

(c) Consider the following class hierarchy : **[2]**

```
A
|
B
|
C
```

If an object of Class C is created, then explain the order of execution of constructor of Class A, B and C.

If object of Class C is created, order of execution of construction of class A, B&C will be first A, then B, then C.

This order is in itself intuitive approach as the variables of the Super class must be initialized before that of subclass because it's the normal approach that a subclass uses Super class variables. So Super class variables must be initialized at first.

(d) Find the error(s), if any, in the following statement [Also correct the error(s)] :

int a = 5;

a = a* 10; **[3]**

No error

(e) What are the Applets in the Java ? How do they differ from application program ? **[2+2]**

Java can be used to create two types of programs: applications and applets. An *application* is a program that runs on your computer, under the operating system of that computer. When used to create applications, Java is not much different from any other computer language. Rather, it is Java's ability to create applets that makes it important. An *applet* is an application designed to be transmitted over the Internet and executed by a Java-compatible Web browser. An applet is actually a tiny Java program, dynamically downloaded across the network, just like an image, sound file, or video clip. The important difference is that an applet is an *intelligent program*, not just an animation or media file. In other words, an applet is a program that can react to user input and dynamically change-not just run the same animation or sound over and over.

As exciting as applets are, they would be nothing more than wishful thinking if Java were not able to address the two fundamental problems associated with them: security and portability. Let us define difference between them.

Java Application	Java Applet
1. GUI (Graphical User Interface) Optional	Inherently graphical
2. Memory Requirements Minimal Java Application requirements	Java Application requirements plus web browser requirements

3. Distribution

Loaded from the file system or by a custom class loading process	Linked via HTML and transported via HTTP.

4. Environmental Input

Command-Line Parameters	Browser client location and size; para-meters embedded in the host HTML document.

5. Method Expected by Virtual Machine

"main( )"- startup method.	int( ) - initialize method. start( ) - startup method stop( ) - pause/deactivate method destroy( ) - termination method paint( ) - drawing method.

6. Typical Applications

Network server; multimedia kiosks,	public-access order-entry system for the developer tools; appliance and consumer web; online multimedia presentations; electronics control. web based animations and navigations.

4(a) How do you define a package in Java ? How do you prevent a class from being accessed from one package to another package ? [3]

Packages are containers for classes that are used to keep the class name space compartmentalized. Packages are stored in a hierarchical manner and are explicitly imported into new class definitions. You can define classes inside a package that are not accessible by code outside that package. You can also define class members that are only exposed to other members of the same package.

To create a package, Java source file (.java) need to include a **package** statement. The **package** statement has the following syntax:

```
package <packagename>;
```

How to create packages?

Java uses file system directories to store packages. The following statement creates a package called MyPackage.

```
package MyPackage;
```

Access Protection

In the preceding chapters, you learned about various aspects of Java's access control mechanism and its access specifies. For example, you already know that access to a **private** member of a class is granted only to other members of that class. Packages add another dimension to access control. As you will see, Java provides many levels of protection to allow fine-grained control over the visibility of variables and methods within classes, subclasses, and packages. Classes and packages are both means of encapsulating and containing the name space and scope of variables and methods. Packages act as containers for classes and other subordinate packages. Classes act as containers for data and code. The class is Java's smallest unit of abstraction. Because of the interplay between classes and packages, Java addresses four categories of visibility for class members:

- Subclasses in the same package
- Non-subclasses in the same package
- Subclasses in different packages
- Classes that are neither in the same package nor subclasses

The three access specifies **private, public,** and **protected** provide a variety of ways to produce the many levels of access required by these categories. Following table sums up the interactions.

While Java's access control mechanism may seem complicated, we can simplify it as follows. Anything declared **public** can be accessed from anywhere. Anything declared **private** cannot be seem outside of its class. When a member does not have an explicit access specification, it is visible to subs classes as well as to other classes in the same package. This is the default access. If you want to allow an element to be seen outside your current package, but only to classes that subclass you directly, then declare that element **protected.**

	Private	No modifier	Protected	Public
Same class	☑	☑	☑	☑
Same package subclass	☒	☒	☒	☒
Same package non-subclass	☒	☒	☒	☒
Different package subclass	☒	☒	☒	☒
Different package non-subclass	☒	☒	☒	☒

Table : Class Member Access

Table applies only to members of classes. A has only two possible access levels: default and pubic. When a class is declared as **public**, it is accessible by any other code. If a class has default access, then it can only be accessed by other code within its same package.

(b) Write a program to find the number of and sum of all integers greater than 50 and less than 350 that are divisible by 3. **[7]**

```
class number{
public static void main(String args[])
{
int count=0,sum=0;
for(int i=51;i<=350;i+=3)

{
count++;
sum+=i;
}
System.out.println("No:s are "+count+" and sum="+sum);
}
}
```

(c) What is type casting ? Why is it required in programming ? Give three examples. **[5]**

It is fairly common to assign a value of one type to a variable of another type. If the two types are compatible then Java will perform the conversion automatically. For example, it is always possible to assign an int value to a long variable. However, not all types are compatible, and thus, not all type conversions are implicitly allowed. For instance, there is no conversion defined from double to byte. Fortunately, it is still possible to obtain a conversion between incompatible types. To do so, you must use a cast, which perform an explicit conversion between incompatible types. This phenomenon is called typecasting.

Need for type casting ⇒ Although the automatic type conversions are helpful, they will not fulfill all needs. For example, what if you want to assign an int value to a byte variable? This conversion will not be performed automatically, because a byte is smaller than an int. This kind of conversion is sometimes called a narrowing conversion, since you are explicitly making the value narrower so that it will fit into the target type.

To create a conversion between two incompatible types, you must use a cast. A cast is simply an explicit type conversion. It has this general form:

```
(target-type) value
```

Here, target-type specifies the desired type to convert the specified value to. For example, the following fragment casts an int to a byte. If the integer's value is larger than the range of a byte, it will be reduced modulo (the remainder of an integer division by) the byte's range.

```
int a;
byte b;
// ...
b = (byte)a;
```

(i) Admission to a professional course is subject to the following conditions:
(a) Marks in Maths >= 75
(b) Marks in Physics >= 60
(c) Marks in Chemistry >= 70
Write a program in Java to process the application and list the eligible candidates. Take appropriate examples. [9]

```
import java.io.*;
class eligible
{
public static void main(String args[])throws IOException
{
System.out.println("Please enter the marks in maths,physics & chemistry resp.");

BufferedReader br=new BufferedReader(new InputStreamReader(System.in));
```

```
String str;
int i,j,k;
System.out.println("Maths:");
str=br.readLine();
i=Integer.parseInt(str);

System.out.println("Physics:");
str=br.readLine();
j=Integer.parseInt(str);

System.out.println("Chemistry:");
str=br.readLine();
k=Integer.parseInt(str);

if(i>=75&&j>=60&&k>=70)
System.out.println("Candidate is eligible");
else
System.out.println("Candidate is not eligible");

}
}
```

(ii) Explain the following Java buzzwords : [6]
- **Java is multithreaded**
- **Java is secure**
- **Java is distributed**

Java is multithreaded ⇒ Java was designed to meet the real-world requirement of creating interactive, networked programs. To accomplish this, Java supports multithreaded programming, which allows you to write programs that do many things simultaneously. The Java run-time system comes with an elegant yet sophisticated solution for multiprocess synchronization that enables you to construct smoothly running interactive systems. Java's easy-to-use approach to multithreading allows you to think about the specific behavior of your program, not the multitasking subsystem

Java is secure ⇒ As you are likely aware, every time that you download a "normal" program, you are risking a viral infection. Prior to Java, most users did not download executable programs frequently, and those who did scanned them for viruses prior to execution. Even so, most users still worried about the possibility of infecting their systems with a virus. In addition to viruses, another type of malicious program exists that must be guarded against. This type of program can gather private information, such as credit card numbers, bank account balances, and passwords, by searching the contents of your computer's local file system.

When you use a Java-compatible Web browser, you can safety download Java applets without fear of viral infection or malicious intent. Java achieves this protection by confining a Java program to the Java execution environment and not allowing it access to other parts of the computer. The ability to download applets with confidence that no harm will be done and that no security will be breached is considered by many to be the single most important aspect of Java.

Java is distributed ⇒ Java is designed for the distributed environment of the Internet, because it handles TCP/IP protocols. In fact, accessing a resource using a URL is not much different from accessing a file. The original version of Java (Oak) included features for intra-address-spaces messaging. This allowed objects on two different computers to execute procedure remotely. Java has recently revived these interfaces in a package called *Remote Method Invocation* (*RMI*). This feature brings an unparalleled level of abstraction to client/server programming.

CS-74 : INTRODUCTION TO INTERNET PROGRAMMING
DEC-2005

Note: Question number 1 is compulsory. Answer any three questions from the rest.

1(a). Write a program in java to perform the addition of two complex numbers. **[10]**

Ans. Refer to Dec-2006, Q2 (a)

(b). Explain what happens if private is applied to a method in a class. Give an example. **[5]**

Ans. Private is the most restrictive access level. A private member is accessible only to the class in which it is defined. This includes variables that contain information which, accessed by an outsider could put the object in an inconsistent state or methods, if invoked by an outsider, could jeopardize the state of the object or the program in which it is running. Private members are like secrets you never tell anybody.

To declare a private member, use the private keyword in its declaration. The following class contains one private member variable and one private method:

```
Class First
{
private int  Myprivate; //private data member
private void  privateMethod() //private member function
{
System.out.println("Inside private method");
}
}
```

Objects of class First can access or modify the Myprivate variable and can invoke privateMethod. Objects other than class First cannot access or modify Myprivate variable, and cannot invoke privateMethod.

For example:

Second class defined here:

```
class Second{
void accessMethod(){
First a =new First();
a.Myprivate=51; //illegal
```

```
a.privateMethod(); //illegal
}
}
```

cannot access the Myprivate variable or invoke privateMethod of the object of class First

(c). Write the output of the following statements where
int a = - 8, b = 4 ;

(i) + + b < < 1
Ans. 10

(ii) a > > 2 **[4]**
Ans. -2

(d). What are final variable, final method and final class? **[3]**
Ans. Final variable: A variable can be declared as final. Doing so prevents its contents from being modified. A final variable has to be initialized when it is declared (in this usage , final is similar to const in C / C++ / C#).
final int size= 350 ;
Variables declared as final do not occupy memory on a per instance basis. Thus a final variable is essentially a constant.

Final method: While method overriding is one of the Java's most powerful features, there will be times when you will want to prevent it from occurring. To disallow a method from being overridden, specify final as a modifier at the start of declaration. Methods declared as final cannot be overridden.

```
 class  A {
  final void meth() {
    System.out.println("This is a final method.");
   }
}

class  B extends A {
void meth() { // ERROR! Can't override.
      System.out.println("ILLEGAL");
}
}
```

Final class: When you want to prevent a class from being inherited, then precede the class declaration with final. Declaring a class as final implicitly declares all of its method as final.

```
final class A {
        //...
}

// The following code is illegal.
 class B extends A {
 //ERROR!  Can't subclass A
   //....
}
```

The above code implies it is illegal for B to inherit A since A is declared as final.

(e). Write a program in java that asks the user to choose circle or rectangle on choosing circle she has to enter its radius if rectangle is chosen she is prompted to input the length of its sides.
Use an overloaded method to calculate the area and output the value on the screen,. [8]

Ans.
```
import java.io.*;
class figure
{
public static void main(String args[])
{
char c;
figure f=new figure();
int ch=0,ch1=0, ch2=0;
System.out.println("Main menu");
System.out.println("1. rectangle");
System.out.println("2.circle");
System.out.println("enter your choice 1 or 2");
try
{
ch=System.in.read();
}
catch(Exception e){}
if(ch==49)
{
System.out.println("Enter the lengths of its sides");
try
{
ch1=System.in.read();
```

```
ch2=System.in.read();
}
catch(Exception e){}
f.area(ch1,ch2);
}//if
else if(ch==50)
{

System.out.println("Enter the radius of the circle");
try
{
ch1=System.in.read();
}
catch(Exception e){}
f.area(ch1);
}// else if
}//psvm

void  area(int a)
{
System.out.println("The area of the circle is : "+ 3.14*a*a);
}

void area(int a, int b)
{
System.out.println("The area of the rectangle is : "+ a*b);
}
}//class  figure
```

2(a). Write a program that prompts the user to enter an integer divisor and an integer dividend. The program should output the quotient and the remainder. Catch any arithmetic exception and output the suitable message. **[9]**

Ans. class h

```
{
public static void main(String args[])
{
h o=new h();
int x=Integer.parseInt(args[0]);
int y=Integer.parseInt(args[1]);
```

```
o.solve(x,y);
}

void solve(int a, int b)
{
int quo=0;
int rem=0;
try
{
 quo=b/a;
 rem=b%a;
}

catch(ArithmeticException e)
{
System.out.println("Divide by zero");
}

System.out.println("The quotient is "+ quo);
System.out.println("The remainder is "+rem);
}
}//class
```

command prompt:
javac h.java
java h 3 79
The quotient is 26
The remainder is 1

(b). Define a constructor. Is it possible to overload a constructor? Justify your answer using an example. [6]

Ans. Refer to Chapter-5, Q-2, Page-56

3(a). What is finally blocks in Java? How many finally blocks can be associated with a try block? Give an appropriate example and explain. [8]

Ans. Refer to Chapter-7, Q-5, Page-81

(b). Describe the accessibility of unnamed, private, protected and public members with in a package, subclass and globally. [7]

Ans. Refer to Chapter-8, Q-1, Page-85

4(a). Consider the following class definition:
public lass excellent extends Good

```
{       public   Excellent (int I)

        {

        }
        public   Excellent ( int I, int j }

        {       super (I, k);

        }

}
```

In how many ways can the instances of Excellent class to be created? Write the corresponding statements. [8]

Ans. The program is as follows:

```
class Good
{
Good()
{
}
Good(int i,int j)
{
System.out.println("" +i +j);
}
}

public class  Excellent extends Good
{
public Excellent(int i)
{
System.out.println(""+i);
}

public Excellent(int i,int j)
{
super(i,j);
System.out.println("I am in subclass");
```

```
}

public static void main(String args[])
{
 Excellent e= new Excellent(45);
 Excellent e1= new Excellent(45,37);
}
}
```

In the above program there are two ways by which instances of Excellent class can be created.

1. Excellent e= new Excellent(45);

Now the constructor public Excellent(int i) {} will be called.

2. Excellent e1= new Excellent(45,37);

Now the constructor public Excellent(int i,int j) {} will be called. Inside the constructor when the super keyword is encountered, the constructor of the base class is called by the compiler.

(b). Write a program to find the Least Common Multiple (LCM) of two integers. **[7]**

Ans. class lcmclass

```
{
public static void main(String args[]){
lcmclass l=new lcmclass();
long x,y;
long g=l.lcm(30,27);
System.out.println("Least common multiple is"+g);
}

long gcd(long a,long b)
{
 if(a>b)
{
long t;
t=a;
a=b;
b=t;
}
while(b>0)
{
long rem=a%b;
```

```
a=b;
b=rem;
}
return a;
}

long lcm(long a,long b)
{
return((a*b)/gcd(a,b));
}
}//class
```

5(a). Write a program to input characters for the Keyword and output a table giving the different number of vowels. [10]

Ans.

```
import java.util.*;
import java.io.*;
class abc
{
public static void main(String args[])
{
String s =" ";
int a=0,e=0,i=0,o=0,u=0;
char ch;
try
{
BufferedReader br;
br=new BufferedReader(new InputStreamReader(System.in));
s=br.readLine();
}//try
catch(Exception exc){}
int num=0;
try
{
while(s!=null)
{
ch=s.charAt(num);
String ss= ch+ "";
num++;
if(ss.equals("a"))
a++;
```

```
else if(ss.equals("e"))
e++;
else if(ss.equals("i"))
i++;
else if(ss.equals("o"))
o++;
else if(ss.equals("u"))
u++;
}
}
catch(Exception exc){}
System.out.println(" a " +a);
System.out.println(" e " +e);
System.out.println(" i " +i);
System.out.println(" o " +o);
System.out.println(" u " +u);
}//psvm
}//class
```

(b). Is every Java program platform independent ? Justify your answer. [5]

Ans. Refer to Dec -2004, Q1(a), Page-205

CS-74 : INTRODUCTION TO INTERNET PROGRAMMING
JUNE-2006

Note: Question number 1 is compulsory. Answer any three questions from the rest.

1(a). Differentiate between nested and inner classes. Explain this through appropriate examples of each.
Ans. Refer to Chapter-6, Q-4, Page-74

(b). "We can have void as return type for the constructor of a class". Is this true or false? Give reasons for your answer.
Ans. We cannot have void as return type for the constructor of a class. Constructor
Are identified by the following rules:
1. The method name must exactly match the class name.
2. There must not be a return type declared for the method, not even void.
As constructor with return type will be treated as a different method, and will not be called implicitly. The compiler in some cases, for example ,where you have defined a constructor with a return type and call it to initialize an object will flag an error stating incorrect number of arguments.

(c). Answer the following questions in brief :

(i) finalize ( ) is always followed by which access specifier?
Ans. Specifier protected is used with finalize() that prevents access to finalize() by code defined outside its class.

(ii) Which special class is a super class of all other classes in Java?
Ans. Object is a superclass of all other classes in java.

(iii) join ( ) method belongs to which class ?
Ans. join () method belongs to Thread class.

(iv) Which operator is used for unsigned right shift ?
Ans. >>> is unsigned right shift operator.

(v) How many bits does short data type contain?
Ans. Short data type contain 16 bits .

(d). Super ( ) must be the first statement executed inside the subclass constructor. Why ? Explain uses of the keyword 'super', with an example.

Ans. Refer to Chapter-6, Q-2, Page-69

(e). What is the role of a default exception handler in Java? Differentiate between 'throw' and throws'.

Ans.
```
class exc {
public static void main(String args[]){
int d=0;
int a=42/d;
}
}
```
When we have not supplied any exception handler of our own, the exception is caught by the default exception handler provided by the java runtime system. Any exception that is not caught by our program will ultimately be processed by the default handler. The default handler displays a string describing the exception, prints a stack trace from the point at which the exception occurred, and terminates the program.

The output of the above program :

Java.lang.AirthmeticException: / by zero
At exc.main(exc.java:4)

Refer to Chapter-7, Q-4, Page-79

(f). Write an applet that reads two floating point numbers, and displays their sum.

Ans.
```
import java.awt.*;
import java.applet.*;
import java.awt.event.*;

public class Userin extends Applet implements ActionListener
{
TextField text1,text2;
public void init()
{
text1=new TextField(8);
text2=new TextField(8);
add(text1);
add(text2);
text1.setText("");
text2.setText("");
```

```
text1.addActionListener(this);
text2.addActionListener(this);
}

public void paint(Graphics g)
{
float x=0,y=0,z=0;
String s1,s2,s;
g.drawString("Input a number in each box",10,50);
try
{
s1=text1.getText();
x=Float.parseFloat(s1);
s2=text2.getText();
y=Float.parseFloat(s2);
}
catch(Exception e){}
z=x+y;
s=String.valueOf(z);
g.drawString("The sum is ",10,75);
g.drawString(s,100,75);
}

public void actionPerformed(ActionEvent ae)
{
repaint();
}
}//class
```

2(a). Differentiate between the following, using examples:

(i) Transient and Volatile keywords.

Ans. When an instance variable is declared as Transient, and then its value need not persist when an object is stored.

For e.g.:

```
Class T{
transient int a; //will not persist
int b; //will persist
```

Here, if an object of type T is written to a persistent storage area, the contents of "a" would not be saved, but the contents of "b" would.

The volatile modifier tells the compiler that the variable modified by the volatile modifier can be changed unexpectedly by other parts of the program. One of these situations involves multithreaded programs. In a multithreaded program, sometimes two or more threads share the same instance variable. For efficiency considerations, each thread can keep its own, private copy of such a shared variable. The real copy of the variable is updated at various times. While this approach works fine, it may be inefficient at times. In some cases all that really matters is that the master copy of a always reflects its current state. To ensure this, simply specify the variable as volatile, which tells the compiler that it must always use the master copy of the volatile variable .

(ii) = = and equals( )

Ans. equals() method compares the characters inside a String object. The = = operator compares two object references to see whether they refer to the same instance.

```
// equals() vs = =
class EqualsnotEqualto{
public static void main(String args[])
{
String s1="Hello";
String s2=new String (s1);
System.out.println( s1 + "equals " +s2  + " —" + s1.equals(s2));
System.out.println(s1  +  " = = "    +s2  +"—"   + (s1 == s2));
}
}
```

output:
Hello equals Hello — true
Hello == Hello —false

(iii) abstract class and interface

Ans. Refer to June-2005, Q2(a), Page-192

(b). What is a package in Java ? Also write steps to create a package in Java.

Ans. Refer to Chapter-8, Q-1, Page-85

(c). Assume that a class A extends a class B, which further extends class C. Also all the three classes implement the method test( ). How can a method in class A invoke the test ( ) method defined in class C (without creating a new instance of class C)? Explain.

Ans.
```
interface abc
{
public void test();
}
class C implements abc
{
public void test()
{
System.out.println("I am in class C");
}
}

class B extends C implements abc
{
}

class A extends B implements abc
{
void meth()
{
super.test();
}
}

class ab
{
public static void main(String args[])
{
A a =new A();
a.meth();
}
}
```
Here super keyword is used to access a member(test() method of class C) of the superclass(class C) that has been hidden (overloaded) by a member of a subclass.(class A). We have not created a new instance of class C.

3(a). What are threads ? What are the two ways in which threads can be created in Java? Explain each one through an appropriate program.

Ans. Threads are light weight. They share the same address space and cooperatively share the same heavyweight process.

Multithreading enables you to write very efficient programs that make maximum use of the CPU, because idle time can be kept to a minimum. This is especially important for the interactive, networked environment in which java operates, because idle time is common. .

A thread is similar to the sequential programs. A single thread also has a beginning, a sequence, and an end. At any given time during the runtime of the thread, there is a single point of execution. However, a thread itself is not a program; a thread cannot run on its own. Rather, it runs within a program. The following figure shows this relationship.

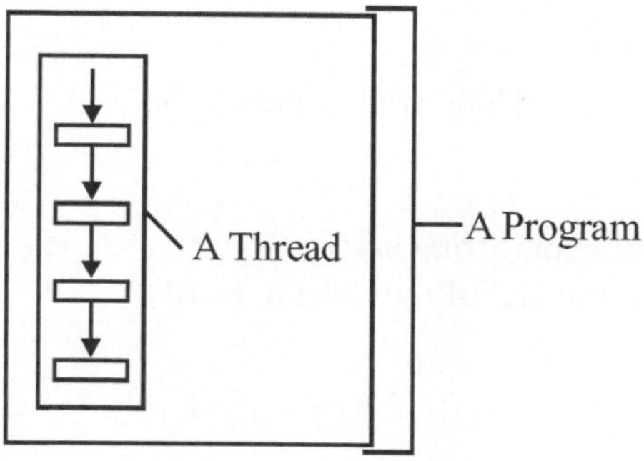

Definition: A *thread* is a single sequential flow of control within a program The real excitement surrounding threads is not about a single sequential thread. Rather, it's about the use of multiple threads running at the same time and performing different tasks in a single program. This use is illustrated in the next figure.

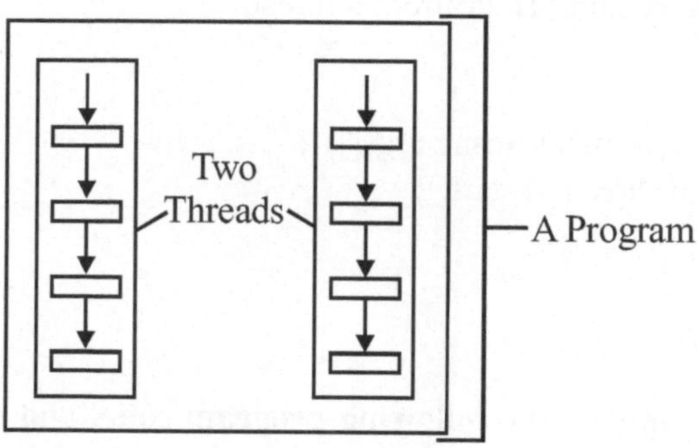

A Web browser is an example of a multithreaded application. Within a typical browser, you can scroll a page while it's downloading an applet or an image, play animation and sound concurrently, print a page in the background while you download a new page, or watch three sorting algorithms race to the finish.

An application that creates an instance of Thread must provide the code that will run in that thread. There are two ways to do this:

1. Provide a Runnable object. The Runnable interface defines a single method, run, meant to contain the code executed in the thread. The Runnable object is passed to the Thread constructor, as in the HelloRunnable example:

```
·public class HelloRunnable implements Runnable {

    public void run() {
        System.out.println("Hello from a thread!");
    }

    public static void main(String args[]) {
        (new Thread(new HelloRunnable())).start();
    }

}
```

2. Subclass Thread. The Thread class itself implements Runnable, though its run method does nothing. An application can subclass Thread, providing its own implementation of run, as in the HelloThread example:

```
public class HelloThread extends Thread {

    public void run() {
        System.out.println("Hello from a thread!");
    }

    public static void main(String args[]) {
        (new HelloThread()).start();
    }

}
```

(b). Give the output of the following program code, and an explanation of its functioning

```
public static void main (string args[ ]) {
int i,j=1;
i=(j>1)?2:1;
```

```
switch(i) {

case 0 :  System.out.println("0"); break;

case 1 :  System.out.println ("1");

 case 2  :   System.out.println("2");

  case 3 :    System.out.println("3");break;
```

Ans. Output:
1
2
3
Java includes a special ternary operator.
It has general form:
Expression1 ? expression2: expression3
Here, expression1 can be any expression that evaluates to a Boolean value. If expression 1 is true, then expression2 is evaluated; otherwise, expression3 is evaluated. In the above example j>1 statement is false so value of is 1. The control then goes to case1 and then case2 , and case3 in a sequence as there is no break.

(c). Write a program that reads the data from one file and writes into another file.

Ans.
```
import java.io.*;
class Display
{
FileInputStream fi;
FileOutputStream fo;
int t;
char ch;
public static void main(String args[])
{
Display d=new Display();
d.copy();
}

void copy()
{
try{
```

```
 fi=new FileInputStream("a1.txt");
 fo=new FileOutputStream("a2.txt");
while((t=fi.read())!=-1)
{
ch=(char)t;
fo.write(ch);
}
}
catch(Exception e){}
}
}//class
```

4(a). Explain the following terms in AWT package :

(i) Frame

Refer to June -2001, Q3(ii), Page 179

(ii) Panel

Refer to June -2001 ,Q3(ii), Page 179

(iii) Component

Ans. Refer to Chapter-9, Page 91

(iv) Container

Refer to June -2001, Q3(ii), Page 179

(b). Explain the String Buffer length and capacity methods, using an example.

Ans. StringBuffer is a peer class of String that provides much of the functionality of strings. StringBuffer defines these three constructors.

StringBuffer()
StringBuffer(int size)
StringBuffer(String str)

The default constructor reserves room for 16 characters without reallocation. The second version accepts an integer argument that explicitly sets the size of the buffer. The third version accepts a String argument that sets the initial contents of the StringBuffer object and reserves room for 16 more characters without reallocation. StringBuffer allocates room for 16 additional characters when no specific buffer length is requested, because reallocation is a costly process in terms of time. Also, frequent allocation can fragment memory .By allocating room for a few characters; StringBuffer reduces the number of reallocations that take place

The current length of a StringBuffer can be found via the length() method , while the total allocated capacity can be found through the capacity() method. They have following forms:

```
int length()
int capacity()
```

Here is an example:

```
class StringBufferDemo{
public static void main(String args[])
{
StringBuffer sb=new   StringBuffer("hello");
System.out.println("buffer ="+ sb);
System.out.println("length =" +sb.length());
System.out.println("capacity= "+ sb.capacity());
}
}
```

output:

```
buffer = hello
length = 5
capacity =21
```

(c). Differentiate between method overloading and method overriding. Explain dynamic method dispatch in this context.

Ans. Refer to Chapter-5, Q-3, Page-59

(d). Explain the Event Delegation Model.

Ans. The Event Delegation Model came into existence with JDK1.1. In this model, events are sent to the component from where the events originated. The component registers a listener object with the program. The listener object contains appropriate event-handlers that receive and process the events. By registering a listener object with the program, the component enables the delegation of events to the listener object for processing.

The following diagram illustrates the JDK1.2 event model:

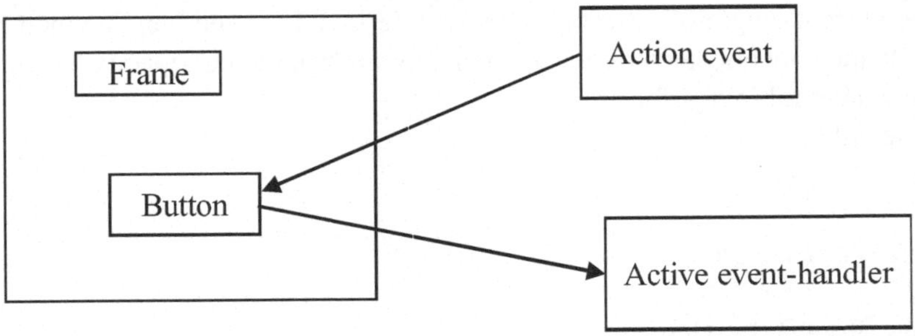

Every event has a corresponding listener interface that specifies the methods that are required to handle the event. Event object are reported to registered listeners. To enable a component to handle events, you must register an appropriate listener for that component. The java.awt.event package contains definitions of all the event classes and listener interfaces.

5(a). Explain static methods and static variables. What are the restrictions on static methods?

Ans. Refer to Chapter-5, Page-63

(b). Write a program in Java to print the following pattern for a given integer n.

```
      1
    1 2 1
  1 2 3 2 1
1 2 3 4 3 2 1
..........................
```

n = number of lines.

Ans

```
class pat
{
public static void main(String args[])
{
pat p =new pat();
p.pattern(4);
}//psvm

void pattern(int n)
{
int i,j,ncount,k;
for(i=1;i<=n;i++)
```

```
{
ncount=((n*2)-(i*2));
do
{
System.out.print(" ");
ncount—;
}while(ncount>=0);
     for(j=1;j<=i;j++)
     {
            System.out.print(" "+j);
     }
      for(k=j-2;k>0;k—)
      {
       System.out.print(" "+k);
      }
     System.out.print("\n");
}//for
}//pattern
}//class
```

(c). What are applets in Java ? Explain the 'applet skeleton', using an example.

Ans. An applet is an application designed to be transmitted over the Internet and executed by a java compatible web browser. An applet is actually a tiny java program , dynamically downloaded across the network, just like an image ,sound file, or video clip.

When an applet begins, the AWT calls the following methods in this sequence:

1 init()
2 start()
3 paint()

When an applet is terminated, the following methods in this sequence are called:

1 stop()
2 destroy()

init()

The init() method is first to be called. This is where you should initialize variables. This method is called only once during the run time of your applet.

start()
The start() method is called after init(). It is also called to restart an applet after it has been stopped.

paint()
The paint() method is called each time your applet's output must be redrawn.

stop()
The stop() method is called when a web browser leaves the HTML document containing the applet.

destroy()
The destroy() method is called when the environment determines that your applet needs to be removed completely from memory.

```
//an applet skeleton
import java.awt.*;
import java.applet.*;
/*
<applet code="appletskel" width=300 height=100>
</applet>
*/

public class appletskel extends Applet{
//called first
public void init(){
//initialization
}

//called second after init(). Also called whenever the applet is restarted
public void start(){
//start or resume execution
}

//called when the applet is stopped
public void stop(){
//suspends execution
}

/*called when applet is terminated. This is the last method executed.*/
public void destroy(){
```

```
//performs shutdown activities
}

//called when an applet's window must be restored.
public void paint(Graphics g){
//redisplay contents of window
}
}
```

CS-74 : INTRODUCTION TO INTERNET PROGRAMMING
DEC-2006

Note: Question number 1 is compulsory. Answer any three questions from the rest.

1(a). What is the difference in run-time polymorphism and compile-time polymorphism? Explain with the help of suitable example. [10]

Ans. Refer to June-2004, Q6 (b), Page-116

(b). What is the difference between Applets and an Application program in Java? Explain. [5]

Ans. Refer to June -2003, Q1 (iv), Page-130

(c). What is the advantage of finally block in Java? Explain with suitable example. [6]

Ans. Refer to Chapter-7, Q-5, Page-81

(d). Write a Program for I/O operation using Buffered Input Stream and Buffered Output Stream. [5]

Ans.
```
import java.io.*;
Public class StreamsIODemo
{
public static void main(String args[ ])
{
try
{
 int a=1;
FileOutputstream  fileout = new File Output stream("out.txt");
BufferedOutputstream  buffout =new Buffered Output stream(fileout);
While(a<=25)
{ buffout.write(a);
a=a+3;
}
buffout.close;
FileInputstream  filein = new FileInputstream("out.txt");
BufferedInputstream  buffin =new BufferedInputstream(filein);
int i=0;
```

```
Do
{
i=buffin.read();
if(i!=-1)
System.out.println(""+ i);
}while( i!= -1);
buffin.close();
}
catch(IOException e)
{
System.out.println("Error opening the file" +e);
}
}
}
```

Output:
1
4
7
10
13
16
19
22
25

(e). Will an error occur if a class with the same name exists in two different packages that you import using * from? How can the error be avoided? [4]

Ans. Yes, an error will occur if a class with the same name exists in two different packages that you import using * form. The error can be avoided by referring to the member(class) by its fully qualified name which includes the package name. Here is the fully qualified name for the Rectangle class declared in the graphics package .

graphics.Rectangle

You could use this qualified name to create an instance of graphics.Rectangle:

graphics.Rectangle myRect = new graphics.Rectangle();

Qualified names are all right for infrequent use. When a name is used repetitively, however, typing the name repeatedly becomes tedious and the code becomes difficult to read.

2(a). Write a program in java to design a class complex for complex number of the form a+ib. write an overload operator + to add two complex numbers. [8]

Ans.
```
import java.io.*;
public class Complex implements Comparable
{
        private double im;
        private double re;

        public Complex() {
        im = 0;
        re = 0;
        }

        public Complex (double a, double b ){
         im = b;
         re = a;
        }

 public Complex add(Complex a){
   return (new Complex(re+a.re,im+a.im));
        }

 public Complex sub(Complex a){
   return (new Complex(re-a.re,im-a.im));
        }

        public Complex mul(Complex a){
     return (new Complex(re * a.re - im * a.im, re * a.im + im *
a.re));
        }
        public Complex div(Complex a) throws EmptyException{
        if ((a.re == 0)||(a.im*a.im == 0)) throw new
EmptyException("Impossibile Eseguire la Divisione: Divisione per
Zero");
                        return (new Complex((re * a.re + im *
a.im)/(a.re*a.re+a.im*a.im),(im * a.re -
re*a.im)/(a.re*a.re+a.im*a.im)));
```

```
}

public double getRe(){
return re;
}
public double getIm(){
return im;
}
public Complex getOpposite() {
return (new Complex(-1*re,-1*im));
}

public String toString() {
        String s = "Real: " + re + " Imm: i * " + im;
        return s;
        }

public boolean equals(Object o) {
 if (o instanceof Complex) {
        Complex c = (Complex)o;
        return ((c.re == this.re)&&(c.im == this.im));
        }
        else { return false; }
}

public int compareTo(Object o) {
        if (o instanceof Complex) {
  Complex c = (Complex)o;
        if (this.re > c.re) return 1;
  else if (equals(c)) return 0;
  else return -1;
 } return 0;
 }
}
```

(b). What is finalize () method in java? Explain. **[3]**

Ans. Refer to Chapter-5, Page-65

(c). Explain the use of "This" keyword in java with the help of suitable example. **[4]**

Ans. Refer to Chapter-6, Q-2, Page-68

3(a). Write a program in java to generate the following output. Using two-dimensional array. [6]

0

1 2

3 4 5

6 7 8 9

Ans.
```
class Design
{
public static void main(String args[])
{
int i,j,k=0;
int twod[][]=new int[4][];
 twod[0]=new int[1];
 twod[1]=new int[2];
 twod[2]=new int[3];
 twod[3]=new int[4];
for(i=0;i<4;i++)
 {
        for(j=0;j<i+1;j++)
        {
                twod[i][j]=k;
                System.out.print(twod[i][j] + "   ");
                k++;

        }
System.out.println();
}
}//main
}//class
```

(b). What is the use of "Super" keyword in java? Explain with suitable example. [5]

Ans. Refer to Chapter-6, Q-2, Page-68

(c). What is package in java? If a class with default access is defined in a package p1, discuss the access rights of this class in another package p2. [4]

Ans. Refer to Chapter-8, Q-1, Page-85

4(a). Differentiate between interfaces and abstract classes in java with the help of suitable example. [8]

Ans. Refer to June-2005, Q2(a), Page-192

(b). Write a program in java to display a text file where name of the file is given at command line. [7]

Ans.
```
import java.io.*;
class Display
{
FileInputStream fi;
int t;
char ch;
public static void main(String args[])
{
Display d=new Display();
d.readfile(args[0]);
}
void readfile(String a)
{
try
{
 fi=new FileInputStream(a);
while((t=fi.read())!=-1)
{
ch=(char)t;
System.out.print(""+ch);
}
}//try
catch(Exception e){}
}
}//class
```

5(a). Write a program in java to sort a list of numbers using any sorting method for a given input n. [6]

Ans.
```
class sorting
{
public static void main(String args[])
{

int a[]={17,99,67,45,0};
int i,j,temp;
```

```
for(i=0;i<a.length;i++)
{
for(j=i;j<a.length;j++)
{
if(a[i]>a[j])
{
temp=a[i];
a[i]=a[j];
a[j]=temp;
}
}
}
System.out.println("Array sorted in Ascending order");
for(i=0;i<a.length;i++)
{
System.out.println(a[i]);
}
}
}
```

(b). Find the output of the following :

(i)

```
Class X {
        static int a = 4;
    static int b;
    static void f (int x)
    {system.out.println ("x ="+x);
    system.out.println ("a ="+a);
    system.out.println ("b ="+b);
    }
    static{
    b =a*2;
    }
public static void main (string args [ ])
    {
        f(20);
    }
}
```

[5]

Ans. x=20

a=4

b=8

(ii) Class Break Demo {
public static void main (string args [ ])
{
outer : for (int i = 0;i< 3; i++)
{
system.out.print ("Pass" + i+ " : ");
for (int j = 0; j< 100; j++)
{ if (j ==10) break outer;
system.out.println (j + " ");
}
system.out.println ("Break Demo");
}
system.out.printIn ("Loops Complete");
}
} **[4]**

Ans. output:

Pass 0:
0
1
2
3
4
5
6
7
8
9
Loops complete

CS-74 : INTRODUCTION TO INTERNET PROGRAMMING
June, 2007

Note : (i) Question number 1 is **compulsory.**
(ii) Attempt any **three** questions from the rest.
(iii) Use Java, wherever necessary.

1. (a) Write any four differences between a Java Applet and a Java Application. Also, write any two common properties of them. Explain through an example for each.

Ans. First Refer : Chapter-2, Q.No.-1, Page No.-12

Two common properties : The main similarities between an applet, and an application is that they both contain their corresponding Java source code and are compiled using e.g. 'javac.exe' (which is installed when you install the 'JDK'), which gives as an output a .class file. And a Java Virtual Machine needs to be installed (this follows also with the installation of the JDK on that computer) on each computer (be it client or server computer) they are running, in order to interpret this .class file to processor dependent machine code.

(b) Indicate the name, type, size and range of values of any four primitive data type in Java.

Ans. Refer to Chapter-3, Q.No.-1, Page No.-22

(c) Write any three advantages of multi–threaded programming.

Ans. The main advantage of multithreaded programming is the ability to spawn off some code to run in the "background" while the rest of the program does something else. For example, consider the typical order-entry program described in the following flowchart. It shows a single path of execution

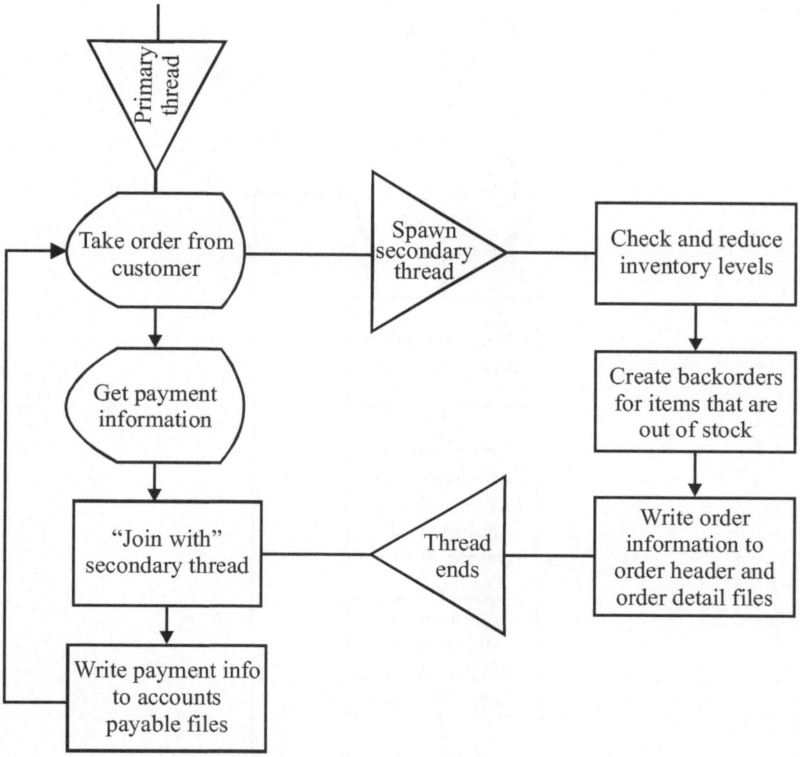

Now consider the next flowchart. It is the same application, but this time it is split into two paths of execution that will execute simultaneously. The first path is called the primary thread. It allows the user to enter the customer's order. When the order is complete, it spawns off a secondary thread that will run in the "background" to update the inventory files, process backorders for any items that are out of stock, and write the order to the order-entry files.

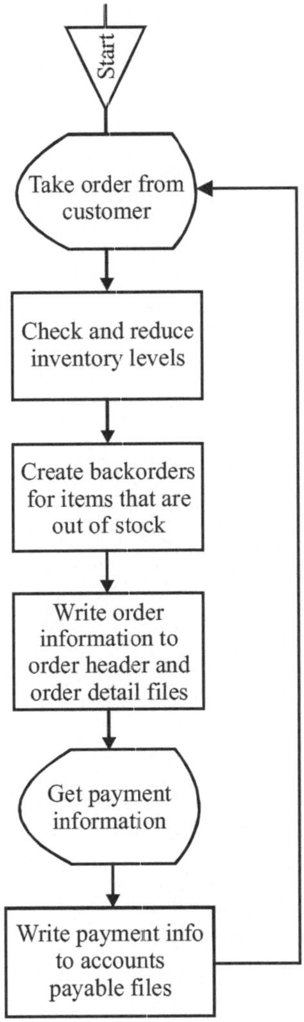

Meanwhile, the primary thread allows the user to immediately enter the customer's payment information (e.g., credit card number, COD, terms, etc.). When that is complete, the primary thread joins with the secondary thread; that is, it waits for the secondary thread to end, which will probably already be finished in this case.

This is advantageous because it allows the user to work uninterruptedly, instead of waiting while the program is processing something else. We'll take a look at the mechanics of multithreaded programming next time.

(d) Write a program in Java for I/O operations using

BufferedInputStream and BufferedOutputStream. Define the problem on your own.

Ans. Refer to Dec-2006, Q.No.-1(d), Page No.-242

2 (a) What is meant by Java Virtual Machine ? Explain.

Ans. Refer to Chapter-2, Q.No.-3, Page No.-13

(b) Explain any six bitwise operators of Java. Also, demonstrate each operator with an example.

Ans. Refer to Chapter-3, Q.No.-5 Page No.-26

3 (a) Write a program in Java that accepts the name of a text file as input and prints the content of that file to standard output.

Ans. Refer to Dec-2006, Q.No.-4(b), Page No.-247

(b) Explain the architecture of a Java Applet with the help of a figure.

Ans. An applet is a program written in the Java programming language that can be included in an HTML page, much in the same way an image is included in a page. When you use a Java technology-enabled browser to view a page that contains an applet, the applet's code is transferred to your system and executed by the browser's Java Virtual Machine (JVM).

Event driven

· An applet waits until an event occurs.

· The AWT notifies the applet about an event by calling event handler that has been provided by the applet. The applet takes appropriate action and then quickly return control to AWT.

· All Swing components descend from the AWT Container class.

User initiates interaction with an Applet

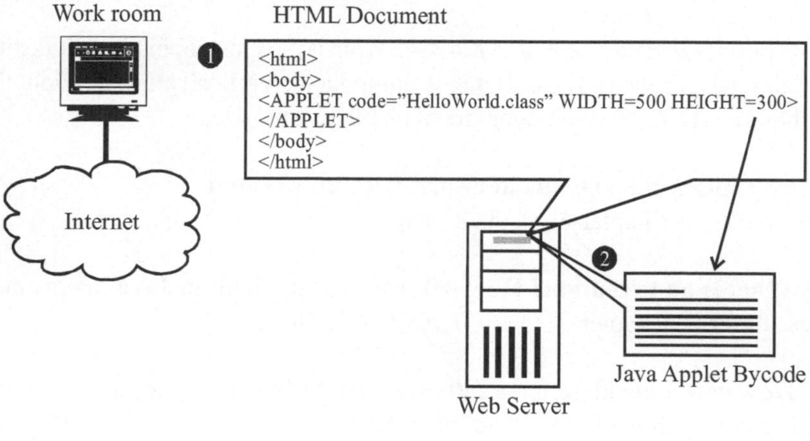

(c) What is the default layout manager in Java? Explain it.

Ans. Every Container, by default, has a layout manager (an object conforming to the LayoutManager protocol). If a Container's default layout manager doesn't suit your needs, you can easily replace it with another one. A layout managers range from the very simple (Container's default layout manager doesn't suit your needs, you can easily replace it with another one. A layout managers range from the very simple (FlowLayout and GridLayout) to the special purpose (BorderLayout and CardLayout) to the ultra-flexible (GridBagLayout).

Each applet brings up a window that you can resize to see how resizing affects the layout.

For a java.applet.Applet, the default layout manager is FlowLayout.

For the content pane of a javax.swing.JApplet, the default layout manager is a BorderLayout.

Various types of layout manager in Java and how to use them :

How to Use BorderLayout : BorderLayout is the default layout manager for all Windows, such as Frames and Dialogs. It uses five areas to hold components: north, south, east, west, and center. All extra space is placed in the center area. Here's an applet that puts one button in each area.

How to Use CardLayout : Use the CardLayout class when you have an area that can contain different Components at different times. CardLayouts are commonly tied to Choices, with the state of the Choice determining which Panel (group of Components) the CardLayout displays.

How to Use FlowLayout : FlowLayout is the default layout manager for all Panels. It simply lays out components from left to right, centering them within their row and, if necessary, starting new rows.

How to Use GridLayout : GridLayouts simply make a bunch of Components have equal size, displaying them in the requested number of rows and columns. Here's a picture of a program with a Panel that uses a GridLayout to control the display of 5 buttons.

How to Use GridBagLayout : GridBagLayout is the most sophisticated, flexible layout manager we provide. It aligns components vertically and horizontally, without requiring that the components be the same size.

4. (a) Explain the extends keyword with an example.

Ans. Refer to Chapter-6, Q.No.-1, Page No.-66

(b) What is an exception? How will you handle them in Java programs ?

Ans. Refer to Chapter-7, Q.No.-1, Page No.-76

(c) How can a package be created in Java? Give an example.

Ans. Refer to June-2004, Q.No.-4(a), Page No.-112

5. (a) Do you agree with the statement that any *Java program is 100% platform independent* ? Justify your answer.

Ans. Yes, I agree with the given statement. Java's architecture facilitates the creation of platform-independent software, but also allows you to create software that is platform-specific. When you write a Java program, platform independence is an option.

The degree of platform independence of any Java program depends on several factors. As a developer, some of these factors are beyond your control, but most are within your control. Primarily, the degree of platform independence of any Java program you write depends on how you write it.

Now Refer : Dec-2004, Q.No.-1(a), Page No.-205

(b) Explain the three categories of an Event.

Ans. Event Categories: For the AWT package, there are a number of events supported. These events are broken down into categories that loosely represent the types of actions that a GUI application needs to process. The events and their listener interfaces are actually defined in another package, awt.event.

Three categories are :

(i) Events : The classes with names ending in "Event" represent specific types of events, generated by the AWT or by one of the AWT components.

(ii) Listeners : The interfaces in this package are all "event listeners"; their names end with "Listener." These interfaces define the methods that must be implemented by any object that wants to be notified when a particular event occurs. Note that there is a Listener interface for each Event class.

(iii) Adapters : Each of the classes with a name ending in "Adapter" provides a no-op implementation for an event listener interface that defines more than one method. When you are only interested in a single method of an event listener interface, it is easier to subclass an Adapter class than to implement all of the methods of the corresponding Listener interface.

(c) Write a program in Java that accepts a list of strings as input and prints all those strings to standard output which consist of all vowels in them.

Ans.
```
class vowelstring
{
public static void main(String args[ ]) throws, IOException
{
BufferedReader br = new BufferedReader(new InputstreamReader(system.in));
string str[10];
System.out.println("Enter 10 strings");
for(int i = 0; i < 10; i++)
```

```
{
str[i] = br.readLine( );
}
System.out.println("Strings contains all vowels");
for(i = 0; i < 10; i++)
{
if(str[i].indexOf('a') >= 0 & str[i].indexOf('e') >= 0 &
str[i].indexOf('i') >= 0 & str[i].indexOf('o') >= 0 &
str[i].indexOf('u') >=0)
{
System.out.println(str[i]);
}
}
}
}
```

CS-74 : INTRODUCTION TO INTERNET PROGRAMMING
December, 2007

Note : (i) Question number 1 is **compulsory.**
(ii) Attempt any **three** questions from the rest.

1. (a) What is bytecode in Java? Explain.
Ans. Refer to Chapter-2, Q.No.-4, Page No.-14

(b) What are the differences between abstract classes and interfaces in Java? Explain.
Ans. Refer to June-2005, Q.No.-2(a), Page No.-192

(c) What are the native methods in Java? Explain.
Ans. A native method is a Java method (either an instance method or a class method) whose implementation is written in another programming language such as C. There are two components to a native method: the declaration, and the implementation. A native method can be declared like other methods, in a Java class. A native method can be implemented in another programming language in a different source file. Typically, the implementation of a native method is a function.
Java Native Interface (JNI) is a standard programming interface for writing Java native methods and embedding the Java virtual machine into native applications. The primary goal is binary compatibility of native method libraries across all Java virtual machine implementations on a given platform.

(d) How does repaint ( ) method work for the applet?
Ans. The repaint() method is the one invoked by a program to do drawing. Their are 4 versions of this method but the one with no arguments is usually used. Drawing via repaint() most often takes place in response to user input.
repaint() ==> update() ==> paint()
repaint() does not invoke paint() directly. It schedules a call to an intermediate method, update(). Finally, update() calls paint().
Using repaint() can be tricky for at least three reasons.
1. the interaction between repaint() and the spontaneous painting done by the GUI thread
2. the fact that repaint() just asks the thread system to schedule a call to update()/paint() and then exits. The repaint() method is asynchronous.
3. the problem of preventing your drawing from being erased when being updated.

repaint() merely requests the AWT thread to call update(). It then returns immediately. This type of behaviour is called asynchronous. How the AWT thread reacts to the request is up to it. This behavour can lead to problems if you are not careful.

(e) Find the error(s) if. Also correct the error(s) and give the output.

```
Class Scope {    int y = 10;
                 { int x = 5;
system.out.println("x=" +x);
system.out.println("y=" +y);
{int x = 10;
system.out.println ("x=" +x);
system.out.println("y=" +y);
}
}
}
```

Ans. Errors:

1. First letter of 'class', i.e. 'c' must be lower 'c'.

2. First letter of 'system', i.e. 's' must be upper 's'.

3. There should be main function.

Corrected code:

```
class scope
{
public static void main(String args[])
{
int y = 10;
{
int x = 5;
System.println("x =" + x);
System.out.println("y =" + y);
{
int x = 10;
System.out.println("x =" + x);
System.out.println("y =" + y);
}
}
}
}
```

(f) What are the command line arguments in Java? Explain with example.

Ans. Any number of arguments can be passed to the java program through command line. While running the program anything written after the name of the class are the command line arguments. Arguments are delimited by the space.

This sample code prints all the command line arguments to the console.

```
public class CmdLnArgmntExp {

public static void main(String[] args) {
System.out.println("d");
for (int i = 0; i < args.length; i++)
System.out.println(args[i]);
}
}
```

Run the program as the follows.

Java CmdLnArgmntExp arg1 arg2 arg3 arg4

Output:

arg1
arg2
arg3
arg4

(g) What is this pointer? Explain.

Ans. First Refer : Chapter-6, Q.No.-2, Page No.-68

"this" is a keyword in java which represents the current object. "this" is a reference to the object in which for example this piece of code

2. (a) Write a program to print all the contents of a text file on screen. Name of the file is entered by the user.

Ans. Refer Dec-2006, Q.No.-4(b), Page No.-247

(b) What is the difference between run-time and compile-time polymorphism? Explain with examples.

Ans. Overloading is **compile time polymorphism**, because compiler checks the method signatures while compiling itself.(i.e. Method names, Argument types, argument creation order, etc...)

In **run time polymorphism** compiler does't know about way of execution of program that mean decide way of execution at run time, while in compile time polymorphism compiler know about the way of execution of program.

e.g. compile time polymorphism -- method overloading
run time polymorphism -- method overriding

Now Refer : June-2004, Q.No.-6(b), Page No.-116

3. (a) Write a Java program to display a button labelled "IGNOU".

Ans.
```
import java.awt.*;
import java.awt.event.*;
import java.applet.*;
/*
<applet code = ButtonDemo" width = 250 height = 150>
</applet>
*/
public class ButtonDemo extends Applet implements Action Listener
{
Button b1;
public void init ( )
{
b1 = new Button("IGNOU");
add(b1);
b1.addActionListener(this);
}
public void actionPerformed(ActionEvent ae)
{
repaint( );
}
}
```

(b) What is exception handling in java? What is the advantage of finally block? Explain.

Ans. Refer to Chapter-7, Q.No.-1, Page No.-76
& Refer to Chapter-7, Q.No.-5, Page No.-81

(c) package p1;
public class X{
int I = 10;
public int j =5;
protected int k = 7;
private int w x2;
}
if there is another package called p2, what are the variables of class X that can be accessed in a class in p2?

Ans. The variable 'j' can be accessed in a class in P2. The variable 'k' can also be accessed in a class in P2 if it is a subclass of class X.

4. (a) What are the thread priorities in java? Explain with the help of a

suitable example.

Ans. Execution of multiple threads on a single CPU, in some order, is called scheduling. The Java runtime supports a very simple, deterministic scheduling algorithm known as fixed priority scheduling. This algorithm schedules threads based on their priority relative to other runnable threads.

When a Java thread is created, it inherits its priority from the thread that created it. You can also modify a thread's priority at any time after its creation using the setPriority method. Thread priorities are integers ranging between MIN_PRIORITY and MAX_PRIORITY (constants defined in the Thread class). The higher the integer, the higher the priority. At any given time, when multiple threads are ready to be executed, the runtime system chooses the runnable thread with the highest priority for execution. Only when that thread stops, yields, or becomes not runnable for some reason will a lower priority thread start executing. If two threads of the same priority are waiting for the CPU, the scheduler chooses one of them to run in a round-robin fashion. The chosen thread will run until one of the following conditions is true:

- A higher priority thread becomes runnable.
- It yields, or its run method exits.
- On systems that support time-slicing, its time allotment has expired.

Then the second thread is given a chance to run, and so on, until the interpreter exits.

At any given time, the highest priority thread is running. However, this is not guaranteed. The thread scheduler may choose to run a lower priority thread to avoid starvation. For this reason, use priority only to affect scheduling policy for efficiency purposes. Do not rely on thread priority for algorithm correctness.

Example :

```
class MyThread implements Runnable {
Thread t;
private volatile boolean running = true;
public MyThread (int p, String tName) {
t = new Thread(this,tName);
t.setPriority (p);
}
public void run() {
System.out.println(t.getName() + " running.");
}
public void stop() {
running = false;
System.out.println(t.getName() + " stopped.");
}
public void start() {
```

```
System.out.println(t.getName() + " started");
t.start();
}
}
class Demo {
public static void main(String args[] ) {
Thread.currentThread().setPriority(10);
MyThread lowPriority =
new MyThread (3, "low priority");
MyThread highPriority =
new MyThread (7, "high priority");
lowPriority.start();
highPriority.start();
try {
Thread.sleep(1000);
} catch ( InterruptedException e) {
System.out.println("Main thread interrupted.");
}
lowPriority.stop();
highPriority.stop();
try {
highPriority.t.join();
lowPriority.t.join();
} catch (InterruptedException e) {
System.out.println(
"InterruptedException caught");
}
}
}
```

Output of the program will be :

```
low priority started
high priority started
high priority running.
low priority running.
low priority stopped.
high priority stopped.
```

(b) What is NumberFormatException( ) in java? When is it used? Explain with example.

Ans. It is a type of exception in Java. To catch a NumberFormatException, put a try statement block around the code that may cause the exception and a catch clause after the try block that describes what to do if the exception occurs. Here's a code fragment that shows how to catch a NumberFormatException that may occur when the parseInt method is called on a String:

```
System.out.print( "Enter an integer: " );
String input = stdin.readLine();

try
{
int x = Integer.parseInt( input );
}
catch ( NumberFormatException e )
{
System.out.println( e.getMessage()
+ " is not a valid format for an integer." );
}
```

In this example, the user is prompted for an integer. The program then tries to parse that string into an int value. If the string of characters has a decimal point or letters or some other invalid int format, then a NumberFormatException is thrown. If that happens, the flow of control transfers to the catch (NumberFormatException e) {...} block of code. In this example, a message is displayed to the user and the program then continues after the catch block without crashing.

The code fragment above will keep your program from crashing if the user enters an invalid int format, but it does not give the user another chance to enter a valid integer format. A repetition statement is necessary, if you wish to repeat the prompt and let the user have another chance to enter a valid integer.

(c) What are the following:
(i) final class
(ii) final variable
(iii) final method

Ans. Refer to Dec-2005, Q.No.-1(d), Page No.-220

5. (a) How does one use multiple inheritance in java? Explain with example.

Ans. Java was designed without multiple inheritance. Java supports multiple inheritance indirectly through the use of interface. In case we are able to extend more than one class then there would be a confusion of which method to process in case both classes have same method name(Same method signature also).

In case of using interfaces to support multiple inheritance we escape this problem as we define the methods that are needed only.
Example :
'class' class_name ['extends' superclass_name]
['implements' interface_name [',' interface_name ...]]

(b) What is a toString( ) function in Java? Explain with example.
Ans. Java's Object class provides a method called toString() that returns the string representation of the object on which it is called. The method signature for toString() is:

public String toString ();

The toString() method is useful for debugging. By default, when an object is printed out in a print stream like System.out, the toString() method of the object is automatically called. For example, in the following code, the string representation of myObject is printed out:

MyClass myObject = new MyClass();
System.out.println"myObject=" + myObject);

The problem with just printing out myObject is that the default toString() method of the supeclass (Object) is called unless myObject overrides the toString() method. As a result, if myObject does not override the toString() method, just the reference value of myObject (not its contents) is printed out.

(c) What is static data in a class? Explain.
Ans. Static Data : This is a field that belongs to the class, not a field that is stored in each individual object.
Static data belongs to the class, not an individual object of the class. There is exactly one instance of static data, regardless of how many objects of the class there are. To make a field "per-class," apply the keyword "static," as shown here.

```
class Employee {
    int   id;               // per-object field
    int   salary;           // per-object field

    static int total;       // per-class field (one only)
        ...
}
```

Every Employee object will have the employee_id and salary fields. There will be one field called totalPayroll stored elsewhere in an object representing the Employee class.

Because static data is declared in the class right next to the instance data, it's all too easy to overlook that static data is not kept in each object with its instance data.

CS – 74: INTRODUCTION TO INTERNET PROGRAMME
June, 2008

Note: Question number 1 is **compulsory**. Answer any **three** questions from the rest.

Q1. (a) Explain the following keywords with example (any four):
(i) this
(ii) throw
(iii) super
(iv) protected
(v) transient

Ans. (i) Refer to Page No.-68
(ii) Refer to Q4, Page No.-79
(iii) Refer to Q2, Page No.-68,69
(iv) Refer to Q2(iv), Page No.-153
(v) Refer to Q2(a) Page No.-230, 231

(b) Create a class named "Employee" with fields: "Employee Name", "Age", "Address". Using the concept of serialization, store and retrieve the states of "Employee" object.

Ans.

```
class Employee implements serializable
{
string Name;
string Age;
string Address;
void display ( )
{
System.out.println("The name of the Employee is:" + Name);
System.out.println("The Age of the Employee is:" + Age);
System.out.println("The Address of the Employee is:" + Address);
}
}
class result

public static void main (String args [ ])
{
Employee a = new Employee ( );
a.Name = "Vikas";
a.Age = "25";
```

```
a.Address = "Delhi";
a.display ( );
}
}
```

(c) Explain the different access specifiers and their scope.

Refer to Q5(i), Page No.-128

(d) Explain the event delegation model in AWT. What are the components of an event?

Ans. The Concept of Event Delegation Model: This model allows special classes known as "adapter classes" to be built and registered with a component in order to handle certain events.

Steps required to use this model:

• Implement the desired listener interface in your adapter class. These include: Action Listener, Window Listener, Mouse Listener, etc.

• Register the adapter listener with the desired component(s). Example: add ActionListener ( ).

• Implement the listener interface's methods in your adapter class. It is in this code that you will actually handle the event.

Components of an Event:

• **Event Object:** When the user interacts with the application by clicking a mouse button or pressing a key, an event is generated.

• **Event Source:** An event source is the object that generated the event, for example, if you click a button, an ActionEvent object is generated.

• **Event Handler:** This is a method that understands the event and processes it. The event handler method takes the event object as a parameter.

Q2. (a) Explain the concept of method over-riding. Can we over-ride method within the same class? Explain.

Refer to Q3, Page No.-57

(b) What is inheritance? Explain with an example.

Refer to Q2(b), Page No.-209, 210

(c) Write a program in Java that inputs a natural number and displays whether or not that number is prime.

Ans.

```
import javax.swing.JOptionPane;
public class PrimeOrNot {
static boolean NumberIsPrime(int number) {
if (number < 2) {
```

```
return false; // must be 2 or greater to be prime
}

int stoppingPoint = (int)Math.sqrt(number);

for (int i = 2; i <= stoppingPoint; i++) {
if ((number % i) == 0) {
return false; // number is divisible by i
}
}
return true; // No factors found so the number is prime
}

public static void main(String[] args) {
String answer = JOptionPane.showInputDialog( "Enter a natural number");
int theNumber = Integer.parseInt(answer);
boolean result = NumberIsPrime(theNumber);
JOptionPane.showMessageDialog( null, theNumber + "'s primeship is " +
result);
}

}
```

Q3. (a) What is a stream? Write a program that reads the contents of a file and writes it into another file.

Ans. A stream is a sequence of bytes travelling from a source to a destination over a communication path.

Now Refer to Q(c), Page No.-235

(b) What is a thread? Explain different methods of thread class.

Refer to Q3(a), Page No.-232, 233, 234

Q4. (a) What is a static method? Why can't a static method use 'this' and 'super'? Explain with example.

Refer to Q5(c), Page No.-265, 266
Now Refer to Chapter-6, Q.No.-2, Page No.-68

(b) Explain any four features of Java.

Refer to Q5, Page No.-14 to 17

Q5. (a) Create a Java applet with a button "Display". On click of button

it should display Rectangle, Oval and Circle within the Applet.

Ans. import java.awt.*;

```
import java.applet.*;
public class ShapeApplet extends Applet
{
   int shape;
   Button button;

   public void init()
   {
      shape = 0;
      button = new Button("Display");
      add(button);
   }

   public void paint(Graphics g)
   {
      int numPts = 3;
      switch(shape)
      {
         case 0:
            g.drawRect(35, 50, 125, 180);
            break;
         case 1:
            g.drawOval(35, 50, 125, 180);
            break;
         case 2:
            g.drawCircle(35, 50, 125, 125);
            break;
      }
   }

   public boolean action(Event event, Object arg)
   {
      ++shape;
      if (shape == 3)
         shape = 0;
      repaint();
      return true;
   }
}
```

(b) What are wrapper classes? Why are they used?

Ans. Wrapper class is a wrapper around a primitive data type. It represents primitive data types in their corresponding class instances e.g. a boolean data type can be represented as a Boolean class instance. All of the primitive wrapper classes in Java are immutable i.e. once assigned a value to a wrapper class instance cannot be changed further.

Wrapper Classes are used broadly with Collection classes in the ***java.util*** package and with the classes in the ***java.lang.reflect*** reflection package.

Following table lists the primitive types and the corresponding wrapper classes:

Type is:	Wrapper Type is:
boolean	java.lang.Boolean
byte	java.lang.Byte
char	java.lang.Character
double	java.lang.Double
float	java.lang.Float
int	java.lang.Integer
long	java.lang.Long
short	java.lang.Short
void	java.lang.Void

(c) Explain the concept of an interface. What is scope and nature of variables and methods defined in an interface?

Refer to Chapter-8, Q3, Page No.-90

CS – 74: INTRODUCTION TO INTERNET PROGRAMME
December, 2008

Note: Question number 1 is **compulsory**. Answer any **three** questions from the rest.

Q1. (a) What is Java Virtual Machine (JVM)? Explain.
Refer Q3, Page No.-13

(b) Why do we use interfaces in java? Explain with example.
Refer Q3, Page No.-90

(c) What happens if an abstract modifier is applied to a class? Explain.
Refer Page No.-72

(d) What do you mean by static data in a class?
Refer Page No.-135

(e) Differentiate between:
(i) Thread and process
(i) Refer (e), Page No.-141

(ii) Applet and application program
(ii) Refer JUNE-03, Q1(iv), Page no.-130

(iii) Final and finalize
Ans. final is used for making a class no-subclassable, and making a member variable as a constant which cannot be modified. finally is usually used to release all the resources utilized inside the try block. All the resources present in the finalize method will be garbage collected whenever GC is called. Though finally and finalize seem to be for a similar task there is an interesting difference here. This is because the code in finally block is guaranteed of execution irrespective of occurrence of exception, while execution of finalize is not guaranteed. finalize method is called by the garbage collector on an object when the garbage collector determines that there are no more references to the object.

Q2. (a) Write a program in java that prompts the user to enter an integer number. It should throw a user-defined exception Invalid Number if number is negative. Also write the code for creating the user-defined function.

Ans. Import java.io.DataInputStream:

```
class number {
public static void main(string args[ ])
{ int n;
try
{
System.out.println("Enter an integer:");
n = Integer.parseInt(inreadline [ ]);
throw new Exception(n);
}
catch(Exception e)
{
if(e < 0)
{
System.out.println("The number is -ve:" + e);
}
}
User-defined Function:
static int fact(int n)
{ if (n = = 1)
return 1;
else
return n * fact(n);
}
```

(b) Will an error occur if a class with the same name exists in two different packages that you import using star form? How can the error be avoided?

Ans. If a class with the same name exists in two different packages that you import using the star form, the compiler will remain silent, unless you try to use one of the classes. In that case, you will get a compile time error and have to explicitly name the class specifying its package.

At any place you use a class name, it can be used with its fully qualified name only, which includes its full package hierarchy.

(c) When do we use parseInt ( ) function? Explain.

Ans. public static int parseInt(String s) throws NumberFormatException

Parses the string argument as a signed decimal integer. The characters in the string must all be decimal digits, except that the first character may be an ASCII minus sign '-' ('\u002D') to indicate a negative value. The resulting integer value is returned, exactly as if the argument and the radix 10 were

given as arguments to the parseInt(java.lang.String, int) method.
Parameters: s - a String containing the int representation to be parsed
Returns: the integer value represented by the argument in decimal.
Throws: NumberFormatException - if the string does not contain a parsable integer.

Q3. (a) What is synchronized block in java? Why do we use it?

Ans. You might not see the problem behavior on your machines, which suggests that the problem occurs with low probability. However, though it might first appear counterintutive, bugs that manifest rarely are worse than those that occur frequently. By this standard, data corruption in a threaded program is a bug of the nastiest sort: it is hard to spot the problem by reading the code, it occurs only rarely in the field, and it may disappear entirely when you run the code in a debugger!

Use a synchronized block to avoid basic data corruption problems in threaded Java programs. The synchronized block looks like this:

```
        synchronized (someObject) {
                //code to be protected
  }
```

Each object in the Java language is associated with its own concurrency protection object, called a monitor. When a thread encounters a synchronized block, it must acquire the monitor associated with someObject before proceeding into the block. When the thread exits a synchronized block, it releases the monitor. Only one thread at a time may acquire a monitor, which guarantees that there will never be more than one thread at a time inside the block. If several blocks of code synchronize on the same object, then only one thread can be in the entire set of blocks.

So, to protect data, you need to (1) identify which pieces of data might be touched by multiple threads, and (2) protect that data in a synchronized block. In the Stocks example, the endangered data is the balances array. The balances array is accessed from both the transfer and checkSystem methods, so both methods will need synchronized blocks:

```
  static void transfer(Transfer t) {
    synchronized (balances) {
        balances[t.fundFrom] -= t.amount;
        balances[t.fundTo] += t.amount;
```

```
        }
    }
    static void checkSystem() {
        int actual = 0;
        synchronized (balances) {
            for (int n=0; n<noOfStocks; n++) {
                actual += balances[n];
            }
        }
        System.out.println("Actual balance is
                        " + actual);
    }
```

Try running the program again. This time the balance will be correct throughout the progam's run.

(b) What are predefined streams in java?

Ans. All JAVA programs automatically import the java.lang package. This package defines a class called System. It contains several methods that can be used to obtain the current time and the settings of various properties associated with the system. System also contains three predefined stream variables, in, out and err. These fields are declared as public and static within System. This means that they can be used by any other part of the program without reference to a specific System object.

System.out referes to the standard output stream. By default, this is the console. System.in refers to the standard input, which is keyboard by default. System.err refers to the standard error stream, which is also console by default. However, these streams may be redirected to any compatible I/O device.

System.in is an object of type InputStream; System.out and System.err are objects of type PrintStream. These are byte streams, even though they typically are used to read and write characters from and to the console.

(c) Describe the various mouse events in MouseEvent class in brief.

Ans. Mouse events are triggered by the computers mouse. Mouse events are actually handled by two interfaces - MouseListener and MouseMotionListener. The MouseListener interface is used to detect the clicking of mouse buttons or the moving of a mouse into or out of a listener's area. The MouseMotionListener interface is used to detect the movement of the mouse.

Methods of the MouseListener interface:

mouseClicked(MouseEvent e)

This method is called when a mouse button is clicked.
mouseEntered(MouseEvent e)
This method is called when the mouse enters a source components area.
Methods of the MouseMotionListener interface:
mouseMoved(MouseEvent e)
This method is called when the mouse is moved while in a components area.
mouseDragged(MouseEvent e)
This method is called when the mouse moves while a mouse button is down while within a components area.

(d) Write the output of the following statements:
int a = -4 b = 8
(i) a^b
(ii) a << 2
Ans. (i) = (1100) ^ (1000) = (0100)
(ii) = 16

Q4. (a) Explain the use of super keyword in java with the help of suitable example.
Refer Page No.-69

(b) Write a recursive function in java to find sum of n terms of the following series :

$$1+\frac{1}{2}+\frac{1}{3}+\frac{1}{4}\ldots$$

Ans.
```
static float sum(float n)
{
if(n = = 1)
return 1;
else
return(1/n) + sum(n - 1);
}
```

(c) Give the output of the following code :
```
class numeric {
static int fact (int n)
{
int p = 1;
int i = n;
while (i >= 2)
{
i- -;
```

```
p = p*i;
}
return p;
}
public static void main (String args [ ])
{
int X = 4;
System.out.println (fact (X));
}
```

Ans. output: 6

Q5. (a) What is the difference between throwing an exception and catching an exception? Explain with example.

Ans. The following is an example of throwing an instance of the ExceptionClass.
throw new ExceptionClass("Something happened, the main program flow has to be interrupted, the caller has to be informed about this");

At the above line the current method execution is interrupted and the created exception object is thrown back to the caller. The exception object should contain the information about the reason of the interruption.

The caller of the method catches the exception by the catch keyword.

```
catch (ExceptionClass e)
{ // --- What to do with this interruption ??? --- }
```

To catch an exception, surround code that might produce it with a try { ... } catch block as follows.

```
try {    code that might produce the exception    } catch (exceptionName variableName)
{      code to handle the exceptional situation    }
```

For example, here's a piece of code that's intended to read a date appearing alone on a line of keyboard input:

```
dayOfYear = 0;
try {
  dayOfYear = Integer.parseInt (keyboard.readLine ( ));
} catch (NumberFormatException e) {
  System.err.println ("error: day of year had wrong format");
} catch (IOException e) {
  System.err.printf ("error: input error encountered: %s%n",
                  e.getMessage ());
}
```

This code is reading what is supposed to be a day of the year from the keyboard. Error situations to look out for include general input errors, say, resulting from a damaged keyboard, or inappropriately formatted input, say, the string "mike". In either case, the above code prints some kind of error message and leaves dayOfYear at 0.

As you can see, the "tried" code can be simpler since it is coded as if nothing will go wrong, separating it clearly from the error cases. The "catch" clauses are also known as exception handlers, because they handle the exceptional, non-routine, cases.

You can catch multiple exceptions, as in the code above, and handle them separately by supplying multiple catch blocks.

If your code may produce a checked exception, you have two choices. One is to catch the exception. The other is to "pass the buck" by saying throws exceptionName in the method header. This puts responsibility on the calling method either to handle the exception or to pass the buck to its caller.

To throw an exception, we use the throw operator and give it an exception object as argument. For example, if the number read above must be positive, we could have the following:

```
dayOfYear = Integer.parseInt (keyboard.readLine ( ));
if (dayOfYear <= 0) {
    throw new IllegalArgumentException ("day of year must be positive");
}
```

In the exception-catching code, we may access the String argument to the Exception constructor via the getMessage ( ) method, as shown in the day-reading example above.

(b) Write a program in java that displays all Command Line arguments in reverse order.

Ans. class commandline {

```
public static void main(string args[ ]) {
for(int i = 0; i < args.length; i++)
System.out.println("args[" + i + "]:" + args[i]);
}
}
```

(c) Static functions can only access static data. Why?

Ans. Static function can only access static data because since static function can be used without having to instantiate an object, the data that it accesses has to be readily and statically available. In other words, if a data / field is not declared 'static', it won't be available until an object is instantiated. And if this data is not available until an object is instantiated, then when a static function tries to access a non-static data, it won't be available to the function. Thus, it is a rule that static function can only access static data.

CS-74: INTRODUCTION TO INTERNET PROGRAMMING
June, 2009

Note: Question No. **1** is **compulsory**. Attempt **any three** from the rest. Use Java As Prog. Language.

Q1. (a) Why is Java called Architecture- neutral? Explain.
Refer to Chapter-2, Page-16

(b) What is automatic type conversion in Java? Explain.
Refer to June-2005, Q.No.-4(c), Page-201

(c) int a = 3, b = 6;
int c = a &b

int d = a^b

int e = $(\sim a \,\&\, b) | (a \,\&\, \sim b)$

Calculate and print the values of c, d & e
Ans. c=2 d=5 e=5

(d) $a = -10,\ b = 2 \cdot\ a >> b + 3$ **print value of a after performing this operation.**
Ans. value = -1

(e) Static function can only use static data of the class. Justify your answer.
Ans. Static methods use no instance variables of any object of the class they are defined in. If you define a method to be static, you will be given a rude message by the compiler if you try to access any instance variables.
Now Refer to December-2004, Q.No.-1(b), Page 205

(f) Write a program that accepts name of a file at command line and displays its contents.
Refer to December, 2006, Q.No.-4(b), Page-247

(g) Differentiate between if-else and switch statement in Java with the help of suitable example.
Refer to Chapter-4, Page-37 & 38

Q2. (a) Can try be used without catch? Explain with the help of suitable example.

Ans. Yes, we can use try block with following final block without catch, like this:

```
try {
        int i = 10;
        //....
        // do smth. here
} finally {
        int i = -10
        //....
        // finalize smth here
}
```

avoiding catch block. Maybe you do need it at all, you simply do not mind about it. It is a fact that many programmers have no code in catch block So, why bother about it all. If you do not have a strategy for error handling do not do it all! Just continue.

Now the question arises that why we need try if we do not catch? Is not it simpler to run just plain code without any blocks. Please do not forget that we use try to try something, if it does not go we can continue anyway. Plain code just will stop and cause runtime error, which will break the program flow.

(b) Does Java Support Multiple Inheritance? Can we use interfaces to achieve the same result? Explain.

Refer to December, 2007, Q.No.-5(a), Page-264

(c) What are the points to ensure while writing a method that is intended to override another method?

Ans. Refer to June-2004, Page-117

Defining a Method with the Same Signature as a Superclass's Method		
	Superclass Instance Method	**Superclass Static Method**
Subclass Instance Method	Overrides	Generates a compile-time error
Subclass Static Method	Generates a compile-time error	Hides

Q3. (a) Differentiate between interfaces and abstract classes with the help of suitable examples.

Refer to June, 2005, Q.No.-2(a), Page-192

(b) Write an applet the displays the sequence of execution of various applet initialization termination function.

Refer to December-2002, Q.No.-4(ii), Page-144

(c) Write a program fragment to show the use of a break statement.
Refer to December-2003, Q.No.-1(iv), Page-123

Q4. (a) How thread priorities are used in Java? Explain with suitable example.
Refer to December-2007, Q.No.-4(a), Page-261

(b) Why is toString( ) used in Java? Write a program fragment to show its usage.
Refer to December-2007, Q.No.-5(b), Page-265

(c) How are Key Events generated in Java? Describe the features of the class used to handle Key Events.

Ans. Java keyboard events are generated when the user presses or releases a key. There are two standard keyboard event-handler methods supported by the Component class: keyDown and keyUp. These two methods are defined as:

```
public boolean keyDown(Event evt, int key)
public boolean keyUp(Event evt, int key)
```

The keyDown method is called in response to the user pressing a key, and the keyUp method is called in response to the user releasing a key. Both methods are passed an Event object and an integer key value parameter. The key value parameter, key, specifies which key was pressed or released. The Event object parameter contains extra information relating to the keyboard event, such as whether the Shift key was held down when the key was pressed.

The Event object contains constants representing the different keys that can be specified in the key parameter.

To check if the key pressed or released is one of these keys, you override keyDown or keyUp and compare the value of key to one of the constants. Following is an example of overriding keyDown to check for the user pressing one of the arrow keys:

```
public boolean keyDown(Event evt, int key) {
  switch (key) {
  case Event.LEFT:
    // left arrow key pressed
    break;
  case Event.RIGHT:
    // right arrow key pressed
    break;
  case Event.UP:
    // up arrow key pressed
```

```
  break;
 case Event.DOWN:
  // down arrow key pressed
  break;
 }
 return true;
}
```

This code shows that handling different key presses is as easy as providing a switch statement with case clauses for each key. Although the example here used the keyDown method for handling key presses, the keyUp method works in the same fashion.

Q5. (a) Write a recursive function in java to print the contents of an array.

Refer to June-2004, Q.No.-6(a), Page-116

(b) How are packages imported? Explain the benefits of using packages and the benefit of importing a package into your program.

Refer to June-2004, Q.No.-4(a), Page-112

(c) Why do we use super ( ) in Java? Explain.

Refer to Chapter-6, Page-69

CS-74: INTRODUCTION TO INTERNET PROGRAMMING
December, 2009

Note: Question No. **I** is **compulsory**. Attempt any three from the rest.

Q1. (a) What is abstraction? Explain through an example.
Refer to Chapter-1, Q.no.-9, Page-9

(b) Differentiate between call-by-value and call-by-reference with the help of suitable example.

Refer to December-2001, Q.no.-4(ii), Page-168

(c) When are the members of a class declared static? What are the restrictions on a static method?
Refer to December-2004, Q.no.-1. (b), Page- 205

(d) Discuss in brief two methods used for a applet execution.
Refer to December-2002, Q.No.-4(ii), Page-144

(e) Write a recursive function in Java to print the gcd of two given integer numbers.
Refer to December-2002, Q.no.-5(i), Page-145

(f) Write the out put of the following:
(i) int n = OX FFFFFFE
For (int i = 0; i<3; i ++)
{ n = n << 1;
System –out- print Ih (n);}
Ans. Output:-

536870908
1073741816
2147483632

(ii) int a = -10; a>>2;
Ans. Output:-

No output

Q2. (a) Differentiate between throw and throws with the help of suitable example.
Refer to Chapter-7, Q.no.-4, Page-79

(b) What is dynamic method dispatch? Explain.

Ans. Dynamic method dispatch is the mechanism by which a call to an overridden method is resolved at run time rather than compile time. Dynamic method dispatch is important because this is how Java implements run-time polymorphism.

Example:-

```
                class A
                {
                        public void m1()
                        {
                        }
                }
                class B extends A
                {
                        public void m1()
                        {
                        }
                        Public static void main(String args[])
                        {
                                A a=new B();
                //B reference will be assigned at run time
a.      m1().
                }
        }
```

(c) What is object serialization? Write a program fragment to show how an object can be saved to and retrieved from file storage.

Ans. Serialization is the process of saving an object's state to a sequence of bytes, as well as the process of rebuilding those bytes into a live object at some future time.

To persist an object in Java, we must have a persistent object. An object is marked serializable by implementing the java.io.Serializable interface, which signifies to the underlying API that the object can be flattened into bytes and subsequently inflated in the future.

Let's look at a persistent class we'll use to demonstrate the serialization mechanism:

```
import java.io.Serializable;
import java.util.Date;
import java.util.Calendar;
public class PersistentTime implements Serializable
```

```
{
private Date time;

public PersistentTime()
{
    time = Calendar.getInstance().getTime();
  }

  public Date getTime()
  {
    return time;
  }
 }
```

As you can see, the only thing we had to do differently from creating a normal class is implement the java.io.Serializable interface on line 4 in the above code. The completely empty Serializable is only a marker interface — it simply allows the serialization mechanism to verify that the class is able to be persisted. Thus, we turn to the first rule of serialization

Q3. (a) Can you extend an Interface in Java? Explain with the help of a program fragment.

Refer to December-2001, Q.no.-2.(e), Page-165

(b) Write a program to show the use of isAlive () and join () in Java.

Ans. Java provides us with a better solution in threads by which we can find out whether all other child threads have finished executing before the main thread and it is done in two ways as mentioned:

1. We can call the isAlive( ) method which will return the value as "true" if the thread is running on which it is called else will give " false" as it's returning value.

2. Another method is to implement join ( ) function. this method will wait until the thread on which it is called is terminated.Both these methods are explained in detail with the examples below.

Example of isAlive:-

```
public class IsAliveExample
{
        public static void main(String[] args)
        {
                Thread th = new MyOwnThread("A");
```

```
            th.start();
            while(th.isAlive());
            System.out.println("Thread is not alive anymore.");
    }
}

class MyOwnThread extends Thread
{
    private String threadName;
    public MyOwnThread(String name)
    {
            threadName = name;
    }
    public void run()
    {
            for(int i = 0; i < 1000; i++)
            {
            System.out.println("Thread " + threadName + " : " + i);
            }
    }
}
```

Example of join:-

```
public class JoinExample
{
    public static void main(String[] args)
    {
            Thread th1 = new MyOwnThread("A");
            Thread th2 = new MyOwnThread("B");
            try
            {
                    th1.start();
                    th1.join();
                    th2.start();
            }
            catch(InterruptedException e)
            {
            }
    }
}
```

```
class MyOwnThread extends Thread
{
        private String threadName;
        public MyOwnThread(String name)
        {
                threadName = name;
        }
        public void run()
        {
                for (int i = 0; i < 1000; i++)
                {
                        System.out.println("Thread " + threadName + " : "
+ i);
                }
        }
}
```

(c) Write a program to show the use of multiple catch statements with single try block?

Refer to Chapter-7, Q.No.-3, Page-78

Q4. (a) Write a program to copy one file to another file. Name of files are given at command line.

Refer to June-2006, Q.no.-3. (c), Page-235

(b) What is an inner class? Explain with an example.

Refer to June-2005 Q.no.-1.(e), Page-189

(c) Why do we use packages in Java? How packages are created in Java? Explain. List 5 important packages of Java.

Refer to Chapter-8, Q.no.-1, Page-85 and now

5 important packages of java:-

import java.awt.*;	Common GUI elements.
import java.awt.event.*;	The most common GUI event listeners.
import javax.swing.*;	More common GUI elements. Note "javax".
import java.util.*;	Data structures (Collections), time, Scanner, etc classes.
import java.io.*;	Input-output classes.

Q5. (a) What are the error (S) in the following code? Also correct the error(s).

```
Class Demo {Public static void main (string args [ ] )
{       int x;
        x=10;
        if (x = = 10) {int y = 20;
         y = * 2
        System. out. print ln ("x=" + y);
        }
        System. out. print In ("y=" + y);
}       }
```

Ans. Error:-

```
3: <identifier> expected
      Public static void main(string args[])
        ^

7: ';' expected
            x=y*2
               ^

8: ';' expected
            System.out.print ln(x="+x);
                              ^

8: unclosed string literal
            System.out.print ln(x="+x);
                                ^

10: ';' expected
      System.out.print ln("y="+y);
                      ^

10: not a statement
      System.out.print ln("y="+y);
                          ^

10: ';' expected
      System.out.print ln("y="+y);
                          ^
```

7 errors

After correcting the errors:-

```
class Demo
{       {
        public static void main(string args[])
        {
                int x;
```

```
            if(x==10){y=20;
            x=y*2;
            System.out.println(x="+x);
            }
            System.out.println("y="+y);
    }       }
```

(b) Is it possible to overload constructors? Why would it be done? Give suitable examples.

Refer to Chapter-5, Q.no.-2, Page-56

(c) If we have to prevent a class from being inherited, how can, we do it? Explain.

Refer to June-2005, Q.No.-4(a), Page-199

(d)Write the output of the following code:
String S= "This is my first Java Prgoram";
System. out. println ("index of (S) = " + S.index of ('S'));
System. out. println ("index of (S) = " + S.index of ('S', 6));
Ans. Output:-

```
index of(S)=-1
index of(S)=-1
```

CS-74: INTRODUCTION TO INTERNET PROGRAMMING
June, 2010

Note: *Question No.* ***1*** *is* ***compulsory****. Attempt* ***any two*** *from the rest. Use* ***Java*** *as programming language.*

Q1.(a) Differentiate between nested and inner classes. Explain with an example.

Ans. Refer to Page No.-74, Chapter-6, Q.No.-4

(b) Write a program for I/O operation using Buffered Input Stream and Buffered Output Stream that accepts user name, age and address from the user and displays it on the console.

Ans.
```
import.java.io.*;
class student
{       public static void main (Srring args [ ])
        {String name;
        int age;
        String address:
        BufferedInputStream sin = new BufferedInputStream (in)
        BufferedOutputStream sout=new BufferedOutputStream (out);
        name = sin.read ( );
        age = sin.read ( );
        address = sin.read ( )
        sout.write (name);
        sout.write (age);
        sout.write (address);
        }
}
```

(c) Write an applet that reads two strings and displays the larger string among them.

Ans.
```
import java.awt.x;
import java.applet.x;
import java.awt.event.x;
public class Userin extends Applet implements Action listener
{       Text Field text1, text 2;
public void init( )
text1 = new Text Field ( );
text2= new TextField ( );
text1.AddActionListener (this);
text2.AddActionListener (this);
}
public void point (Graphics g)
{       String S1, S2, S3;
        S1= text1.getText ( );
        S2= text2.getText ( );
if (S1>S2)
        S3=S1;
else
```

```
S3=S1;
g.drawString (S3, 10, 50);
}
public void actionPerformed (ActionEvent are)
{       repaint ( );
}
}
}
```

Q2. (a) What is run-time polymorphism? How does it differ from compile-time polymorphism? Explain with an example.
Ans. Refer to Page No.-116 & 260

(b) What are threads? How can they be created?
Ans. Refer to Page No.-232, June-06, Q.No.-3(a)

Q3. (a) Write a program in Java to generate the following output, using two-dimensional array:

a
a b
a b c
a b c d

Ans.
```
class Diagram
{       public static void main (string args [ ])
        {       int I, j;
                char td [ ] [ ] = new char [4] [ ];
                td[0]= new char [1];
                td[1]=new char [2];
                td[2]= new char [3];
                td[3]=new char [4]; char ch;
                for (i=0, i<4; i++)
                {       eh= 'a';
                        for (i=0;j<=i<j++)
                        {       td [i] [j]= ch++;
                                System.out.println (td[i][j]+ "  ");
                        }
                        System.out.println( );}}}
```

(b) What is the role of a default exception handler in Java? Differentiate between 'throw' and 'throws'.
Ans. Refer to Page No.-229, June-06, Q.No.-1(e)

Q4. (a) Write a program that accepts two files as input and appends the content of first file to second file.

Ans.
```
import java .io.*;
class fileopp
{       public static void main (String args [ ])
        {       fileInputStream. fin= new fileInputStream ("first");
                fileOutputStream. fout= new fileOutputStream ("second");
                while (fin. available ( ) !=0)
                {       fout.write (fin.read ( )
                }
                fin.close ( );
                fout.close ( ):
```

```
        }
}
```

(b) Explain the advantages of *super* keyword in Java.

Ans. Refer to Page No.-68, Chapter-6, Q.No.-2

Q5. (a) Write GUI Java application to simulate the simple calculator. The calculator should be able to do the basic operations.

Ans.

```
import javax.swing.*;
import javax.swing.JOptionPane;
import java.awt.*;
import java.awt.event.*;
//<applet code=Calculator height=300 width=200></applet>
public class Calculator extends JApplet {
  public void init() {
     CalculatorPanel calc=new CalculatorPanel();
      getContentPane().add(calc);
      }
  }
class CalculatorPanel extends JPanel implements ActionListener {
   JButton n1,n2,n3,n4,n5,n6,n7,n8,n9,n0, plus,minus,mul,div,dot,equal;
     static JTextField result=new JTextField("0",45);
     static String lastCommand=null;
     JOptionPane p=new JOptionPane();
     double preRes=0,secVal=0,res;
     private static void assign(String no)
     {
        if((result.getText()).equals("0"))
          result.setText(no);
        else if(lastCommand=="=")
          {
                  result.setText(no);
                  lastCommand=null;
          }
        else
          result.setText(result.getText()+no);
     }
    public CalculatorPanel() {
       setLayout(new BorderLayout());
       result.setEditable(false);
       result.setSize(300,200);
       add(result,BorderLayout.NORTH);
       JPanel panel=new JPanel();
       panel.setLayout(new GridLayout(4,4));
       n7=new JButton("7");
       panel.add(n7);
       n7.addActionListener(this);
       n8=new JButton("8");
       panel.add(n8);
       n8.addActionListener(this);
       n9=new JButton("9");
```

```
panel.add(n9);
n9.addActionListener(this);
div=new JButton("/");
panel.add(div);
div.addActionListener(this);
n4=new JButton("4");
panel.add(n4);
n4.addActionListener(this);
n5=new JButton("5");
panel.add(n5);
n5.addActionListener(this);
n6=new JButton("6");
panel.add(n6);
n6.addActionListener(this);
mul=new JButton("*");
panel.add(mul);
mul.addActionListener(this);
n1=new JButton("1");
panel.add(n1);
n1.addActionListener(this);
n2=new JButton("2");
panel.add(n2);
n2.addActionListener(this);
n3=new JButton("3");
panel.add(n3);
n3.addActionListener(this);
minus=new JButton("-");
panel.add(minus);
minus.addActionListener(this);
dot=new JButton(".");
panel.add(dot);
dot.addActionListener(this);
n0=new JButton("0");
panel.add(n0);
n0.addActionListener(this);
equal=new JButton("=");
panel.add(equal);
equal.addActionListener(this);
plus=new JButton("+");
panel.add(plus);
plus.addActionListener(this);
add(panel,BorderLayout.CENTER);
}
public void actionPerformed(ActionEvent ae)
{
if(ae.getSource()==n1) assign("1");
else if(ae.getSource()==n2) assign("2");
else if(ae.getSource()==n3) assign("3");
else if(ae.getSource()==n4) assign("4");
else if(ae.getSource()==n5) assign("5");
else if(ae.getSource()==n6) assign("6");
```

```
else if(ae.getSource()==n7) assign("7");
else if(ae.getSource()==n8) assign("8");
else if(ae.getSource()==n9) assign("9");
else if(ae.getSource()==n0) assign("0");
else if(ae.getSource()==dot)
    {
     if(((result.getText()).indexOf("."))==-1)
        result.setText(result.getText()+".");
    }
else if(ae.getSource()==minus)
    {
    preRes=Double.parseDouble(result.getText());
    lastCommand="-";
    result.setText("0");
    }
else if(ae.getSource()==div)
    {
    preRes=Double.parseDouble(result.getText());
    lastCommand="/";
    result.setText("0");
    }
else if(ae.getSource()==equal)
    {
    secVal=Double.parseDouble(result.getText());
    if(lastCommand.equals("/"))
        res=preRes/secVal;
    else if(lastCommand.equals("*"))
        res=preRes*secVal;
    else if(lastCommand.equals("-"))
        res=preRes-secVal;
    else if(lastCommand.equals("+"))
        res=preRes+secVal;
    result.setText(" "+res);
    lastCommand="=";
    }
else if(ae.getSource()==mul)
    {
    preRes=Double.parseDouble(result.getText());
    lastCommand="*";
    result.setText("0");
    }
else if(ae.getSource()==plus)
    {
    preRes=Double.parseDouble(result.getText());
    lastCommand="+";
    result.setText("0");
    }
  }
}
```

(b) Explain static methods and static variables in Java.

Ans. Refer to Page No.-63, Chapter-5

CS-74: INTRODUCTION TO INTERNET PROGRAMMING
December, 2010

Note: *Question No.* ***1*** *is* ***compulsory****. Attempt* ***any two*** *from the rest. Use* ***Java*** *as programming language.*

Q1. (a) Compare the following :

(i) transient and volatile

Ans. Refer to Page No.-230, June-06, Q.No.-2(a)(i)

(ii) = = and equals ( )

Ans. Refer to Page No.-231, June-06, Q.No.-2(a)(ii)

(ii) Interface and Abstract class

Ans. Refer to Page No.-231, June-06, Q.No.-2(a)(iii)

(b) Write a program in Java that accepts a file as input and prints its contents to standard output in reverse order. That is, the last line of the file is printed as first line.

Ans.
```
import java.io.*;
class Display
{       fileInputStream fi;
        String S=new String [500];
        int i=0;
public static void main (String args [ ])
{       fi= new fileInputStream ("ai.txt");
        while (fi. Available ( ) : = 0)
                {       s[i] = fi. readLine ( );
                        i++;
                }
                        int j = i;
                        while (j > = 0)
                                {       system.out.println (s[ j]);
                                        j- -;
                                }
}
}
```

(c) Write a program in Java to add two complex numbers.

Ans. Refer to Page No.-244, Dec-06, Q.No.-2(a)

(d) What do you mean by a layout manager? Explain Grid Bag layout in detail with an example.

Ans. Refer to Page No.-255, June-07, Q.No.-3(c)

Q2. (a) What is overloading? What is overriding? Explain the differences between them.

Ans. Refer to Page No.-57, Q.No.-3 & Page No.-59, Q.No.-4, Chapter-5

(b) What is the function of this keyword in Java?

Ans. Refer to Page No.-68, Chapter-6, Q.No.-2

Q3. (a) Explain *join* ( ) method with an example. To which class in Java does it belong to?

Ans. Refer to Page No.-285, Q.No.-3(b) & Page No.-288, Q.No.-1(c)(iii)

(b) Explain the function of *finalize* ( ) in Java with an example.

Ans. Refer to Page No.-110, June-04, Q.No.-2(b)

Q4. (a) Write a program in Java that accept 5 strings as input and prints those strings as output which consist of atleast one vowel.

Ans.
```
class vowelstring
{       public static void main (String args [ ]) throws 1OException
{BufferedReader br = bew BufferedReader (new InputStreamReader
(system.in));
        String str[10];
        System.out.println ("Enter 5 strings");
        for (int i=0; ic 10; i++)
                {str [i] = br.readLine( );}
        System.out.println ("Strings contain atleast one vowel");
        for (int i = 0; i<10; i++)
{if (str[i]. indexof ('a')>=0 || str [i].indexof ('e')>=0 || str [i]. indexof ('i')
        >=0 || str [i]. indexof ('o') >=0 || str [i]. index of ('n'))
                                {System.out.println (str[i]);
                                }
                }
        }
}
```

(b) Is Java, a platform independent language? Justify your answer.

Ans. Refer to Page No.-205, Dec-04, Q.No.-1(a)

Q5. (a) Explain the differences between AWT, and swing. Why do you prefer to use swing over AWT?

Swing is preferred over AWT, and there are many differences between both which are as follows :

1.Swing is also called as JFC's (Java Foundation classes) and AWT stands for Abstract windows toolkit.

2.AWT components are called Heavyweight component and Swings are called light weight component because swing components sits on the top of AWT components and do the work.

3. Swing components require javax.swing package where as AWT components require java.awt package .

4.swings components are made in purely java and they are platform independent whereas AWT components are platform dependent.

5.we can have different look and feel in Swing whereas this feature is not supported in AWT.

6.Swing has many advanced features like JTabel, Jtabbed pane which is not available in AWT. Also. Swing components are called "lightweight" because they do not require a native OS object to implement their functionality. JDialog and JFrame are heavyweight, because they do have a peer. So components like JButton, JTextArea, etc., are lightweight because they do not have an OS peer.

7.With AWT, you have 21 "peers" (one for each control and one for the dialog itself). A "peer" is a widget provided by the operating system, such as a button object or an entry field object.

8.With Swing, you would have only one peer, the operating system's window object. All of the buttons, entry fields, etc. are drawn by the Swing package on the drawing surface provided by the window object. This is the reason that Swing has more code. It has to draw the button or other control and implement its behavior instead of relying on the host operating system to perform those functions.

9.Several consequences result from this difference between AWT and Swing. AWT is a thin layer of code on top of the OS, whereas Swing is much larger. Swing also has very much richer functionality.

10.Using AWT, you have to implement a lot of things yourself, while Swing has them built in. For GUI-intensive work, AWT feels very primitive to work with compared to Swing. Because Swing implements GUI functionality itself rather than relying on the host OS, it can offer a richer environment on all platforms Java runs on.

(b) Write a program in java that accepts a string as input and checks whether it is a palindrome or not.

Ans. Refer to Page No.-154, June-02, Q.No.-4(i)

CS-74: INTRODUCTION TO INTERNET PROGRAMMING
June, 2011

Note: *Question No.* ***1*** *is* ***compulsory****. Attempt* ***any two*** *from the rest. Use* ***Java*** *as programming language.*

Q1. (a) How does Java Programme support robustness?

Ans. Refer to Page No.-140, Dec-02, Q.No.-1(e)

(b) Write the precedence of the following operators. < > [ ] ~ > > ( )

Ans. Highest: ( ) [ ] ~ >> > < Lowest

(c) Is it possible to convert string into numbers? Explain with the help of suitable example.

Ans. Yes. It is possible to convert a string into numbers. Demo.java:

```
public class Demo
{
public static void main (string[ ] args)
{
//this program requires two arguments on the command line if (args.length= =2)
{
//Convert strings into numbers
float a=(float.valueOf(args[o])).floatValue( );
float b=(float.valueOf(args[f])).floatValue( );
//do some arithmetic operations.
system.out.println("a+b="+(a+b));
system.out.println("a–b="+(a–b));
system.out.println("a×b="+(a×b));
system.out.println("a/b="+(a/b));
system.out.println("a%b="+(a%b));
}
else
{
system.out.println("This program"+ "requires two command line arguments.");
}
}
}
```

Output:

If we uses:

a=4.5

b=87.2

then,

a+b=91.7

a–b=–82.7

a×b=392.4

a/b=0.0516055

a%b=4.5

(d) State whether True or False for the following statements:

(i) A subclass cannot call the constructor of it's super class.

Ans. False

(ii) The Array size in Java is fixed after it is declared.

Ans. False

(iii) A default member function of a class can not be accessed outside the package in which this class is declared.

Ans. True

(iv) If no exception is thrown from a try block, then control passes to finally block after the closing braces of the try block.

Ans. True

(v) A Native method is a method which is not written in Java.

Ans. True

(e) Differentiate between transient and volatile keyword in Java.

Ans. Refer to Page No.-230, June-06, Q.No.-2(a)

(f) What are the various ways to execute an Applet?

Ans. Refer to Page No.-152 [Browser and Applet viewer]

(g) Write an Applet showing the sequence of method executed during the life cycle of an Applet.

Ans.
```
import java.applet.Applet;
import java.awt.Graphics;
/* Applet can either run by browser or appletviewer application & Define
<applet> tag within comments as given below to speed up the testing.*/
/*<applet code="AppletLifeCycle" width=100 height=100>
</applet>
*/
public class AppletLifeCycle extends Applet
{
//init method is called first.
//It is used to initialize variables & called only once.
public void init( )
{
super.init( );
}
```

```
//start method in the second method to be called.
//start method is called every time the applet has been stopped.
public void start( )
{
super.start( )
}
//stop method is called when the user navigates
//away from html page containing the applet.
public void stop( )
{
super.stop( );
}
/* Paint method is called every time applet has to redraw its output */
public void paint(Graphics g)
{
super.paint(g);
}
/* destroy method is called when browser completely removes the applet
from memory. It should free any resources initialized during the init method.*/
public void destroy( )
{
super.destroy( );
}
}
```

Q2. (a) When do we use protected specifier in a Java program? Explain with example.

Ans. Protected methods & fields can only be accessed within the same class to which the methods & fields belong, within its subclass & within classes of the same package but not from anywhere else. You use the protected access level when it is appropriate for a class's sub classes to have access to the method or field, but not for unrelated classes.Example: Protection.java

```
package gullybaba;
public class Protection
{
int n=1;
private int n_pri=2
protected int n_pro=3;
public int n_pub=4;
public Protection( )
        {
```

```
System.out.println("Base Constructor");
System.out.println("n="+n);
System.out.println("n_pri="+n_pri);
System.out.println("n_pro="+n_pro);
System.out.println("n_pub="+n_pub);
}
}
```

Derived.java

```
package gullybaba;
class Derived extends Protection
{
Derived( )
{
System.out.println("Derived Constructor");
System.out.println("n="+n);
//Class only
System.out.println("n_pri="+n_pri);
System.out.println("n_pro="+n_pro);
System.out.println("n_pub="+n_pub);
}
}
```

(b) What is method overloading? Explain.

Ans. Refer to Page No.-188, June-05, Q.No.-1(d)

(c) How Garbage Collection is performed in Java?

Ans. Refer to Page No.-64 [Garbage Collection]

Q3. (a) What is a package? Why do we need package? Explain.

Ans. Refer to Page No.-112, June-04, Q.No.-4(a)

(b) Differentiate between while and do-while with the help of suitable example.

Ans. while **STATEMENT** or while Loop: Simplest of all the looping structures in Java.

→ Syntax of While Loop:

```
Initialization;
while (test condition)
{
body of the loop
}
```

→ While is an entry-controlled loop statement.

→ In while loop, the test condition is evaluated & if the condition is true, then the body of the loop is executed.

→ After execution of the body of while loop, the test condition is once again evaluated & if it is true, the body is executed once again.

This process of repeated execution of the body continues until the test condition finally becomes false & the control is transferred out of the loop.

→ The body of the while loop may have one or more statements.

Do **STATEMENT**: on some occasions it might be necessary to execute the body of the loop before the test is performed. Such situations can be handled with the help of do statement.

→ Syntax of do statement/do-while loop:

```
Initialization;
do
{
body of the loop
}
while (test condition);
```

→ On reaching the do statement, the program proceeds to evaluate the body of the loop first.

→ At the end of the loop, the test condition in the while statement is evaluated.

→ If the condition is true, the program continues to evaluate the body of the loop once again.

This process continues as long as the condition becomes false, the loop will be terminated & the control goes to the statement that appears immediately after the while statement.

→ Since the test condition is evaluated at the bottom of the loop, the do-while construct provides an exit controlled loop & therefore the body of the loop is always executed atleast once. Difference b/w while & do-while loops:

while	do-while
It is a looping construct that will execute only if the test condition is true.	It is looping construct that will execute at least once even if the test condition is false.
It is an entry-controlled loop.	It is an exit-controlled loop.
It is generally used for implementing common looping situations.	It is typically used for implementing menu-based programs where the menu is required to be printed at least once.

(c) Write a program to accept two numbers at the command line and print out their product.

Ans. public class commandLine

```
	{
public static void main(string[ ] args)
	{
//this program requires two arguments on the command line.
	if (args.length= =2)
```

```
        {
//Convert strings into numbers
float a= (float.valueOf(args[o])).floatValue( );
float b=(float.valueOf(args[f])).floatValue( );
//do arithmetic operation (product)
System.out.println("a * b="+(a * b));
        }
else
        {
        System.out.println("This program"+ "requires 2 command Line
arguments");
                }
        }
}
```

Output:

a=2
b=4
a * b=2 * 4=8

Q4. (a) Can you extend interfaces in Java? Explain with example.

Ans. Refer to Page No.-165, Dec-01, Q.No.-2(e)

(b) What is the method to retrieve the colour of the text? Write a program to retrieve the RGB values of a colour.

Ans. getColour.java

```
import java.io.*;
import java.awt.*;
import java.imageio.ImageIO;
import java.awt.image.BufferedImage;
public class getcolour
{
public static void main (string args[ ]) throws
IOException
{
File, file=new File ("rockface.jpg");
Buffered Image image= ImageIO.read(file);
//Getting pixel colour by position x=100 & y=40
int clr=image.getRGB(100,40);
int red=(clr & 0×00ff0000)>>16;
int green=(clr & 0×0000ff00)>>8;
int blue=(clr & 0×000000ff);
System.out.println("Red colour value="+red);
```

```
System.out.println ("Green colour value="green);
System.out.println ("Blue colour value="+blue);
        }
}
```

Output:

Red Colour value=33
Green Colour value=50
Blue Colour value=60

(c) What is a stream? Differentiate between stream source and stream destination.

Ans. Stream: A stream is a sequence of bytes of undetermined length that travel from one place to another over a communication path. Stream has two types:
(1) Stream Source: Places from where the streams are picked up are known as stream sources. A source may be a file, input devices etc.
(2) Stream Destination: Places where the streams are received or stored are known as stream destination. A stream destination may be a file or output devices or a network places ready to receive stream. In other words, we can say that. A stream in Java is a path along which data flows. Stream has a source or a destination & both source, & a destination may be physical devices or program or other streams in the same program.

Q5. (a) What will happen if main thread finishes before the child thread? How do you make sure that child thread gets terminated first?

Ans. In older Java-runtime system, if the main thread finishes before a child thread had completed, there was a possibility that the Java run-time system would "hang". This problem is not exhibited by the modern Java runtime system. However, since this behaviour was exhibited by some older Java run time system, it seems better to be safe rather than sorry, since you don't always know the environment in which your program may run. The main thread is also a convenient place to perform the orderly shutdown of your program. Such as the closing of files. Therefore, it often just makes sense for it to finish last. Fortunately, it is trivially easy for the main thread to wait until the child threads hare completed.

(b) What is built-in Exceptions in Java? Explain the use of any one of them with the help of suitable example.

Ans. Built-in Exception: The built-in exception in Java are of following types classified on the basis of exception handled by the Java compiler:
(1) Checked Exception (2) Unchecked Exception.
→ Basically, Built-in Exceptions are logical errors that are identified & thrown by the system but trapping and handling them is the responsibility of the programmer. Some of the Built-in-Exceptions are:
→ Arithmetic Exception: Raised when a number is divided by zero.
→ ClassNotFoundException: Raised when a specified class file is not found.

→ NullPointerException: Raised when a variable is used without initializing.
→ IOException: It deals with file related errors.

Example of Arithmetic Exception:

```
public class Exceptionjava
        {
public static void main (string[ ] args)
        {
                division (100, 0);
        }
public static void division (int numerator, int denominator)
        {
        try
        {
int average=numerator/denominator;
System.out.println ("Average"+average);
        }
Catch (Exception ex)
        {
System.out.println("Divide" +ex.getmessage ( ) + "Exception" + "\n" + "Please
Check the denominator"),
                }
        }
}
```

Output:

Divide by zero
Exception
Please Check the denominator.

(c) How many Listeners are there for trapping mouse movements? Explain briefly.

Ans. Following are the listeners for trapping mouse movements:

- mousePressed (MouseEvent e)
- mouseReleased (MouseEvent e)
- mouseClicked (MouseEvent e)
- mouseEntered (MouseEvent e)
- mouseExit (MouseEvent e)

CS-74: INTRODUCTION TO INTERNET PROGRAMMING
December, 2011

Note: *Question No. 1 is **compulsory**. Attempt **any two** from the rest. Use **Java** as programming language.*

Q1. (a) What is Java Virtual Machine (JVM)? Explain.

Ans. Refer to Page No.-13, Chapter-2, Q.No.-3

(b) Write a program in Java to display the following pattern for a given number n.

1
2 2
3 3 3 $n = 4$
4 4 4 4

Ans.
```
import java.awt. *;
Class series
{
Public static void main (string[] args)
{
int i j ;
int j ;
System.out.println ("The series is ");
for (i=1; i<=4; i++)
{
for (j=1; j<=i; j++)
            {
            System.out.println(i);
            }
      }
}
```

(c) Explain the use of conditional operator with the help of an example.

Ans. Conditional operator (?): Java includes a special ternary (three-way) operator that can replace certain types of if-then-else statements. This operator is the ? and it works in Java much like it does in C & C++. It can seem somewhat confusing at first, but the ? can be used very effectively once mastered. The ? has this general form

expression1? expression2: expression3

Here, expression1 can be any expression that evaluates to a Boolean value. If expression1 is true, then expression2 is evaluated; otherwise, expression3 is evaluated. The result of the ? operation is that of the expression evaluated.

Both expression2 & expression3 are required to return the same type, which can't be void. Example:

Class Ternary

```
{
Public static void main (String args[ ])
        {
        int i, k;
        i = 10;
        k=i < 0 ? - i : i;                    //get absolute value of i
System.out.println(i+ "is"+k);
        }
}
```

Output:

Absolute value of 10 is 10
Absolute value of -10 is 10

(d) What is call-by-value and call-by-reference in Java? Explain with example.

Ans. Refer to Page No.-168, Dec-01, Q.No.-4(ii)

(e) Explain the need of various access specifiers with the help of suitable examples.

Ans. Refer to Page No.-128, Dec-03, Q.No.-5(i)

(f) What is an inner class in Java? Explain.

Ans. Refer to Page No.-74, Chapter-6, Q.No.-4

Q2. (a) What is user-defined exception in Java? Explain with example.

Ans. Refer to Page No.-82, Chapter-7, Q.No.-6

(b) Why can't we have more than one public class in the same file? Explain.

Ans. Refer to Page No.-195, June-05, Q.No.-2(c)

(c) What do you understand by the term late binding? Explain.

Ans. Late Binding is a computer programming mechanism in which the method being called upon an object is looked up by name at run-time. It is also known as Dynamic Binding. It refers to the case where computer is not able to resolve the call & the binding is done at runtime only.

Q3. (a) Find the error(s) if any in the following code. Also correct the error(s).

```
Interface A {
                void call( );
                void call( );
            }
class demo implements A {
        void call( ) {
                system.out.println("first version invoked");
                    }
void call( ) {
system.out.println("second version invoked);
    }
}
```

Ans. Interface A

```
{
void call1( );
void call2( );
}
class demo implements A
{
public void call1( )
        {
        system.out.println("first version/call1( )invoked");
        }
}
public void call2( )
        {
        system.out.println("second version/call2( )invoked");
        }
}
Class B
        {
public static void main (String args( ))
                {
        demo ob=new demo( );
                ob.call1 ( );
                ob.call2 ( );
        }
}
```

(b) How are priorities used in Java? Explain with an example.

Ans. Refer to Page No.-261, Dec-07, Q.No.-4(a)

(c) What is default access in Java? Explain.

Ans. Refer to Page No.-104, June-04, Q.No.-1(b)

Q4. (a) Why do we use static data? Explain.

Ans. Refer to Page No.-265, Dec-07, Q.No.-5(c)

(b) Write a program using recursion to compute sum of first n terms of the following series:

$$x-\frac{x^3}{3!}+\frac{x^5}{5!}-\frac{x^7}{7!}+...$$

Ans. import java.util.*;

```
public class sumofseries
        {
public static double sum(int n)
        {
```

```
        if(n==1)
        return 1.0;
        return sum(n-1) + 1.0/n;
        }
public static void main (String[ ] args)
        {
scanner input=new Scanner (system.in);
System.out.println("Enter no. of terms");
int num=input.newInt( );
System.out.println(sum(num));
        }
}
```

(c) Write a program in Java to count number of words, chars and lines in a file. Name of the file is accepted at command line.

Ans.import java.io.*;

```
public class WordCount{
private static void linecount(String fName, BufferedReader in)
throws IOException{
long numChar=0;
long numLine=0;
long numWords=0;
String line;
do{
line = in.readLine();
if(line!= null)
{
numChar += line.length();
numWords += wordcount(line);
numLine++;
}
}while(line!= null);
System.out.println("File Name: " + fName);
System.out.println("Number of characters: " + numChar);
System.out.println("Number of words: " + numWords);
System.out.println("Number of Lines: " + numLine);
}
private static void linecount(String fileName){
BufferedReader in = null;
try
{
FileReader fileReader = new FileReader(fileName);
in = new BufferedReader(fileReader);
linecount(fileName,in);
```

```
}
catch(IOException e){
e.printStackTrace();
}
}
private static long wordcount(String line)
{
long numWords = 0;
int index = 0;
boolean prevWhiteSpace = true;
while(index < line.length()){
char c = line.charAt(index++);
boolean currWhiteSpace = Character.isWhitespace(c);
if(prevWhiteSpace && !currWhiteSpace){
numWords++;
}
prevWhiteSpace = currWhiteSpace;
}
return numWords;
}
public static void main(String[] args){
long numChar = 0;
long numLine=0;
String line;
try{
if (args.length == 0)
{
BufferedReader in = new BufferedReader(new InputStreamReader(System.in));
line = in.readLine();
numChar = line.length();
if (numChar!= 0){
numLine=1;
}
System.out.println("Number of characters: " + numChar);
System.out.println("Number of words: " + wordcount(line));
System.out.println("Number of lines: " + numLine);
}else{
for(int i = 0; i < args.length; i++){
linecount(args[i]);
}
}
}
catch(IOException e){
```

```
e.printStackTrace();
}
}
}
```

Q5. (a) Give the output of the following:

```
public class temp {
        public int f( )
        {
         try
{
return 0;
}
 catch (Exception e)
{
  return 2;
}
        }
public int g( )
{
    try
      {
            return 3;
      }
finally
        {
return 4;
        }
}
Public static void main(string args[ ])
{
  Take 0 = new temp( );
system.out.println("f( )returns" +0.f( ) );
system.out.println("g( )returns" +0.g( ) );
    }
}
```

Ans. Visit us at www.Gullybaba.com\bca\CS-74

(b)

```
for (int i = 31, i >= 0, i—)
if(((i<<j)&i)!= 0)
system.out.println("*");
else
system.out.println("?");
```

if i = 42 what is the output of the above code?

Ans. for (int i=42; i>=0, i—)

```
if(((i<<j) & i)!=0)
{
System.out.println(" * ");
        }
else
        {
        System.out.println ("?");
        }
```

Output:

```
        *
        *
        *
        *
        *
        *
        *
        *
        *
        *
        *
```

(c) What are abstract classes in Java? Why do we need them?

Ans. Abstract Classes: In some cases, you will find that a super class can't have any instance (object) & those of such classes are called abstract classes. Abstract classes usually contain abstract method. abstract method is a method signature (declaration) without implementation. Basically these abstract method provides a common interface with different classes.

Need of Abstract Classes: Abstract Classes are generally used to provide common interface derived classes.

Example:

```
        abstract class A
        {
        int i;
        void show( )
        {
        system.out.println("Hello: This is A");
        }
}
class B extends A
        {
        int j ;
        void show( )
```

```
        {
        system.out.println("Value of j="+j);
        }
}
        class mainclass
        {
public static void main(string[ ] args)
        {
        B objB=new B( );
A objA;
obj A=obj B;                //obj A references to obj B
obj A.i=6;                  // obj A can now access A's member
obj A.show( );              //show ( ) of B: Run-Time Polymorphism
objB.j=5;
obj A.show( );              //show ( ) of B: Run-Time Polymorphism
        }
}
```

Output:

value of j=0
value of j=5

(d) What are various colour constructors? Explain briefly.

Ans. Java defines two constructors for the colour class, of which, one constructor takes three integer arguments & another takes three float arguments.

public colour (int r, int g, int b)

Creates a colour based on red, green & blue components expressed as integers from 0 to 255. Here the r, g, b means red, green, & blue contents respectively.

public colour (float r, float g, float b)

Creates a colour based on red, green & blue components expressed as floating-point values from 0.0 to 1.0. here, the r, g, b means red, green & blue contents respectively.

CS-74: INTRODUCTION TO INTERNET PROGRAMMING
June, 2012

Note: *Question No.1 is* ***compulsory****. Attempt* ***any two*** *questions from the rest. Use* ***Java*** *as programming language in your answers.*

Q1. (a) What is class in oop? Write a Java program which create a student object and display students basic information by appropriate method call. Make and state necessary assumptions.

Ans. Refer to Page No.-6, Chapter-1, Q.No.-4 & Page No.-136, June-2003, Q.No.-6(i)

(b) What is a switch statement? Give an example of a situation where it cannot be used. Write a program fragment to show how that situation can be coded.

Ans. Refer Page No.-39[Switch Statement]

Switch statement can't be used when we need to write some variable in conditional part.

Switch statement only uses constant as cases to compare the values.

Program

```
# include <iostream.h>
# include <conio.h>
void main ( )
{
        int a, b, c;
        printf("Enter value of a & b);
        scanf("%d %d", &a, &b);
        if (a > b)
        c = a – b;
        else
        c = b – a;
        getch( );
}
```

Note: If else blocks can be used instead of switch if we want to evaluate on the basis of variables or conditions.

(c) What is an applet program? Write any three differences between Applet and Application program.

Ans. Applets are written in Java and they are viewed using Applet Viewer or a Java enabled browser. Applets are included in HTML page using <APPLET> tag, and then these can be viewed by the users having Java enabled browser.

Thing to note is that Applets are not executed on the server side. They are transferred to user's machine and then executed by the browser's Java Virtual Machine (JVM).

Now, Refer to Page No.-124, Dec-2003, Q.No.-3(i)

(d) Write a Java program to add two matrices.

Ans. import java.io.*;

```
public class MatrixAddition
{
	static int[][] matrix1 = new int[3][];
	static int[][] matrix2 = new int[3][];
	static int[][] matrix3 = new int[3][];
	public static void main(String[] args)
	{
		try
		{
			int tempVal = 3, cols = 3;
			BufferedReader in = new BufferedReader(new Input
			StreamReader(System.in));
			/** System.out.println("Please enter the number of
			rows required.");
			* tempVal = Integer.parseInt(in.readLine());
			*
			* System.out.println("Please enter the number of cols
			required.");
			* cols = Integer.parseInt(in.readLine());
			*/
			matrix1[0] = new int[3];
			matrix1[1] = new int[3];
			matrix1[2] = new int[3];
			matrix2[0] = new int[3];
			matrix2[1] = new int[3];
			matrix2[2] = new int[3];
			matrix3[0] = new int[3];
			matrix3[1] = new int[3];
			matrix3[2] = new int[3];
			System.out.println("enter values for ("+tempVal+ "
			x " + cols + ") matrix 1:");
			int input;
			for (int i = 0; i < tempVal; i++)
			{
				for (int j = 0; j < cols; j++)
				{
```

```
                input =
                Integer.parseInt(in.readLine());
                matrix1[i][j] = input;
        }
}
System.out.println("enter values for (" + tempVal +
" x " + cols + ") matrix 2:");
for (int i = 0; i < tempVal; i++)
{
        for (int j = 0; j < cols; j++)
        {
                input =
                Integer.parseInt(in.readLine());
                matrix2[i][j] = input;
        }
}
System.out.print("\n\n");
//Printing the entered matrix.
System.out.println("Matrix 1 is as follows:");
for (int i = 0; i < tempVal; i++)
{
        for (int j = 0; j < cols; j++)
        {
                System.out.print(matrix1[i][j] +
                "\t");
        }
        System.out.print("\n\n");
}
System.out.println("Matrix 2 is as follows:");
for (int i = 0; i < tempVal; i++)
{
        for (int j = 0; j < cols; j++)
        {
                System.out.print(matrix2[i][j] +
                "\t");
        }
        System.out.print("\n\n");
}
//now lets add the two matrix.
for (int i = 0; i < tempVal; i++)
{
        for (int j = 0; j < cols; j++)
        {
```

```
                    matrix3[i][j] = matrix1[i][j] +
                    matrix2[i][j];
                }
            }
            System.out.println("The answer is as follows:");
            for (int i = 0; i < tempVal; i++)
            {
                for (int j = 0; j < cols; j++)
                {
                    System.out.print(matrix3[i][j] +
                    "\t");
                }
                System.out.print("\n\n");
            }
        }
        catch (Exception ex)
        {
            System.out.print("Ooopsie! We've had an Exception:
            " + ex.getMessage());
        }
    }
}
```

Q2. (a) What is inheritance? How it is implemented in Java? Create a class named Account and create another class named Saving Account by extending the Account Class.

Ans. Refer to Page No.-8, Chapter-1, Q.No.-7

Example showing implementation of Inheritance in Java:

```
packageTEST_JAVA_INHERITANCE_PACKAGE;
class Java_Inheritance_Base_Class
{
    public void Java_Inheritance_Base_Method()
    {
        System.out.println("Executing
        Java_Inheritance_Base_Method of
        Java_Inheritance_Base_Class");
    }
}
class Java_Inheritance_Derived_Class extends Java_Inheritance_Base_Class
{
}
class Test_Inheritance
{
```

```
        public static void main(String[] args)
        {
                Java_Inheritance_Derived_Class derivedObj = new
                Java_Inheritance_Derived_Class();
                derivedObj.Java_Inheritance_Base_Method();
        }
}
Cass Account
{
        int bal;
        void show_bal ( )
        {
                system.out.printIn("Balance is =" +bal);
        }
}
Class SavingAccount extends Account
{
        int Save_bal;
        void set_saving (int a, int b)
        {
                Super.bal = a;
                Save_bal = b;
        }
        Class mainClass
        {
                public static void main (String args [ ])
                {
                        SavingAccount S = new SavingAccount( );
                        S. set_saving (2000, 3000);
                        S.show_bal ( );
                }
        }
}
```

(b) What is static in Java? Explain why the main method in Java is always static.

Ans. Refer to Page 135[Static] & Page No.-205, Dec-2004, Q.No.-1(b)

Q3. (a) Write an applet program which draw a circle inside a rectangle. Fill the circle with blue color.

Ans. import java.awt.*;

```
import java.applet.*;
public class shape extends Applet
{
```

```
        int shape;
        public void init ( )
        {
                shape = 0;
        }
        public void paint (Graphics g)
        {
                g.draw Rect (35, 50, 125, 180);
                g.draw Circle (40,60);
                g.fill Circle (blue);
        }
}
Public boolean action (Event e, object arg)
{
        repaint ( );
        return true;
}
```

(b) What is a bitwise operator? List any five bitwise operators of Java. Give an example of use of bit wise operator.

Ans. Refer to Page No.- 26[Bitwise Operator]

Q4. (a) Does Java support multiple Inheritance? Can Interfaces be used to achieve the multiple Inheritance in Java? Explain with an example.

Ans. Refer to Page No.-264, Dec-2007, Q.No.-5(a)

Interfaces can be used to implement multiple inheritance like hierarchies.

Example:

```
Interface InterfaceName
{
        // "constant" declarations
        // method declarations
}
// inheritance between interfaces
Interface Interface Name extends InterfaceName
{
        ...
}
// not possible
Interface InterfaceName extends InterfaceName1, InterfaceName2
{
        ...
}
// not possible
```

```
Interface InterfaceName extends ClassName
{
        ...
}
// implements instead of extends
Class ClassName implements InterfaceName
{
        ...
}
// multiple inheritance like]
Class ClassName implements InterfaceName 1, InterfaceName 2
{
        ...
}
//combine inheritance and interface implementation
Class ClassName extends SuperClass implements InterfaceName
{
        ...
}
//multiple inheritance like again
Class ClassName extends SuperClass
Implements InterfaceName1, InterfaceName2
{
        ...
}
```

(b) What is a package? Which package is by default imported in a Java program? Explain the benefit of using pakage with an example.
Ans. Refer to Page No.-112, June-2004, Q.No.-4(a)

Q5. (a) What is a multithreading? Give two advantages of multithreading. Explain one way of creating thread in Java. Also explain how a thread priority is set in Java?
Ans. Refer to Page No.-180, June-2001, Q.No.-4(a), Page No.-232, June-2006, Q.No.-3(a), & Page No.-251, June-2007, Q.No.-1(c)

(b) What is Layout Manager? Explain Flow Layout and show how Flow Layout is set in Java through an example program?
Ans. A layout manager allows the java programmer to develop graphical interfaces that will have a common appearance across the heterogeneous internet.
Now, Page No.-164, Dec-2001, Q.No.-1(iv)

CS-74: Introduction to Internet Programming
December, 2012

Note: *Question No.1 is **compulsory**. Attempt **any two** questions from the rest. Use **Java** as programming language in your answers.*

Q1. (a) Explain any five Java basic features briefly.
Ans. Refer to Page No.-14, Chapter-2, Q.No.-5

(b) What is a constructor? Write a java program to implement a Rectangle class that has constructors with 0, 1 or 2 parameters.
Ans. Refer to Page No.-126, Dec-2003, Q.No.-4(i)

```
Class shape
{
        int a, b;
        Shape (int i, int j)
        {
                a = i;
                b = j;
        }
        Shape (int i)
        {
        a = b = i;
        }
        Shape ( )
        {
        a = b = 1;
        }
}
Class mainClass
{
        public static void main (string args [ ])
        {
                // Default Constructor with zero parameter
                Shape r1 = new Shape ( );
                System.out.println(r1.l+"," + r1.b);
                //Constructor with one parameter
                Shape r2 = new Shape (10);
                System.out.println(r2.l+"," + r2.b);
                //Constructor with two parameter
                Shape r3 = new Shape (5, 7);
                System.out.println(r3.l+"," + r3.b);
        }
}
```

(c) What is a Thread? Explain various states of a thread with the help of a suitable diagram.

Ans. Refer to Page No.-232, June-2006, Q.No.-3(a)

States of Thread are:

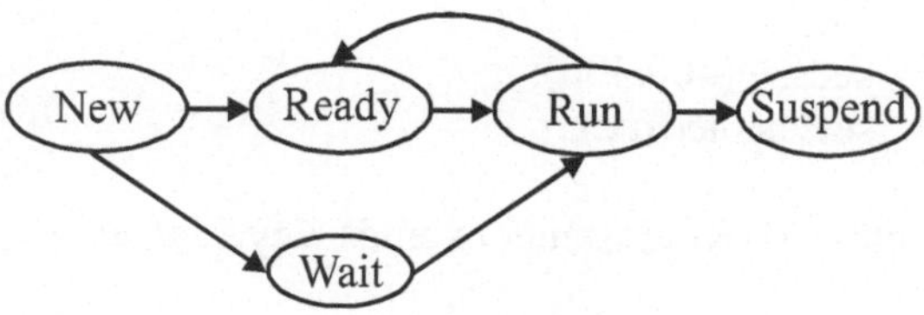

(d) What is an event in GUI programming? Write a program to print "Key Pressed" whenever a key is pressed on the keyboard.

Ans. In Graphical User Interface (GUI) programming, there's the concept of event. For example, moving the mouse, clicking a mouse button, switching to a different window, hitting a key. The software needs to respond to these things.

The programmer writes code that draw buttons, menus, windows etc. The programmer write his program so that it knows the mouse position, mouse click, keyboard press, or any other signal from input devices. The programmer also writes code so that for example if a mouse click happened, and its position is inside a button, then some function is called as a reaction.

```
import java.awt.*;
import java.awt.event.*;
public class KeyPress extends Frame
{
        Label label;
        TextField txtField;
        public static void main(String[] args)
        {
                KeyPress k = new KeyPress();
        }
        public KeyPress()
        {
                super("Key Press Event Frame");
                Panel panel = new Panel();
                label = new Label();
                txtField = new TextField(20);
                txtField.addKeyListener(new MyKeyListener());
                add(label, BorderLayout.NORTH);
                panel.add(txtField, BorderLayout.CENTER);
                add(panel, BorderLayout.CENTER);
                addWindowListener(new WindowAdapter()
```

```
            {
                    public void windowClosing(WindowEvent we)
                    {
                            System.exit(0);
                    }
            });
            setSize(400,400);
            setVisible(true);
    }
    public class MyKeyListener extends KeyAdapter
    {
            public void keyPressed(KeyEvent ke)
            {
            char i = ke.getKeyChar();
            String str = Character.toString(i);
            label.setText(str);
            }
    }
}
```

(e) What is inheritance? Write the declarations for the classes and methods of a hierarchy consisting of vehicle, car and petrol car.

Ans. Refer to Page No.-209, Dec-2004, Q.No.-2(b)

```
Class vehicle
{
        int category;
        void show ( )
        {
                system.out.println("Category"+category);
        }
}
class car extend vehicle
{
        string model;
        void show_model ( )
        {
                system.out.println("Model is:" + model);
        }
}
class petrol_car extends car
{
        string color;
        void display ( )
```

```
        {
                System.out.println("Colour of vehicle" + color);
        }
}
```

Q2. (a) What is interface? Differentiate between interfaces and abstract classes with the help of an example.

Ans. Refer to Page No.-90, Chapter-8, Q.No.-3 & Page No.-192, June-2005, Q.No.-2(a)

(b) What is an exception? Explain with an example how multiple exceptions are handled in Java. If there are multiple catch clauses, which one is called? Also explain the use of finally in exception handling.

Ans. Refer to Page No.-76, Chapter-7, Q.No.-1, Page No.-78[Multiple catch Clauses] & Page No.-81, Q.No.-5

Q3. (a) Write a Java program which read the contents of a file and display it on screen with each line appearing in reverse order.

Ans. Same as Page No.-295, Dec-2010, Q.No.-1(b)

(b) What is Graphics class in Java? Explain why drawstring() method is used. Also explain how you will get color of a Graphics object in java.

Ans. Syntax –

public abstract class Graphics
extends Object

The Graphics class is the abstract base class for all graphics contexts that allow an application to draw onto components that are realised on various devices, as well as onto off-screen images.

A Graphics object encapsulates state information needed for the basic rendering operations that Java supports. This state information includes the following properties:

- The Component object on which to draw.
- A translation origin for rendering and clipping coordinates.
- The current clip.
- The current color.
- The current font.
- The current logical pixel operation function (XOR or Paint).
- The current XOR alternation color (see setXORMode(java.awt.Color)).

drawString(AttributedCharacterIterator iterator, int x, int y)

Draws the text given by the specified iterator, using this graphics context's current color.

drawString(String str, int x, int y)

Draws the text given by the specified string, using this graphics context's current font and color.
If g is a graphics context, you can change the current drawing color for g using the method g.setColor(c), where c is a Color.
For example, if you want to draw in green, you would just say g.setColor(Color.GREEN) before doing the drawing. The graphics context continues to use the color until you explicitly change it with another setColor() command. If you want to know what the current drawing color is, you can call the function g.getColor(), which returns an object of type Color. This can be useful if you want to change to another drawing color temporarily and then restore the previous drawing color.
Every component has an associated

- foreground color
- background color.

Generally, the component is filled with the background color before anything else is drawn (although some components are "transparent," meaning that the background color is ignored). When a new graphics context is created for a component, the current drawing color is set to the foreground color. Note that the foreground color and background color are properties of the component, not of a graphics context.

Q4. (a) What is access specifier? Explain the need of access specifier. Briefly explain about public, protected and private access specifiers.
Ans. Refer to Page No.-128, Dec-2003, Q.No.-5(i)
They are used to access the values of variable declared in another class.

(b) What is object serialisation? Explain how objects are serialised with an example. Describe how volatile and transient data is serialised.
Ans. Refer to Page No.-284, Dec-2009, Q.No.-2(c) & Page No.-230, June-2006, Q.No.-2(a)(i)

Q5. (a) What is an error in Java? How does it differ from an exception?
Ans. Refer to Page No.-78, Chapter-7, Q.No.-3 & Page No.-76[Introduction]

(b) Explain use of final keyword in Java.
Ans. Refer to Page No.-206, Dec-2004, Q.No.-1(d)

(c) Describe the garbage collection mechanism in Java. How would you use the finalise() method to close all open file handles? Show with an example program.
Ans. Refer to Page No.-64[Garbage Collection] & Page No.-110, June-2004, Q.No.-2(b)

CS-74: Introduction to Internet Programming
June, 2013

Note: *Question No.1 is* ***compulsory****. Attempt* ***any two*** *from the rest.*

Q1. (a) Explain the term polymorphism? How does Java support polymorphism? Explain with the help of examples.

(b) What is the difference between call-by-value and call-by-reference? When does Java use each?

(c) List the main differences between Java applet and application program with the help of suitable example.

(d) When do we use protected access specifier? Explain with example.

(e) Give the reason why main ( ) method in Java is defined as public and static? Also explain why name of class containing main ( ) is same as name of the file in it is stored?

Q2. (a) What are abstract classes in Java? How do they differ from interfaces? Explain.

(b) Write an applet in Java that will display current date.

Q3. (a) What is finally block in Java? How many finally block can be associated with a try block? Explain with the help of an example.

(b) Perform the following operations:
int x = 10, int y = –10

(i) x << 2;	**(ii) x >>2;**
(iii) x^y;	**(iv) y<<2;**

Q4. (a) Write a recursive method in Java to print all the elements of given integer array.

(b) What is static data? When is it used? Explain with example.

(c) Write the output of the following program segment.

```
Class ABC {
Public static void main (string args [ ])
{
        Outer : for (int i = 0; i < 10; i ++)
        {
            for (int j = 0; j < 10; j++)
            {   if (j > i)
            {
                 System. out. Println ( );
                 continue outer;
            }
System. out. print (" " + (i*j) );
                      }
            } system. out. prentln ( );
        }
   }
```

Q5. (a) What is the use of value of ( ) method in Java? Explain with the help of example.

(b) Find the error (s) if any in the following code. Also correct the errors and give the out put:

(i) Class scope

```
        {
            {   int i = 5;
                Int j = 7;
        System. Out. println ("i ="+ i);
        System. Out. println ("j ="+ j);
            }
                  int i = 10;
        System. Out. Println ("i ="+ i);
        System. Out. Println ("j ="+ j);
        }
```

(ii) Short S = 100;

```
S = S*2;
System. Out. Println ("S="+s);
```

(c) What are command line arguments in Java? Explain with example?

CS-74: Introduction to Internet Programming
December, 2013

Note: *Question No.1 is* ***compulsory****. Attempt* ***any two*** *from the rest.*

Q1. (a) What is super key word in Java? Explain with example.

(b) Differentiate between overloading and overriding with the help of suitable example.

(c) Write the output of the following code segments:

(i) int i = 8, j = 1;

i >> j+2;

(ii) int x = 10, y = 5;

```
if (x! = 10 and y + + < 10)
        x= y
    System. out. print ln ("x ="+ x);
    System. out. print ln ("y ="+ y);
```

(d) What is byte code in Java? Explain.

(e) Static function can operate only on static data. Explain.

(f) How does repaint ( ) method work for Applets in Java?

Q2. (a) Write a program in Java to print the following output using 2 – D array for a given integer n.

```
1
2 2
3 3 3
4 4 4 4
.
.
.
n n n n - - - n
```

(b) Write a program in Java to copy one file to another file using command line arguments.

Q3. (a) Differentiate between throw and throws in Java with the help of an example.

(b) Package pac 1 ;

```
public class one {
                int i = 1 ;
        private int j = 2 ;
        protected int k = 3 ;
        public int l = 4 ;
.
.
.
}
```

if class Two is defined in another package pac 2, then what are the variable accessible in Two? Explain with example.

(c) What is Java virtual machine? Explain.

Q4. (a) What is the difference in final and finally in Java? Explain with example.

(b) Write the output of the following:

```
Class Example {
    public static void main (string args [ ])
            { int i, j, k ;
               i = j = k = 1 ;
          If (k = = 1 and J + + <6)
                i = 5 ;
System. out. println (i + " " + j + " " + k) ;
    }
```

Justify your Answer

(c) What is this key word? Explain.